RISK AND RHETORIC IN RELIGION

*Whitehead's Theory of Language
and the Discourse of Faith*

LYMAN T. LUNDEEN

Fortress Press   Philadelphia

RISK AND RHETORIC
IN RELIGION

Quotations from the following books by Alfred North Whitehead are reprinted with the kind permission of the Macmillan Company:

Adventure of Ideas   Copyright 1933 by the Macmillan Company, renewed 1961 by Evelyn Whitehead.

Modes of Thought   Copyright 1938 by the Macmillan Company, renewed 1966 by T. North Whitehead.

Process and Reality   Copyright 1929 by the Macmillan Company, renewed 1957 by Evelyn Whitehead.

Religion in the Making   Copyright 1926 by the Macmillan Company, renewed 1954 by Evelyn Whitehead.

Science and the Modern World   Copyright 1925 by the Macmillan Company, renewed 1953 by Evelyn Whitehead.

Symbolism: Its Meaning and Effects   Copyright 1927 by the Macmillan Company, renewed 1955 by Evelyn Whitehead.

Library of Congress Catalog Card Number 71-171501
ISBN-0-8006-0050-9

2912H71   Printed in the United States of America   *1-50*

For
Anton and Ruth,
pioneers in a great adventure.

"The worship of God is not a rule of safety—it is an adventure of the spirit, a flight after the unattainable." Alfred North Whitehead, *Science and the Modern World*

TABLE OF CONTENTS

ABBREVIATIONS

Throughout this work, the principal works of Alfred North White-head are referred to according to the following standard abbreviations, and all references are to the editions cited.

AE *The Aims of Education and Other Essays*
(New York: The New American Library, 1949)

AI *Adventure of Ideas*
(New York: The Free Press, Crowell Collier
& Macmillan, 1967)

CN *The Concept of Nature*
(Cambridge: Cambridge University Press, 1920)

FR *The Function of Reason*
(Boston: Beacon Press, 1958)

MT *Modes of Thought*
(New York: Capricorn Books, 1958)

PR *Process and Reality*
(New York: Harper & Row Torchbooks, 1960)

RM *Religion in the Making*
(New York: The World Publishing Co., 1960)

SMW *Science and the Modern World*
(New York: The New American Library, 1959)

SP *Science and Philosophy*
(New York: The Philosophical Library, 1948)

Sym *Symbolism: Its Meaning and Effect*
(New York: Capricorn Books, 1959)

Foreword

This study is the result of a long-standing interest in the relationship between faith and reason. Early in life I was introduced to a religious perspective in which total commitment and honest criticism were understood as partners in the enterprise of faith. Not only were faith and reason taken to be compatible, but in some fashion each was construed as dependent on the other. On the one hand, faith was informed, qualified and corrected by a real concern for truth. On the other hand, man's most dependable knowledge was taken to be shaped, gathered and applied by people with fundamental commitments and exclusive interests. Such a point of view seemed capable of integrating all of human existence in a very exciting and satisfying manner.

The problem for me has been to find instruments whereby this kind of perspective could be articulated and perhaps even made plausible. In the contemporary context the combination of apparently subjective faith and the claims of objective inquiry has been especially difficult. The modern mind-body split together with all the parallel distinctions that it generates has kept man's value judgments and faith commitments from touching, let alone influencing, the supposedly objective information of science, common sense and technology. Is it then appropriate to speak of knowing God? Can one claim that faith is a way of dealing with reality in its broadest contours, or must religious commitment be understood as mere personal preference, fantasy, wishful thinking or an escapist opiate? These questions are also raised in more secular ways. How can we decide which technological avenues to develop? Can we afford to let scientists and technicians proceed as though their value judgments were irrelevant to the results of their research or to the application of that research to the human environment? Should we allow purported experts and specialists to make all the important decisions for us as if those conclusions followed necessarily from some efficient technique or esoteric information? Here also is the issue of the relationship of faith and reason in the broad sense. What we want for man needs to be seen as a critically important factor in the pursuit and utilization of knowledge. The question is how we might understand the relationship involved without minimizing commitment to values or emasculating the power of rational endeavor.

One way of getting at these issues is to focus on the religious use of language. Here the relationship of emotion, evaluation and decision to the more objective features of human experience is brought onto center stage. Obviously, this is why the literature in this area has been growing by leaps and bounds. It is a way of dealing with a whole range of problems by zeroing in on one specific area.

In the discussion of religious language, many philosophical resources have been utilized. One possible resource that has received little attention is the philosophy of Alfred North Whitehead. This is unfortunate because his work includes extensive treatment of both language and religion as they contribute to the fabric of human civilization. Whitehead's ability to combine a profound appreciation of religious expressions with a high estimate of empirical concerns suggests that his philosophy may be an important ingredient that needs to be added to the current discussion of religious discourse. The renewed and broad-based interest in process styles of thought enhances the relevance of Whitehead's work. If process approaches are being found useful in other realms of inquiry, it would seem that the potential contribution of process thought to the discussion of religious language needs exploration.

This study claims that Whitehead's understanding of language allows religious statements to have both cognitive and affective significance. Assertions of faith can be legitimate claims about the universe where faith appears at the same time

as they express will, emotion and value. In this respect, Whitehead is seen as keeping open the possibility that faith involves
some kind of knowledge. In the face of persistent and powerful
challenges to this point of view, Whitehead meets the basic
questions with suggestive insights concerning experience and its
relationship to linguistic activity. By treating all knowledge as
dynamic and value-laden, Whitehead calls into question the
normative use of strictly objective criteria in the assessment of
religious assertions. Whitehead's contention that clarity always
means "clear enough" for some qualifying purpose provides a
link between statements of "fact" and expressions of "value."
As a consequence, all knowledge claims are informed to some
degree by exclusive interest. The religious expression of ultimate priorities need not be cut off from more objective claims
just because it is heavy with emotion and evaluation. Both
types of concern are dependent on the same complex of living
experience and can therefore provide healthy correctives for one
another.

A couple of secondary intentions should be made explicit.
This study also attempts to elucidate Whitehead's theory of
language for the sake of its broader implications. That is to say,
the significance of religious discourse need not be the only issue
that Whitehead's approach to language is found to illuminate.
His general theory of language has also been neglected and its
explication alongside of other options may be useful.

Also, since Whitehead is of interest in his own right as an
initiator of process philosophy, the study of his views on language may make the assets of this total approach more apparent
and more accessible. In other words, language in general and
religious language in particular may provide a way into Whitehead's work that can supplement other approaches to his
philosophy.

There are a number of persons who have given assistance to
me in this project and I would acknowledge their contributions
with appreciation. They are not accountable for the end product, but without them I might not have undertaken the task
or finished it in the same way. George Arbaugh, Karl E.

Mattson and Robert Horn all gave me personal encouragement in the pursuit of this type of problem. John Macquarrie, James Alfred Martin, Jr., Bernard Meland and Daniel Day Williams provided insights into the substance of the matter and constructive criticism of the manuscript at various stages. William Lazareth helped sustain my interest in publishing this work when the pressures to do other things were all too plentiful. My wife, Grace, and our four children have also contributed in many ways, but most of all by letting me have a great deal of time which might more properly have been theirs.

1

RELIGIOUS LANGUAGE AS A CONTEMPORARY PROBLEM

The religious use of language to express man's convictions about the meaning of life has been a central problem in our time. Such discourse presents difficulties because it apparently combines the deepest personal evaluations with serious claims about the broadest features of reality. The problem is not only the combination of expressive and assertive functions, but the universal scope of the claims involved. When man attempts to articulate the significance of his own life, he necessarily sets it in relation to the universe. Taken seriously, then, he is not just speaking about his own attitudes but about the widest environment imaginable.

It makes little difference whether religious assertions refer explicitly to God or only imply some universal coordination of values. Using the term "God" in a very general sense, one can understand all religious expressions as having reference to a factor in reality which is the ultimate ground of our existence and relative significance. It need not be concluded that a Western conception of a personal God is a prerequisite for religious expression. God can be seen as the ground and goal of all religions to be characterized in their diverse ways.

Obviously, language does not have to be explicit in its reference to God in order to be taken as religious. Nor is a detailed conception of God required as the precondition of religious discourse. What does seem necessary is that religious expression refer to some factor which calls forth and justifies the individual's response, integrates his interests, and gives his life significance in the context of the universe. One might call this the "religious object," or some more neutral name, but what is important is to recognize both the danger of limited experience and the need for some ontological reference.[1]

Terminology is not the real issue, however. If the term "God" is understood in a very general sense, we can admit its intimate connection with particular religious traditions without destroying its broader interpretive power. On the other hand, even though all religious assertions are seen as having reference to God in a very general way, explicit reference to God does not, by itself, make an expression religious. The term "God" can also be used in a philosophical manner, so that expressions concerning the ultimate coordination of reality and value are put forward, not as intimate, personal conviction, but as the rational and critical description of the most general traits of experience. Similarly, the use of the term "God" to announce anger or injury need not be considered religious. The religious use of language, like so many other types of discourse, is fundamentally a matter of intention and context. As a result, there are borderline cases, which are not to be resolved by an abstract classification.

The central problem with religious discourse has to do with the nature of the claims expressed. Does religious language have a cognitive significance in addition to its obvious affective appeal? How is this use of language related to evidence and confirmation? Are its assertions to be taken seriously, even though they are inextricably entangled with such deep emotion and feeling? The cognitive significance of religious discourse is the unsettled and disturbing question which has kept attention focused on the religious use of language. If there is cognition involved in these expressions, then it should be possible to show how they relate to man's knowledge and methods of inquiry in other areas of human experience. If it is admitted that no knowledge claims are implied, then it is highly ques-

1. John E. Smith, *Experience and God* (New York: Oxford University Press, 1968), p. 16.

tionable whether these same expressions can fulfill their special functions in the religious realm.

Even if, as some claim, the issue has now shifted from whether or not religious assertions are meaningful to how they are used, the problem is not decisively different.[2] There is still a need to explain *how* religious assertions can have cognitive meaning. In other words, to admit that such significance is possible for religious discourse leaves the field open for attempts to explain the way this might happen and what difference it makes. In this sense, even the moves to more moderate forms of linguistic analysis have not taken the question of cognitive significance out of its central place.

This is not just an academic problem. In the wake of successful science and technology, the whole culture has become permeated with secularist attitudes that tend to challenge the importance of articulated religious claims, whatever their content. Thus, while there are probably no self-styled positivists around, the big issues about life's meaning and purpose are still in difficulty. The nagging questions raised explicitly by reductionist approaches to language are still there—imbedded in the very fabric of our culture. In the emphasis on the contingent, the transient, the autonomous, and the relative, concerns that are manifest in religious faith tend to be relegated to some private sphere where the importance of any particular faith claim is in doubt.[3] One can talk about this problem as though it were an esoteric question reserved for theologians and philosophers, but, in fact, it is part of contemporary social reality. All the discussion here should be read with that in mind, even though the focus may seem to be more limited.

Not all religious expressions raise this problem in the same way. For instance, the historical claims of a particular religion like Christianity can be treated much like similar claims that are not in any way seen as religious. The indication that a man

2. Dallas M. High, ed., *New Essays on Religious Language* (New York: Oxford University Press, 1969), p. v.
3. Langdon Gilkey, *Naming the Whirlwind: The Renewal of God-Language* (Indianapolis and New York: The Bobbs-Merrill Company, 1969), pp. 40–61.

called Jesus lived is much easier to understand and evaluate than the claim that this man is somehow the clue to the structure and meaning of the universe. It is essentially the second type of claim that puts religious language in difficulty.

Theological expressions, as one form of religious discourse, articulate the problematic side of the issue the most sharply. Since this use of language is concerned explicitly with the content of the faith, problems that may not be apparent in cultic practice or personal devotion become evident. For this reason, when dealing with the scope and character of religious claims, it is appropriate to give a major share of attention to discourse that is patently theological. At least, one need not spend too much time wrestling with the difference between the language of religious practice and the language of theology. While there are important differences here, the basic commitments involved permeate the entire fabric of religious discourse.

The religious use of language can be distinguished from other types of expression, even though it shares a common structure. It is not identified by unique syntax or vocabulary, but rather by the purposes which inform it. With this in mind, there are some characteristic features of religious discourse that can be noted.

The primary characteristic of religious language is its expression of fundamental personal and corporate convictions about the meaning of life. For an individual, it is language in which he can express those "ultimate concerns" around which other interests are ordered. For a community, religious language makes it possible to share, cultivate, and criticize such concerns. In this sense, religious language has to do with basic attitudes close to the core of a person's identity. The convictions expressed in this form are both intimate and ultimate. They are intimate in that they give an order of relative importance to all the interests of human life, and they are ultimate in that there are no convictions which carry more weight. Such convictions are attitudes toward life itself. They are the focused response of man to those factors that are crucial for his existence. The language of religion expresses these attitudes and provides a structure in which they can be fostered and communicated. In religious language, man articulates those ideas and values which give him identity and purpose. As William Hordern has described it: "Religious language, Christian or otherwise, is unique because it deals with the ultimate convictions of a man's life, . . . the convictions by which he lives and dies."[4]

A second feature of religious language arises out of the kind of reference which ultimate convictions require. Such convictions not only reflect attitudes but also put forth claims about the circumstances which make these attitudes appropriate. They say something about the context in which total commitment has developed. They have an assertive aspect in which claims are made about that which is taken as ultimate. The very centrality of these convictions in the life of an individual extends their reference to the conditions of human existence. Thus, the reference of religious language to a reality beyond the believer and his community cannot be explained away without making the religious attitudes, themselves, problematic. Even when the assertive aspect is not explicit, it needs to be taken into account. The importance of religious convictions implies some claim about the state of affairs in which fundamental commitments are made and sustained. The characteristic significance of the assertive aspect of religious language is made clear by Dorothy Emmet; "religion loses its nerve when it ceases to believe that it expresses in some way truth about our relation to a reality beyond ourselves which ultimately concerns us."[5]

A third characteristic of religious discourse is its highly symbolic use of language. Of course, all language is symbolic, but some discourse is much more dependent on a literal and direct understanding of symbols. Other uses of language involve analogy and more complex symbolism. Words are used to direct

4. William Hordern, *Speaking of God* (New York: The Macmillan Co., 1964), p. 104.
5. Dorothy M. Emmet, *The Nature of Metaphysical Thinking* (London: Macmillan & Co. Ltd., 1957), p. 4.

attention from the literal meaning to some component of experience which can be described only obliquely. In this sense, religious language requires a sophisticated use of symbol. As Ian Ramsey describes it: "Religious language is no set of labels for a group of hard, objective 'facts' glanced at by passive observers."[6]

Complex symbolism is required in religious language because of its combination of profoundly personal attitudes with claims about ultimate reality. Reference to either of these factors by themselves demands the use of metaphor and analogy. Personal feelings are always hard to express adequately, and literal expressions will not suffice. Poetic imagery is necessary to evoke an appreciation of attitudes and feelings. Assertions about ultimate reality must also use analogy. Terms are qualified and stretched in order to describe the most general aspects of experience. As religious language combines these two types of expression which already require complex symbolism, its mode of symbolization is still less "literal" and direct. The result is a kind of studied ambiguity and oddness in religious discourse. This ambiguity is not simply unintelligible, but only marks language used in a radically different way than other more straightforward usage. Religious discourse stretches language to its very limits. Therefore, the radical qualification of univocal symbols is one of its identifying characteristics.

Religious language can be characterized by these three basic features: it expresses man's ultimate convictions, it involves assertions about what is taken as ultimate, and it requires highly complex symbolism. Given these characteristics, then, how is it that such language is a problem? What are the crucial issues that must be faced by any constructive approach to religious discourse?

The problem involved in maintaining the cognitive significance of religious language is actually a set of related difficulties. The division and order used here is not intended to be definitive—only an appropriate framework for further discussion.

6. Ian T. Ramsey, *Religious Language* (London: SCM Press, 1957), p. 26.

A central problem involved in religious discourse is the metaphysical scope of its claims. In asserting that the conditions of existence warrant a particular religious response, this mode of discourse becomes intimately related to metaphysics. The two types of discourse involve similar difficulties when compared to statements that are more readily accepted as clearly meaningful and based on objective knowledge. Thus, an understanding of religious language is somehow wrapped up with the nature of metaphysical expressions.

Metaphysics is the philosophical discipline that seeks to describe the most general features of experience. Where the special sciences are concerned with a selected aspect of experience in which a limited type of facts and relationships can be considered, metaphysics attempts to discern and describe the generic characteristics of all experience; the traits which are implied in any more specialized mode of inquiry or interpretation. In this sense, whenever some relationship is assumed between a system of thought, or symbols, and a reality to which it refers, metaphysical claims and assumptions are involved. The factors with which metaphysics is concerned are the very ones which make thought effective and speech possibile. The generality of metaphysics reaches to the very limits of experience, and, therefore, this type of language is appropriately understood to refer to ultimate reality, insofar as this can be grasped from within the human perspective.

In attempting to understand and express the generic traits of the reality man experiences, metaphysics makes use of concepts drawn from more limited contexts. Metaphysical descriptions are constructed by extrapolating words from special fields—where their meanings have been stabilized—and applying them on the metaphysical level of generality. In this way, the meaning of terms is modified and expanded to give expression to the broadest dimensions of man's experience.

Because religious language is also concerned with the ultimate reality to which all systems of thought and expression must be related, it too has a metaphysical aspect. Religious language at least implies judgments that are universal. It

involves claims and assumptions that are of the same generality
as required by metaphysics. Religious language, however, is not
merely metaphysical discourse. It does not only articulate
illuminating descriptions of the very structure of human
existence, but it also expresses, fosters, and communicates attitudes toward ultimate reality. Without the assertive dimension, with its metaphysical implications, the attitudes which
are essential to religious conviction and expression seem to lose
their authenticity and power. Yet, religious expressions cannot
be reduced to metaphysics, either. They reflect an intimate,
personal, and affective response to the universe. They share in
the difficulties that affect metaphysical discourse, and any constructive interpretation of religious language will require a
concurrent clarification of metaphysical usage

There are those who argue against any connection between
religious claims and metaphysics. Often, they contend that
metaphysics is based on the mere human manipulation and
development of concepts, while religion has its roots in concrete encounter. The contrast is between human speculation
and an engagement with real factors effective in experience. It
parallels the mind-body distinction which has been so influential
in modern thought. As sense-perception provides data for
reflection, so faith claims its own kind of direct intuition. This
tends to isolate revelatory experience from all forms of human
inquiry and discovery. One consequence is that the interdependence of faith and metaphysics is excluded. Even the
generic implications of religious claims can be ignored in the
effort to maintain the privileged status of revelation or to
ensure the priority of divine initiative. Karl Barth has been the
primary influence in this regard, both by explicit statements
and by the overall thrust of his position. A similar opposition
between reason and revelation is evident, in varying degrees, in
many other modern thinkers. Metaphysical inquiry is understood as conflicting with the humility and openness required by
faith. Willem F. Zuurdeeg provides one illustration of this
point of view in his discussion of metaphysics in *An Analytical
Philosophy of Religion*. His identification of metaphysics with

describe reality, is it not necessary to qualify its meaning to the point where any other predicate would have worked as well? These are some of the questions that continue to be raised in regard to the metaphysical use of language. They persist even when metaphysics is seen as unavoidable, and they are at least effective in minimizing metaphysical claims. In other words, the problems inherent in wide-ranging generalization are more serious for the elaborate claims of theism than they are for a procedural metaphysics such as that involved in the concern for evidence and verifiability.

The problems inherent in metaphysical assertions can be seen in the theological context when attempts are made to describe the nature of God. Suppose it is asserted that God loves man. First, the reference of the term "God" to some kind of universal coordination may seem problematic. Second, the choice of predicates also raises serious questions. It is likely that someone will ask why "love" has been chosen to characterize this relationship, rather than "apathy" or even "hatred." Attention to all the facts available does not seem to give compelling support to the utilization of any of these terms. Are there, then, specific things that may be expected if God loves man? Indeed, is there anything that could possibly happen to falsify this assertion? If there is not, then there is evidently some truth in Antony Flew's conclusion that religious language is in danger of "death by a thousand qualifications."[9]

In these ways, the generality of metaphysical language and the level of abstraction required for assertions of such broad scope continue to plague those who would use either religious or metaphysical discourse in a serious way. This remains a pressing problem because it exposes the very nerve of these kinds of language. It challenges their ability to refer to ultimate reality in a meaningful and important manner. Unless one is willing to give up the assertive aspect of religious discourse by restricting it to the expression of subjective states, the meta-

9. Antony Flew, "Theology and Falsification," *New Essays in Philosophical Theology*, ed. by Antony Flew and Alasdair MacIntyre (London: SCM Press Ltd., 1955), p. 107.

physical question must be addressed as an important dimension of the problem of religious language.

A second major problem that faces religious discourse is the relation of religious assertions and empirical statements. It is, of course, an underlying consideration in the problem of metaphysics, but it is so fundamental as to warrant separate attention. This is a linguistic way of formulating the question of how man's sense-experience can be related to religious conviction. In what way does man's bodily perception of the external world provide data for the development of religious claims? Do religious assertions deal with empirical facts? Do they depend upon what is given in the experiences of particular objects, persons, and events? If religious language is seen as completely independent of man's normal powers of perception, then its significance is extremely difficult to comprehend, and the convictions which are expressed tend to fall far short of integrating the "whole" person. If religious assertions are "about the facts" and depend on sense-perception in some fashion, then it is just this kind of relationship that needs to be made clear. Any interpretation of religious language must clarify this relationship.

In the last analysis, it is the data that are available in concrete perception that decide this matter. In other words, what man's bodily experience is thought to offer for conceptual and linguistic development largely determines the kind of relationship that religious discourse can have to that data. If the data of perception are understood as discrete and separable impressions without any suggestion of pattern or connection, then religious discourse, or any language that expresses order and general characteristics, must find some basis other than perception. Unfortunately, these other sources of pattern and order are likely to be so dependent upon the power of the mind to create structure or impose it, that broad generalizations will continue to be suspect. If man's most dependable contact with this world is through his senses, then for religious language to be excluded from any direct relationship to their data seems to make this form of language secondary in importance and highly speculative in its content.

On the other hand, if perception itself should somehow be found to include structure and connections in its data, then assertions of various grades of generality could be developed on the basis of perception. On such grounds, some continuity could be found between detailed factual assertions and language which orders the facts in contexts of meaning. Perhaps even the integration of "all of life" in a religious frame of reference would be possible in a manner that would both derive from perception and illuminate it. In this important way, the understanding of the data of perception is an aspect of the problem of religious language. Any adequate interpretation of religious language must include the treatment and clarification of this issue.

Another problem involved in religious discourse is that of analogy. Again, analogy is implied in the discussion of metaphysics and perception, but it deserves direct consideration. Religious language speaks of God with the confidence that such words have important meaning. Yet, the difference between God and man is so great that these words seem too anthropomorphic to be about God, or so qualified as to be virtually empty expressions of agnosticism. Neither one of these options is in keeping with the convictions on which religion is based. Analogy suggests another alternative in which language is not used in a literal and straightforward way, but neither does it collapse into emptiness. It promises an option that lies between anthropomorphism and agnosticism in religious expression.

Analogy is dependent on a relation of similarity. In its root sense, it is a relationship of proportion in which two sets of different terms exemplify a common pattern or ratio. Used mathematically, analogy allows the precise determination of one unknown quality when the others in the proportion are given. This is not only the primary root meaning, but it is also the most accurate and dependable use of analogy.[10] It is really what Dorothy Emmet calls a "deductive analogy" because it depends on developing only the implications of what is already clearly

10. Emmet, *op. cit.*, p. 6.

given.[11] It suggests, however, more flexible and less precise forms of analogical reasoning in which similarity of structure or pattern enables us to understand characteristics and relationships that are initially vague and obscure in terms of those which are more directly accessible. At some point, the deductive development of implications gives way to the use of analogy to explore and illuminate that which is extremely complex, changing, and beyond exhaustive understanding. In this way, analogy is the basis for probable inference and induction. These modes of reasoning lack the certainty of mathematics, but they make up for this loss by their relevance to concrete data. Even the hypothetical method can be understood as an application of analogy—only in this case it is the pattern of coordination which must be established by imaginative projection and anticipated observations.

The analogical method always assumes that things which are similar in some respects are likely to have other similarities as well. Just as the method of difference is a procedure which enables us to distinguish between factors in experience, the method of analogy sets things in relationship on the basis of some similarity. It is usually understood that the analogy functions to interpret the complex and remote in terms of the simple and familiar. Even though both sides of the analogy must be "given" in some respects, a distinction is made between its familiar and accessible components and those which are to be determined or illuminated by the analogy. Thus, as either an argument or an illustration, analogy gives access through the well-known to that which is less adequately understood. For whatever reason, that which is difficult to grasp directly is clarified and interpreted by putting it in relationship with that which is more directly available.

Because analogy is based on similarity and continuity, it is always necessary to supplement analogies with the discerned differences so that what is analogous in some respects may be seen to retain its own character. This problem, notably, does

11. *Ibid.*, p. 8.

not arise with the mathematical proportion, because such an analogy does not deal with concrete factors having many facets and relationships—but only with the single, abstract feature of quantity. When analogies are used to illuminate and explore the world of concrete experience, they must be continually qualified so that emphasized similarities do not obscure important differences. They then take on a much more tentative, provisional, and partial character.

The linguistic application of analogy uses words that have a familiar and distinct meaning to describe those factors that are not readily expressed by using precise modes of classification and characterization. Either there is something here that has not been seen before, or it is desired that we grasp it in a new way. The contrast is between the literal and the analogical use of language. Words are said to be used literally when their meaning is straightforward or univocal. Their usage has been stabilized in a community so they mean just what they say, something definite and widely recognized. On the other hand, words are understood to be used analogically when they have a kind of dual reference, that is, they carry their accepted meaning but modify it in an oblique reference to that which is somehow similar and yet also decisively different. In this way, analogy is a means of linguistic approximation. It is mid-way between using words with conventional precision and using them in a completely arbitrary and confusing fashion. It is somewhere between univocal and equivocal expression. Its common implicit form is metaphor, but it is used in many ways to extend the reference of language beyond the distinct and the familiar. In the linguistic use of analogy, it is not the mathematical or deductive form of analogy that is the paradigm case, but some more adventuresome probe of concrete, progressive experience. Of course, the terms on both sides of the analogy must somehow be accessible, but they do not need to be completely accessible or simple for the analogies to function.

When analogy is applied to religious discourse, the problems involved in discerning the proper similarities are increased to their very limits. In order for analogy to function at all in this realm, there must be something in common between God and creation, between ultimate reality and finite reality. Yet, it is just this pattern of similarity that is difficult to establish in religious discourse. What does ultimate reality share with finite realities, which are man's intimate associates in everyday experience? Or, what has God in common with man that would justify our anthropomorphic descriptions of his nature and attributes? What similarity is given that enables us to use words that are literally applicable to creatures in order to speak of the mysterious creator?

The problem of analogy on the religious level raises questions about the very possibility of communication and intelligibility. Here it is one side of the analogy that seems to have all its terms as unknowns, and the relationship that is common to the two sides is just what is vague and obscure. It is a little like trying to work out a mathematical proportion when only one or two of the four numbers are given. We can set up the terms in the right relationships as far as the formula is concerned, but we cannot use the analogy to determine any of the unknowns. The analogy is drained of all meaning and power because the basis for the analogy is lacking. Or, consider probable reasoning of a statistical type. The similarity between the terms and their situations must be given at the outset, in order for them to be included as data in statistical calculations. Conclusions can be extended beyond their empirical base, just because such similarities are discernible. If the religious use of analogy is understood in the same fashion, it may well seem that the extension of language to God or ultimate reality requires such a speculative leap that the analogy is rendered useless. If the religious use of analogical predication is to be intelligible, God must be similar to man in some respects or the entire enterprise falters.

There is another aspect to the problem of religious use of analogical language that should be mentioned. If literal predication is understood as precise and direct, so that all analogical predication must be based on univocal elements, there is a clear tendency to evaluate analogical language as an inferior mode of discourse. The greater the dependence on analogy, the less important and the less dependable language seems to be. This difficulty affects religious language by making it one of the least significant and reliable forms of discourse. If precision and univocal simplicity are the norms for meaning, then religious language is in difficulty. The force of that difficulty is apparent in contemporary discussions of the cognitive status of religious assertions. When cognition is identified by literal predication and precise description of "facts" which are directly accessible, then religious language must be denied any cognitive significance, unless its literal basis can be indicated. This is a persistent problem for those who would use religious language in a serious manner. The nature of the religious convictions expressed seems to require not only a cognitive claim but, if anything, a claim held to be more significant than those which can be expressed literally.

The resolution of the problem of analogy seems to depend on some way in which univocal language can be used to bridge the gap between God and man. Some religious convictions, themselves, will not allow such a bridge, because for them, God is "wholly other" and completely beyond univocal description. An alternative point of view would have to show how it is possible to assert something about God in a definite way and still maintain the transcendence required by religious convictions.

Religious language has been described here with a strong emphasis on its assertive character. While the basis of religious discourse has been understood as the realm of personal convictions and interpersonal relationships, the language expressive of these factors has been seen to require an assertive element. Indeed, the problems noted thus far, in respect to religious language, have been directly related to the importance of propositional "content" in religious discourse. These problems could be minimized, if not entirely eliminated, by de-emphasizing the assertive aspect of religious language.

The relationship of the propositional factor to the intimately personal and intentional aspects of religious language is thus one of the central issues that must be faced. It is not enough to recognize that religious language functions to accomplish the purposes of the religiously committed and express their values. Religious language is obviously more than the assertion of propositions or the presentation of descriptions of the context of commitment. Exclamations, imperatives, prayers, liturgical formulae, initiation orders, hymns, and many other forms of religious usage cannot be reduced to statements about "the way things are." But can they function without implied assertions? It has been assumed in this discussion that they cannot. This is appropriate because such an assumption raises the peculiar problems of religious discourse in the sharpest and most direct manner. If, when faced in this way, the problems are not subject to illumination and clarification, then perhaps another definition of religious language will have to be adopted in which the assertive side is minimized or jettisoned. However, it is not clear that such a reduction will allow religious discourse to fulfill its distinctive functions in the life of the individual or society. The absence of the assertive aspect and the loss of emphasis on propositional content may cause religious language to lose its authenticity and power as the expression of total commitment and life-orientation.

The problem, here, is discovering a way in which the personal and performative aspects of religious discourse can be held together with the assertive and propositional. How can the values and decisions of the individual be expressed together with claims that are meant to be objective in content? The tension can be seen in the contrast between expressing personal commitment in the form "I believe in" and describing the content or object of faith in the statement "I believe that." The distinction is an easy one to make, but it is hard to maintain with consistency. In theological circles, this same distinction has been influential in developing the contrast between talking "to" God and talking "about" God, or the difference between immediate religious experience and propositions about that experience.

While there are surely important differences between "believing in" and "believing that," and many things one can do with language other than stating facts, this distinction raises problems of its own. For instance, one can admit that expressing belief in God, in the sense of trust and confidence, is quite different from asserting that God exists. Indeed, the proposition can evidently be accepted as true, without any personal commitment or trust in God. However, is it equally possible to express trust in God without accepting the assertion that there is a God in which to trust?

One is left with the difficulty of putting expressions of personal commitment and propositions in a common context of significance where they do not destroy or distort each other beyond all recognition. A stress on the propositional can mutilate the personal components so as to destroy their effectiveness for the practice of religious faith. As Dallas High has written in a recent attempt to stress the performative and personal side of religious expression: "When we focus upon statements, assertions, or the propositions about *what* we believe, we can overlook the world of persons and interrelations of persons . . . in which statements, assertions, or propositions about what we believe occur."[12] On the other hand, expressions of deep personal conviction are not well-served by isolating them from statements about "facts" and the conditions of "performance." "I baptize thee in the name of the Father, and of the Son, and of the Holy Ghost" may be a performative expression, but can it perform without a background of assertion?

Personal intentions, attitudes, and feelings can surely be distorted by an overemphasis on propositional content; the rules and "hard" data required for objective discourse can get in the way, but can these attitudes and intentions retain their serious and important meaning without some connection with more objective discourse? It seems that we cannot have one without the other, and the problem is then how to keep them together without destroying the personal or neglecting the propositional.

12. Dallas M. High, *Language, Persons, and Belief* (New York: Oxford University Press, 1967), p. 166.

At the root of this difficulty is a metaphysical question. What is the relation of persons and things, values and facts? Can they be distinguished and yet related in ways that preserve both differences and the continuity which human experience requires?

The linguistic forms of potential solutions to this problem hinge on the role of language in experience. Does our language shape and, in some respects, contribute to the very experience which it also expresses? Or, is language strictly the secondary and abstract formulation of an experience that is essentially outside the structure of language and its categories? Does linguistic expression illuminate or distort our fundamental experience? In the context of religious discourse, does the preaching and teaching of religious doctrines in some way elicit personal convictions? Or, is doctrine a secondary distillate of an experience that is immediate and fundamentally incompatible with linguistic formulation? Answers here reflect both religious and metaphysical commitments. Yet, it is just such answers which are decisive for the way in which religious language is understood and interpreted in respect to other forms of discourse. As the language which is expressive of man's capacity to recognize value, religious language must be set in some definite relationship to expressions about facts and conditions which allow the choice of values and their illuminating coordination in worship. What is at stake is not just the language of religion, but the importance and status of the religious dimension of man's life as it affects the individual, other areas of human inquiry, and the whole of human culture.

In the last few years, religious language has been considered from many different perspectives, with the intention of illuminating its special problems and its fundamental significance in the lives of men. In addition to issue-oriented discussions, various philosophical approaches to language have been used to criticize, clarify, and justify the religious use of language. In this context, it is worthwhile to consider an additional philosophical perspective in its bearing on the problem of religious language. The thought of Alfred North Whitehead has been relevant in other approaches to contemporary issues, and it could well make a significant contribution to the discussion of religious language. It will therefore be the aim of this study to explore Whitehead's philosophy in its special relevance to the understanding of religious discourse. Hopefully, such an exploration will also illuminate the nature of man's ultimate commitments and the character of the claims expressed in religious language.

Whitehead's philosophy, as a major contribution to process styles of thought, may also become more readily accessible through his theory of language than it has been by intricate elaboration of the details of his categorical system. If, as Dorothy Emmet has suggested, Whitehead's general approach is more significant than the conceptual scheme he develops, one should be able to grasp key features of Whitehead's thought by considering his treatment of language and its use in the service of faith.[13] One need not be exclusive in this respect—denying the importance of careful treatments of the intricacies of Whitehead's metaphysics—but it may be that there are resources in Whitehead's thought that are not directly dependent on a total command of his system. A process approach, if it is accessible in this way, could be of pragmatic value in the contemporary situation. It would be available to the many people who do not have the patience or inclination to master the details of a total metaphysical scheme. That is to say, the basic concepts and method can be useful, even though the whole system may be inaccessible or in need of detailed refinement.

It is easy to think that Whitehead's major contribution has little to do with the discussion of language. Against the rigorous linguistic investigations characteristic of much contemporary philosophy, Whitehead stands out as a major contributor to speculative metaphysics. He is known for his attempts to deal systematically with the generic features of experience, not for the careful and painstaking analysis of concrete statements.

While it is true that Whitehead was not a linguistic philos-

13. Dorothy M. Emmet, *Whitehead's Philosophy of Organism*, 2nd ed., (New York: St. Martin's Press, 1966), pp. xxxvi, 281.

opher—in the sense that he would consider language apart
from metaphysical issues—he was deeply interested in the
function of language. His philosophy is explicitly concerned
with the nature of language and its capacity to give expression
to the most general features of experience. His writings are
permeated with such discussions and, at certain crucial points,
his metaphysics is grounded in conclusions drawn from various
uses of language. As Wilbur Urban has pointed out, a "critique
of language constitutes in a sense a prolegomenon to his
metaphysics."[14]

Whitehead even has a significant historical relationship with
linguistic philosophy. In his early career, he was interested in
mathematics and logic. He collaborated with Bertrand Russell
in the massive and influential *Principia Mathematica.* In that
work, Whitehead and Russell were able to interpret the whole
of mathematics as a rigorous development of basic logical
assumptions. They thereby demonstrated in detail what other
thinkers had anticipated in less complete form, impressively
demonstrating the power of mathematical logic. This achievement encouraged the application of rigorous and innovative
logical techniques to the main questions of philosophy—
whether those questions were considered to be metaphysical
or merely linguistic.

Whitehead moved from his early interest in mathematics
and logic to a concern for the philosophy of science. In a day
when science was rapidly shifting its orientation, he found himself deeply involved in the philosophical and cultural implications of the transition from Newtonian mechanics to relativity
physics. Whitehead's interest and expertise in the history and
philosophy of science gave him special competence to deal with
issues involved in the relationship of science to other areas of
human concern. It was while dealing with the theories of contemporary science, that he began to develop many of the basic
notions that were to be useful in his later metaphysical effort.

14. Wilbur M. Urban, "Whitehead's Philosophy of Language and its Relation to
his Metaphysics," *The Philosophy of Alfred North Whitehead,* ed. by Paul
Arthur Schilpp (New York: Tudor Publishing Company, 1951), p. 304.

Whitehead's most interesting works, for the purpose of this study, are the products of his third, and last, period of intellectual achievement. In this period, he turned his full attention to the most inclusive interpretation of experience—metaphysics. Drawing on his rich background in mathematics and science, he sought to articulate a single conceptual scheme in which all of man's aesthetic, moral, and religious intuitions could also be included.

Some of the special characteristics of Whitehead's work suggest its potential for illuminating the problem of religious language. It is persistent in the attempt to keep science, religion, and philosophy in productive interaction as facets of human inquiry, which are mutually corrective and complimentary. It reflects a high regard for both the intuitions and the expressions of religion. It interprets value, emotion, and feeling as much more fundamental in the cognitive process than is usually recognized. The scope of Whitehead's mature philosophy, its direct attention to problems of language and its profound appreciation for both science and religion, are all factors which encourage the inclusion of his perspective in the discussion of religious language. Whitehead's own ability to use language about God even as he maintained a consistently high regard for the empirical data makes the exploration of the implications of his thought seem especially promising.

The thesis of this study, then, is that the mature philosophy of Alfred North Whitehead does provide a viable basis for understanding religious language, in the face of the challenge to its cognitive significance. The argument will take the form of a demonstration of the resources in Whitehead's thought which have direct bearing on the problem of religious discourse. It will be argued that this philosophy not only addresses itself to the crucial issues, but that in doing so it suggests a way of understanding these difficulties so that the cognitive significance of religious assertions can be affirmed without isolating the religious mode of cognition from the other aspects of man's experience and knowledge.

The procedure will be to begin with a general outline of

Whitehead's philosophy. Then four selected aspects of his thought will be considered. These will include his treatment of the relation of language and metaphysics, his understanding of the data of perception, his doctrine of symbolic reference, and, finally, his own explicit interpretation of religion and its modes of expression. It is intended that the cumulative exposition of these different aspects of Whitehead's thought will provide support for the general thesis, and illuminate the specific character of some constructive resources in Whitehead's thought which are available for the interpretation of religious language.

Such a use of multiple, expository perspectives in approaching Whitehead's philosophy is justified because it seems to be a method that is consistent with its subject matter. It is more in keeping with the organic character of Whitehead's philosophy than an attempt to proceed in a straight-line development. Nathaniel Lawrence's description of Whitehead's philosophy makes the need for cumulative perspectives evident.

> As opposed to a 'linear' exposition Whitehead's exhibition is more 'radial.' Whitehead spotlights the structure of thinking again and again, each time from a different angle. To read Whitehead is to be taken to a series of elevated lookouts and shown the main outlines of the same vista.[15]

Our purpose here will be to discover what Whitehead discerned in those perspectives which has relevance for the problem of religious discourse.

---

15. Nathaniel Lawrence, *Whitehead's Philosophical Development* (Berkeley: University of California Press, 1956), p. xx.

2

WHITEHEAD'S ORGANIC ALTERNATIVE

This chapter aims to introduce the philosophy of Alfred North Whitehead, giving special attention to his understanding of language. Whitehead's philosophy can be characterized by describing his method and his fundamental metaphysical hypothesis. Our description is not intended to do justice to details, but only to provide a starting point for further discussion.

Whitehead's method is empirical in a broad sense. Reflection must always begin with experience, but it is not assumed at the outset that man's encounter with his environment can only yield certain clear and distinct components. The object of philosophy is to be inclusive, treating experience as a potentially rich source of data. Nothing is to be excluded from experience in an arbitrary way, but, instead, inquiry is directed toward the discovery of the constituent components of experience and their relations.

As Whitehead sees it, experience includes much more than the definite deliverances of the five senses. It is not just a collection of discrete sense-experiences—sound here, colors there and pain within—but it is an amalgam of variegated factors integrated into a single occasion as a part of a continuous sequence, drawing from the past and advancing into the future. The goal of philosophy is to discern and describe as many components of this changing complex of data as possible. Philosophy must begin where all thought finds its resources— in man's immediate encounter with his environment.[1]

1. *PR*, p. 6.

Beginning with this empirical complex, Whitehead proceeds by descriptive generalization to discriminate fundamental factors and characterize patterns of coordination. He combines conceptual analysis and synthesis in a way that compares with the hypothetical method of science. For him, all thought is based on selection, projection, and evaluation. In sophisticated techniques, the steps become more explicit, refined, and developed. In this respect, the methods of science and philosophy are parallel, even though they function for different purposes and focus on different aspects of experience. Whitehead puts it clearly. "No systematic thought has made progress apart from some adequately general working hypothesis, adapted to its special topic. Such an hypothesis directs observation, and decides upon the mutual relevance of various types of evidence."[2]

For Whitehead, understanding always involves the notion of combination, and the analytic exploration of complex experience is the first step in philosophical method. This discrimination of component factors is combined with a synthetic interpretation which places them in meaningful patterns. Such synthesis takes the form of hypothetical projection and anticipates further confirmation. It can be directed toward the one-to-one correspondence of details or toward the discovery of wider and wider systems of coordination. Discriminated factors are not only important for what they are in themselves, but they also present potential clues to the modes of coordination in experience. Finally, they can be used to illuminate and explore the widest dimensions of reality in the search for metaphysical descriptions. However, on every level, analysis and synthesis function together as reciprocal modes of understanding.[3]

Metaphysics, then, is not sheer speculation or dogmatic prescription. It is a search for the most general factors and patterns in our experience. Moving from the occurrences of daily existence, or from man's corporate experience in special-

2. *AI*, p. 222.
3. *MT*, p. 63.

ized fields of inquiry, metaphysics utilizes illuminating notions from narrower contexts in an attempt to form a scheme of interpretation which includes "all the facts." It draws on productive ideas derived from limited modes of experience and extrapolates them for use as metaphysical models. Such a process is best described as discovery, and its method requires the appreciation of details as well as general principles. Whitehead compares it to the flight of an airplane. "It starts from the ground of particular observation; it makes a flight in the thin air of imaginative generalization; and it again lands for renewed observation rendered acute by rational interpretation."[4]

The various sciences are of special importance in this effort because their skill in producing potential models of coordination is highly developed. Ordinary experience is significant in a parallel manner because it is also productive of interpretive notions, and it gives needed balance to the specialized scientific emphasis. Whitehead utilizes both the technical knowledge of scientific inquiry and the practical wisdom of common sense. Even man's ethical, aesthetic, and religious intuitions are contributors to the philosophical scheme, both as interpreted data and as types of coordination.

While philosophy begins with selected areas of experience and with models chosen from these areas, its purpose is to "recover the totality obscured by the selection."[5] It is an attempt to see all of life as *one* world of experience. It seeks those principles which never fail to be exemplified in any experience whatsoever. It describes those generalities which "apply to all the details of practice."[6] Philosophy therefore accepts both the necessity and the risk of a task that includes the broadest possible dimensions. As far as Whitehead is concerned, to ignore metaphysical issues is merely to open the door for uncriticized assumptions of equally wide generality and potentially greater risk.

4. *PR*, p. 7.
5. *Ibid.*, p. 22.
6. *Ibid.*, p. 19.

Whitehead pursues the metaphysical task, intending to avoid both dogmatism and skepticism. A provisional, approximate approach to metaphysical descriptions is what is required—and all that is available. "Metaphysical categories are not dogmatic statements of the obvious; they are tentative formulations of the ultimate generalities."[7] Metaphysical generalization, as Whitehead undersands it, carries with it the risk and promise of inquiry which is imaginative, progressive, and yet never final. "It is an adventure in which even partial success has importance."[8] It should inspire the imagination of specialists, even as it gives them some protection against the narrowness of their own interests. Philosophy keeps all forms of selective analysis rooted in the concrete totality of experience.

Whitehead's use of the term "concrete" should be noted because it emphasizes the particular in its given relationships to an environment. The root meaning of "that which grows together" is decisive, rather than the focus on a single entity which is assumed to be independent of other factors. In respect to "concrete" experience, the term is used to indicate immediate participation with other actualities, not the abstract consideration of factors initially discerned in immediate experience. What is "concrete" is not an easily isolated particular, but the actual involvement in an intricate complex of relationships.

Whitehead's working hypothesis is indicated by the description—the philosophy of organism—which he frequently gives to his own system. This hypothesis attributes a kind of organic "life" and "experience" to all reality. Generalizing from the human psychological field and its dynamic combination of focus within a perspective, Whitehead conceives the ultimate realities as organisms characterized by affective experience. Such experience does not usually involve either consciousness or sense-perception. Whitehead calls the components of this experience "prehensions." They are the means whereby realities are related to one another in various degrees of inclusion and exclusion. In their positive role, prehensions are termed "feelings." These

7. *Ibid.*, p. 12.
8. *Ibid.*, p. 14.

inclusive prehensions give a definite shape to the experience and reality of the fundamental organisms.

By attributing some form of experience to all actualities, Whitehead asserts that the emergence (concrescence) of these ultimate realities is based on a selective activity analogous to purpose.[9] The final realities are events of selective integration in the very process of their origination. Whitehead calls these events "actual entities" and contends that all explanation must be rooted in them.

> 'Actual entities'—also termed 'actual occasions'—are the final real things of which the world is made up. There is no going behind actual entities to find anything more real. They differ among themselves: God is an actual entity, and so is the most trivial puff of existence in far-off empty space. But, though there are gradations of importance, and diversities of function, yet in the principles which actuality exemplifies all are on the same level. The final facts are, all alike, actual entities.[10]

God is the one actual entity that deserves special comment. God is not an occasion of experience emerging and perishing. God is the primordial entity that informs the entire process with a definite order of possibility. However, God is not merely a general structure of possibility but a reality which develops, in some respects, in interaction with all other actualities. Taking their achievements into his own reality, God gives an initial purpose (subjective aim) to each entity which is suited to its particular circumstances.[11]

The experience of actual entities involves both physical and mental dimensions. The fundamental realities are di-polar, manifesting the impress of efficient causality and some degree of novel origination. Physical feelings allow for the conformal transmission of pattern and energy which is associated with direct and coercive causality. Conceptual feelings, on the other hand, grasp possibilities that may be seized or dismissed. Phys-

9. *SMW*, p. 101.
10. *PR*, pp. 27–28.
11. *Ibid.*, pp. 521–524.

ical feelings approximate the actualities of the immediate past in an objectified form. Conceptual feelings focus on forms of definiteness which are initially discerned in physical circumstances, but which can be abstracted and considered as possibilities for attainment.[12] Depending on the sophistication of a particular organism—the development of its mental pole— the conceptual entertainment of these "pure potentials" (eternal objects) can contribute to various degrees of freedom and original achievement. By means of conceptual feelings, actual entities can seek a purpose that is strictly inherited, or they can modify that inheritance by some sort of comparison and decision. In this way, conceptual feelings are the instruments by which freedom develops in the organic process.[13]

In Whitehead's scheme, then, causal relations exist with the past in terms of physical prehensions, but such relations do not entirely determine the present. An actuality is tied to its inherited data as other actualities perish and contribute their objectified feelings for further synthesis. But how the emerging entity appropriates its data is not completely determined. The actuality is independent of its contemporaries and has, in principle, the freedom to contribute in some significant manner to its own character. Each actual entity is a unique synthesis of inherited data, informed by a peculiar perspective of interest and purpose. In the immediacy of its own experience, each entity is a novel creation. At the very least, it reflects a standpoint in the universe that is not exactly duplicated by any other entity.

By combining physical and mental activity in a pervasive type of affective experience, the organic hypothesis treats sophisticated special capabilities as emergent factors. Human reflection, consciousness, and sense-perception are all developments from patterns of activity that exist on more primitive

12. In all actual entities, except God, conceptual feelings are derived from physical feelings. God is the notable exception here because in this one case an actual entity functions from the outset with a fully developed conceptual pole. As the primordial entity, God envisions the entire structure of possibility and it is the physical pole, his actuality, which is in the process of development. See *PR*, pp. 522–524.

13. *PR*, pp. 366–369.

levels. A rudimentary conceptual activity pervades all reality so that no dualistic interpretation of the mind-body problem is necessary. As Whitehead describes it: "An occasion of experience which includes a human mentality is an extreme instance, at one end of the scale, of those happenings which constitute nature."[14] There is continuity in organic development, without excluding novel origination and sophisticated development.

What is of decisive importance in this organic hypothesis is the reciprocal influence of "whole" and "part." This, coupled with the asymmetrical progression from a determinate past toward a somewhat unpredictable future, gives to reality the character of pervasive interdependence and creative advance.

The reciprocity of organic coordination involves both individuality and corporate influence. Actual entities are affected by their environments, and they in turn influence those environments. Every organism reflects the context in which it arises, and every level of coordination is shaped by its constituent members. This is the case, whether the coordination is that of an animal body, an enduring object, a weather system or a cultural milieu. As Whitehead puts it, the "plan of the *whole* influences the very characters of the various subordinate organisms which enter into it."[15] Or, conversely, "In the full concrete connection of things, the characters of the things connected enter into the character of the connectivity which joins them."[16]

In this way, the organic hypothesis not only characterizes the ultimate individual realities, but also their participation in larger "wholes" which allow for corporate attainment, the maintenance of identity over different periods, and the sustenance of various grades of experience. Finally, the universe itself is conceived as the collective reality of actual entities in their hierarchical modes of coordination. Whitehead calls this macrocosmic process "transition," but it cannot be understood apart from the microscopic processes which contribute to it.

14. *AI*, p. 184.
15. *SMW*, p. 76.
16. *MT*, p. 81.

"The whole universe is the advancing assemblage of these processes."[17]

The inexorable progression from past to future in the emergence of actual entities allows for the combination of conformity and freedom, the mutual immanence and yet partial transcendence of the various factors. Reality has a living, creative character without loss of continuity.

Creativity is Whitehead's most general category, expressing the "notion that each event is a process issuing in novelty."[18] In respect to the past, there is at work a universal relativity demanding some conformity as each emerging entity takes all inherited factors into account.[19] But, since contemporary events are independent of each other, the actual future is not strictly determined by the past. The connection between the actual and the potential is made on the fine line between the past and the future. This allows unity and plurality, similarity and difference, conformity and freedom, all to be taken seriously.[20] "Each task of creation is a social effort, employing the whole universe. Each novel actuality is a new partner adding a new condition."[21] The individual processes (actual entities) have ontological and explanatory priority, but they combine in social modes of coordination to contribute to broader forms of process.

The creative advance thus combines stability and change in various modes of coordination. "Nothing ever really recurs in exact detail. No two days are identical, no two winters."[22] Yet, one can discern patterns that are stable enough to allow predic-

---

17. *AI*, p. 197.
18. *Ibid.*, p. 236.
19. *PR*, p. 33.
20. Charles Hartshorne has characterized the notion of asymmetrical advance as Whitehead's novel insight in its combination of internal and external relations, the one and the many. ("Whitehead's Novel Intuition," *Alfred North Whitehead: Essays on his Philosophy*, ed. by George L. Kline [Englewood Cliffs, N.J.: Prentice-Hall Inc., 1963], pp. 18–26). The universal relativity of determinate actualities is the expression of internal relations, arising out of an inherited past, and the emphasis on the novel appropriation of that past is the recognition of the importance of external relations. The process of development can combine both of these types of relations because it is asymmetrical. "Relationships to prior entities are internal to the given entity, but not conversely." See *PR*, p. 19.
21. *PR*, pp. 340–341.
22. *SMW*, p. 12.

tion and anticipation. Whitehead makes the point by contrasting the dependable rotation of the heavenly bodies and the unpredictable variations of the weather. "Men expected the sun to rise, but the wind bloweth where it listeth."[23] Understanding then requires the grasp of both stability and change. While the broad patterns allow for general predictions, details always tend to be somewhat surprising. Human knowledge is an attempt to ascertain the patterns of stability and their relative persistence. An appeal to further confirmation takes its place as a continuing aspect of all inquiry.

The consequence of this pervasive and creative interdependence is the relativity of all judgments. Distinctions can be drawn, but they are partially dependent on the purposes they serve, and are ultimately only approximations. This is not simply a retreat into obscurity and vagueness. Approximations are better or worse, and different puposes allow various degrees of useful precision. Organic interdependence allows pragmatic distinctions but qualifies their ultimate accuracy. Whitehead illustrates this point by reference to the human body. We have a sense of our own identity in contrast to the external world, but if we are "fussily exact, we cannot define where a body begins and where external nature ends."[24] In a similar way, the ultimate realities in Whitehead's metaphysical scheme have an overlapping character. Identities are real, but boundaries are difficult to ascertain with precision. On the most fundamental level of reality, actual entities are interdependent and constituted by their relationships to each other.

In this way, the organic hypothesis contributes to a view of inquiry that seeks precision, but never assumes the finality of its distinctions. Victor Lowe has noted that such an appreciation of the approximate character of human knowledge is a consistent strain that runs through all of Whitehead's thought. Lowe, describing Whitehead's approach, says that, "exactness should be pursued but never assumed, . . . humans ought to be aware of the roughness of their knowledge, consider what as-

23. *Ibid.*
24. *MT*, p. 30.

sumptions they are making, and advance by defining routes of approximation."[25]

The relativity involved in the organic hypothesis is foreshadowed in Whitehead's work on the foundations of geometry and science. Early in his career, he developed the method of extensive abstraction to deal with the nature of points, lines, planes, and volumes. This method allowed Whitehead to understand the precision of geometry and the spatial-temporal locations of physics as based on abstractive approximation toward an ideal limit. The point-instant is an important illustration. Using the method of extensive abstraction, Whitehead was able to interpret the point-instant as an abstract symbol for an event that retained an ineradicable extension and duration. By following the convergence properties of sets of abstractions, Whitehead concluded that such a precise symbol, in all its utility, had reference to an aspect of reality which could not be reduced to a corresponding simplicity.[26]

The emphasis on relative distinctions also involves Whitehead's knowledge of broad scientific theories. The "process" metaphysics that develops can be contrasted with philosophies of "substance" in the same way that contemporary physics reflects a shift away from Newton's "matter in motion."

Whitehead rejects the notion of substance as fundamental for metaphysical description. Substance, as the unchanging substratum of accidents or change, is what Whitehead calls "vacuous actuality" or actuality devoid of experience. "It is fundamental to the metaphysical doctrine of the philosophy of organism," Whitehead says that the "notion of an actual entity as the unchanging subject of change is completely abandoned."[27] In the place of substance, the organic model gives to actual entities the universal capacity for some grade of experience or subjective immediacy. Organic relationships become

25. Victor Lowe, *Understanding Whitehead* (Baltimore: The Johns Hopkins Press, 1966), p. 247.
26. For an account of the method see *CN*, pp. 74–98. For criticism of the method see W. Mays, *The Philosophy of Whitehead* (New York: Collier Books, 1962), pp. 115–125.
27. *PR*, p. 43.

decisive in place of independent substances. This shift qualifies all attempts to achieve complete precision.

The impetus for the rejection of vacuous actuality comes, in part, from the radical transformation of modern science, which took place from Newton to Einstein. Whitehead describes the change in this way: "This change of view, occupying four centuries, may be characterized as the transition from Space and Matter as fundamental notions to Process conceived as a complex of activity with internal relations between its various factors."[28] Rather than bits of matter moving in empty space with external relations decisive, modern science has adopted a view of reality in which energy fields and mutual influence are the crucial features. "The notion of empty space, the mere vehicle of spatial interconnections, has been eliminated from recent science. The whole spatial universe is a field of force, or in other words, a field of incessant activity."[29]

Whitehead seeks to translate this modern view into the metaphysics of the philosophy of organism. The world is understood as a complex of functional activity. Everything is constituted by its activity in relation to other actualities. Individuality is the result of a unique synthesis of other actualities.[30]

Whitehead draws on his familiarity with the microscopic events of physics to describe the very fundamental transmission of energy and patterns between actual entities. Such minute flashes of energetic interaction are similar to organisms in their dependence on historic routes of development—their continual interaction with their immediate environment, and their exhibition of a focus of identity within a field of influence. They can also be compared with the fundamental features of an occasion of human experience in which interest combines with given data to grasp the environment in a particular manner. Here Whitehead discerns an important analogy between the physical transmission of energy and the shape of human experience.

28. *MT*, p. 198.
29. *Ibid.*, p. 186.
30. *Sym*, p. 26.

There is thus an analogy between the transference of energy from particular occasion to particular occasion in physical nature and the transference of affective tone, with its emotional energy, from one occasion to another in any human personality. The object-to-subject structure of human experience is reproduced in physical nature by this vector relation of particular to particular.[31]

It is this analogy which is the basis for Whitehead's metaphysical generalization of affective experience.

Man's experience provides a useful metaphysical model because of its familiarity and our inability to apprehend anything apart from it. It can be considered as an organic event in which the polar interplay between focus and context reflects the organic mode of coordination. Each occasion of human experience can be viewed as a selective activity which resembles the "life" of lower organisms and the interchange of energy involved in the events of microphysics. Whitehead's most general description of this interplay treats it in terms of the interdependence of fact and value. These are ultimate notions in the organic hypothesis which are involved in every occasion of experience—and thus in every reality. The very grasp of facts is informed by a sense of importance.[32] For Whitehead, every reality experiences value, even if such value is only a kind of physical feeling—"the sheer final enjoyment of being definitely something."[33] Depending on the development of the conceptual pole, organisms also involve value in their appetition toward potential forms of definiteness which are relevant to their circumstances. Thus value, for Whitehead, is identified with limitation, either actual or potential. On every level of reality, the aim of the creative advance is toward the realization of value in that "species and to that extent which in that instance is possible."[34] The value that each entity has for itself gives it identity in a world of many actualities, but it also binds it into one universe in which many levels of value

31. *AI*, p. 188.
32. *MT*, p. 5.
33. *FR*, p. 31.
34. *MT*, p. 16.

are ordered. The key to this pervasive influence of value is the role of interest and selectivity in the occasions of human experience.

The organic hypothesis, then, combines the energetic activity of electromagnetic events, the life-styles of organisms and the polarity of man's occasions of experience into a metaphysical model. It suggests an underlying continuity of emotion, interaction, and interdependence which can only be expressed in approximate and provisional ways. It allows for novelty as the creative advance moves from the endowment of the past toward a future that has yet to be determined. The dominant notion is that of affective experience, arising out of the settled past and anticipating future realization.

This entire philosophical scheme is bound up with a view of the nature and function of language. For Whitehead, language plays a complex role in man's experience, manifesting the organic interaction and progressive development which characterizes all of reality. It is a powerful instrument utilized by man in his attempts to deal constructively with his environment. It is a tool which can be used to promote novel and creative responses to given circumstances. At the same time, its given structures provide a veritable storehouse of common human experience.[35] In both of these aspects, language exerts a profound influence on the development of man. It is not merely a tool at man's disposal or a repository of cumulative experience on which he may choose to draw, but it is a factor that makes its own impact on those who utilize it, and its given structures contribute to the general basis of all reflection and expression. A similar duality of role is evident in the relation of language to metaphysics. Linguistic capabilities determine the limits of metaphysical description at the same time that language is a primary source of data for metaphysical consideration. Language is both instrument and source of data, contributing directly to the shape and scope of metaphysical description. On every level, man's use of language reflects a relationship of interdependence and mutual contribution.

35. *PR*, pp. 7, 16.

Organic progression and reciprocity are as effective on this cultural level as they are in the order of nature.

A high estimate of the importance of language is evident in all of Whitehead's later works. It is the most important tool available to man; so central that Whitehead describes the souls of men as the "gift from language to mankind."[36] Language is the primary means of recall, comparison, and communication.[37] Serving both the society and the individual, language makes possible the partial sharing of experience as well as the intimate rhetorical conversation, which is such a large part of personal reflection.[38] The social exchange of ideas is dependent on language, along with the possibility of corporate criticism and action. At the same time, language contributes to the individual's sense of identity. By its capacity to give emphasis to both ideas and emotions, language welds communities together, but it also reinforces the identities of the individual members of those communities. Uniting people around a "common treasure," language also provides the articulated memory which is necessary for the individual's reflection and expression.[39] In all of this, language increases the effectiveness of thought, contributing to civilization even as its own structures are the product of civilization.[40]

The power of language lies in its capacity to call attention to selected factors in experience. It frees men to deal with their circumstances in such definite ways that alternatives can be considered, compared, criticized, and evaluated in the light of a specific purpose. Thus, language makes a creative and corporate response to shifting circumstances an effective option. By means of language, men are "released from complete bondage to the immediacies of mood and circumstance."[41] Symbolizing important factors within experience, language enables men

36. *MT*, p. 57.
37. *SP*, p. 134.
38. *MT*, p. 46.
39. *Sym*, p. 68.
40. *MT*, p. 49.
41. *Ibid.*, pp. 49–50.

to move beyond instinctive practices to reflective prediction and action. In this way, it accelerates processes of change and accomodation.

> The symbolic expression of instinctive forces drags them out into the open: it differentiates them and delineates them. There is then opportunity for reason to effect, with comparative speed, what otherwise must be left to the slow operation of the centuries amid ruin and reconstruction.[42]

Selectivity is the key here. The very essence of language is its capacity to give repeated emphasis to assigned empirical components. The handy and flexible elements of experience are used to symbolize other factors relevant to particular purposes, which are not easily accessible or so readily manipulated. By progressive development in an historic community, these symbols become relatively stable and dependable instruments for thought and expression.

Whitehead considers these linguistic forms as abstract because, by themselves, they do not indicate their connection with a concrete perspective, purpose, or process. They are components of experience which have been wrenched from their initial setting and put forward, as though their characteristics were independent of that context of relationships and the personal centers of experience involved. The factors symbolized are also abstract, because, in their identification with certain words, they too are treated as though they were independent of their contextual relationships. The symbolization of language thus reflects a selective process in which certain factors are emphasized while others are ignored. Words call attention to entities, factors, patterns, and relationships which are of special interest in a particular perspective. At the same time, they diminish the apparent relevance of those empirical factors which are not mentioned.[43]

As a technique for representation, language can take very different forms and communicate widely divergent meanings,

---

42. *Sym*, p. 69.   43. *MT*, pp. 48, 53.

depending on the perspectives that inform its development and use. Radically different interests and types of abstraction can be given linguistic expression. For example, language can give emphasis to edible objects that are necessary for man's immediate physical well-being, or it can focus on relationships of wide generality, such as those symbolized in algebra and mathematics. Language is not simply given, but it is a method that reflects the purposes and position of those who use it. It is a technique whereby man increases his ability to cope with the intricacies of his environment by selective emphasis and exclusion. It is eminently effective because it allows the articulation of both determinate features in a particular situation and the possibilities which may be relevant to many situations.

As the process of selectivity underlying the utility of language, abstraction is a simplifying procedure. It is a process which transforms the dynamic complexity of immediate experience into a set of definite factors in a perspective of interest. In this respect, in the semantic relationship of linguistic forms to the concrete components of experience symbolized, language is also a simplifying technique. It excludes consideration of some factors in order to focus more readily and effectively on others. Language, like all other abstractions, "involves emphasis, and emphasis vivifies experience, for good or for evil."[44] It selects and eliminates, enhances and neglects, emphasizes and excludes. By doing so, it enables man to stabilize the concrete flux of experience so that he can deal with clear-cut entities which have definite relationships and distinct characteristics. If the abstractions on which our language is based are well-founded, and if they are not pressed beyond the purposes which inform their own emphases, they do contribute an effective means for dealing with the environment.[45]

Abstraction signifies both the result of an activity and the activity itself. Charles Hartshorne's description makes plain both the type of activity involved and the kind of result that can be expected. "The abstract is what can be considered while

44. SP, p. 120.
45. SMW, p. 58.

various other things are omitted from consideration. The abstract is what can be abstracted, detached in thought and, at least potentially, in actuality, from various relationships or contexts, and yet in this detachment still be the identical entity."[46] Whitehead's point is that such abstraction always excludes some aspects of the entity's character in the process of wrenching it from its organic relationships. Thus, language both emphasizes and excludes, simplifying concrete experience so that it can be handled more easily. While Whitehead does not use the word "simplify" with respect to language, he does use it in regard to other forms of abstraction, so that it is appropriate to speak of language, in his scheme, as an initially simplifying technique.

The kind of simplification that is involved here is best illustrated by Whitehead's category of "transmutation."[47] Transmutation is the activity whereby irrelevant differences are disregarded in favor of the grasp of dominant similarities. "Transmutation is the way in which the actual world is felt as a community, and is so felt in virtue of its prevalent order. For it arises by reason of the analogies between the various members of the prehended nexus, and eliminates their differences."[48] The appearances given by our senses thus present a simplified edition of reality, informed by the needs and interests of our species.[49] In a similar way, sophisticated techniques are also "happy simplifications" which allow us to focus on factors that are relevant to some specific purpose.[50] The recognition of this simplification is especially important on the level of language and thought, because Whitehead sees the great danger here as "over-simplification."[51]

Whitehead is concerned lest the process of selectivity be ignored in the appreciation of the utility of the symbols them-

46. Charles Hartshorne, *The Divine Relativity* (New Haven: Yale Univ. Press, 1948), pp. 67–68.
47. *AT*, p. 213.
48. *PR*, p. 383.
49. *AI*, pp. 261–263.
50. *Ibid.*, p. 221.
51. *Ibid.*, p. 23.

selves. It is at this point that language, because of its very effectiveness, can contribute to a dangerous over-simplification of concrete experience. The symbols can be treated as perfectly definite in their own right, without any reference to the abstractive process in which they have been developed. Consequently, language is understood in separation from the diversity of purposes and perspectives which affect its meaning. In a similar fashion, a single unit of expression may be taken as meaningful, without reference to the wider context of experience. That is to say, it may be assumed that complete abstraction is a possibility, so that abstract factors can be considered apart from any reference to the process of abstraction, or without regard for the totality of relationships from which they have been drawn. Whitehead's philosophy denies the possibility of separating any definite factors from the influence of purpose and interest. It claims that complete abstraction is impossible, so that any abstract factor must ultimately be referred to the organic context in which it arises.

Whitehead's point is that, insofar as language is explicit, it does call attention to some factors, at the expense of others, and this selection ties whatever symbols that result into the context of concrete experience and relationships. What is not mentioned in the ordinary uses of language is the network of coordination which, in Whitehead's organic philosophy, contributes to the character of each entity.[52] Some of these relationships are so general that they can be taken for granted. Others are irrelevant to some special purpose. But the consequences can be quite misleading, if we assume that what words make explicit is the self-sufficient locus of meaning. Whitehead describes a characteristic and common linguistic exclusion in this way: "We habitually speak of stones, and planets, and animals, as though each individual thing could exist, even for a passing moment, in separation from an environment which is in truth a necessary factor in its own nature."[53] Or, to use another illustration, Whitehead's contrast between the word

52. *MT*, p. 77.
53. *AI*, p. 154.

"forest" and an actual forest makes evident the exclusion required by language and its practical advantages.

> We can say the word 'forest' whenever we like; but only under certain conditions can we directly experience an existent forest. To procure such an experience usually involves a problem of transportation only possible on our holidays.[54]

The easily reproduced word leaves out such systematic relationships as geographical location. As a special abstraction, it omits any explicit reference to environmental conditions.[55] As a consequence, the interests involved in the identification of an actual forest and the context necessary for the existence of an actual forest may be forgotten in the emphasis on the apparently independent and definite word.

To say that language simplifies concrete experience is, patently, only one side of the matter. Whitehead also recognizes that language adds to the complexity of experience and makes possible sophisticated syntheses, which are progressive and expansive in character. Once symbols have been established, they are added to the host of factors that constitute human experience. They allow for such flexibility of combination and subtlety of expression that their complicating power must also be taken into account. Whitehead only wants to make sure that we recognize the abstraction involved in the development of language. Once he has made that point, he is quick to indicate that the results of such an abstractive procedure are contributed as potential components for more sophisticated developments. The word that has been assigned a meaning in one perspective is added to the multitude of diverse factors available for further integration in other perspectives. Language forms are thus both the results of selective derivation and data for further development. The utility of linguistic symbols is a rhythmic phenomenon in which careful definition gives way to the qualifications required by different situations of concrete application.

Whitehead's understanding of language parallels his descrip-

54. *PR*, p. 277.   55. *MT*, p. 77.

tion of other factors involved in the creative advance. Given Whitehead's own assertion of the importance of linguistic evidence *for* the metaphysical task, it would seem fair to view his generic characterization of reality in terms of creativity as at least partially dependent on the way language functions. Conversely, then, the asymmetrical advance from a determinate past into a future with real novelty can be used to illuminate the nature of language. "The many become one and are increased by one" is a fundamental insight that has relevance for language, as well as for the rest of experience.[56] Linguistic symbols are based on the integration of a complex of disparate factors in a perspective of interest. Then the definite symbols developed are offered for further synthesis in other perspectives which involve some deviation of interest or point of view. This is, of course, not only a process in which single words are important, but it also characterizes total language systems as progressive social creations.

The definiteness attained by corporate agreement as to the importance of certain types of abstraction is modified and qualified as the language is applied in concrete circumstances. Each language thus manifests both stable systematic features and a "growing edge" of development. It has an evolutionary character which corresponds to the context of varying perspectives in which it is used. There are perspectives in which meanings are established and learned; perspectives in which symbolic formulations are used with specific intentions, general expectations as to the perspectives in which these expressions will be interpreted, and the somewhat unpredictable perspectives in which the symbols are actually understood. A variation in perspective is insured by the historic character of experience, and that variation reduces the definite significance of every linguistic form. The perspectives are as decisive, in Whitehead's view, as the symbols themselves. The meaning of linguistic symbols is not to be separated from the concrete process of interaction in which both a perspective of interest and definite symbols are involved.

56. *PR*, p. 32.

Because of its dependence on an evolutionary context, language never escapes a certain vagueness and indeterminacy. "There is not a sentence, or a word, with a meaning which is independent of the circumstances under which it is uttered."[57] It is the conditions of concrete relevance that the symbols do not make explicit. Language functions by providing a definite syntax and vocabulary, but it also requires the recognition that these symbols are applied in situations which are dynamic and value-laden. What is given explicit expression always requires qualification by factors which are firmly enmeshed in concrete relationships. Abstraction, as the basis of linguistic precision, involves the selection of these factors for emphasis. It can never complete because it is founded on a point of view which ultimately implies a reference to the totality of experience, including those things that have been relegated to the dim background by some prevailing interest.

Language is not an altogether definite means of expression and communication because of its abstractive distance from concrete experience and the multiplication of factors which must always be correlated in its use. Because of this, Whitehead questions the widespread attitude that linguistic statements can give exact expression to propositions.[58] "The vagueness of verbal statements is such that the same form of words is taken to represent a whole set of allied propositions of various grades of abstractness."[59] Which proposition is intended must be indicated by contextual factors which are not explicit in the sentence. The meaning of a particular expression is affected by such things as the intention of the speaker, or the imaginative capabilities and mood of the listener. A variety of emotional factors are directly involved in the development of the symbols themselves. One of the reasons why linguistic expressions cannot be taken as completely definite is that they function in the dynamic interaction of individuals who feel, as well as think. The meaning of their words is not to be discov-

57. *SP*, p. 103.
58. *PR*, p. viii.
59. *Ibid.*, p. 294.

ered simply by concentrating on grammar or on dictionary definitions. Whitehead describes the emotional factors involved in linguistic expression in these words:

> No verbal sentence merely enunciates a proposition. It always includes some incitement for the production of an assigned psychological attitude in the prehension of the proposition indicated. In other words, it endeavors to fix the subjective form which clothes the feeling of the proposition as a datum. There may be an incitement to believe, or to doubt, or to enjoy, or to obey[60]

Propositions, themselves, are understood by Whitehead as being less independent of concrete experience and emotion than is often thought. For him, a proposition is a factor relating an actual entity or nexus of entities to some definite possibility. It is an effective aspect of reality before it is conceptualized or expressed in language. In their concrete relationship of the actual and the potential, propositions exert a powerful emotional influence before they are reduced by radical abstraction to precise intellectual content. Whitehead resists the tendency to identify the proposition with either conceptual or linguistic formulations. He sees the primary function of propositions as "lures for feeling" for they are directly involved in concrete experience, with all its complex relationships. They allow the powerful emotional contrast of the actual and the possible. Here it is not the question of their truth or falsity that is primary, but rather the interest they can generate. Propositions are either true or false as they reflect possibilities exemplified in actuality or those excluded by determinate actualities. Whitehead, however, insists that their interest is of more significance than whether they are true or false. "In the real world it is more important that a proposition be interesting than that it be true."[61] Even the untrue propositions which reflect what might have been realized are powerful in eliciting emotion. It is the contrast of true and false propositions on an emotional and physical level that Whitehead understands as the basis for consciousness, and of the more sophisticated intellectual develop-

60. *AI*, p. 243.   61. *PR*, pp. 395–396.

ment that is established upon it. Therefore, propositions are not "primarily for belief, but for feeling at the physical level of unconsciousness."[62] It is not only language that is abstract and indefinite in its expression of propositions, but thought is also abstract and potentially misleading.

The function of language thus goes beyond the mere expression of ideas. "It is a mistake to think of words as primarily the vehicle of thoughts.[63] A more fundamental function of words is their excitement of feeling, which enhances the relevance of certain factors in our experience. Language has a power and influence that far exceeds its "intellectual content." "Words and phrases carry with them an enveloping suggestiveness and an emotional efficacy."[64] The meaning of a linguistic expression is not only the thought conveyed, but the emotions transmitted. This indicates, again, that the meaning of language cannot be separated from its roots in a concrete situation. It is just such a separation that Whitehead sees as leading to bifurcations of thought and experience, reason and emotion, fact and value. Therefore, Whitehead maintains that language, itself, makes evident the impossibility of such radical separation. Definite thoughts, meanings, and expressions cannot be separated from their grounding in physical and emotional interaction with the environment. Both the symbols used and the meanings intended must be factors in experience, rather than merely thoughts considered apart from experiential connections.

The most important aspect of language, then, is its capacity to elicit the deep feelings and emotions of concrete experience. Words do not merely call to mind abstract concepts for entertainment, they make certain experiences possible. They focus attention on accessible empirical factors that transcend the symbols. As Whitehead describes the spoken word: "Speech consists of noises, or visible shapes, which elicit an experience of things other than themselves."[65] Language functions to enhance the relevance of selected factors in experience. These

62. *Ibid.*, pp. 283–284.   64. *Sym*, p. 67.
63. *Ibid.*, p. 277.   65. *AI*, p. 224.

factors are not primarily intellectual notions, but they carry with them the emotional power of concrete and living connections with our total experience.

Whitehead uses the relationship between language, thought, and experience to illustrate the progressive abstraction involved in linguistic expression. With respect to thought, language can give only partial and truncated expression to the ideas man entertains.[66] This is made evident by the continuing struggle that is required in order for us to express ourselves. As Whitehead sees it, linguistic formulations of that which is entertained in thought must always be treated as partial and provisional.[67] Language is not coterminous with thought because it always leaves out important contextual and dynamic factors that are involved in the intellectual process, and which defy precise expression in definite linguistic forms.[68] Language does not limit our thoughts, but it does limit their expression, and it requires the recognition of non-linguistic factors for its own interpretation. This is why Whitehead is concerned with the over-simplification uncritical acceptance of linguistic precision promotes. "Language cloaks the most profound ideas under its simplest words."[69] By doing so, it excludes subtleties of thought and elusive connections between thought and physical experience. It presents our thoughts in a truncated form.

Whitehead also sees the relationship of thought and concrete experience as one of initial simplification. He describes mentality as an "agent of simplification" which allows man to increase his grasp of selected factors in experience.[70] Thought excludes environmental and emotional factors, which are important constituents of experience. Language carries such abstraction even further as the most effective means available for the expression of thought, but we always know more than we are able to say, and experience more than we can analyze.[71]

---

66. *MT*, p. 49.
67. *Ibid.*
68. *Ibid.*, pp. 48–50.
69. *RM*, p. 75.
70. *AI*, p. 213.
71. *SP*, p. 129 and MT, p. 121.

Thought, like language, adds its own complexity to experience even as it is initially based on abstraction. Whitehead recognizes an interplay between thought and experience that eludes precise analysis, and which will not allow a sharp demarcation between the mental and physical aspects of experience.[72] This lies behind his claim that all reality combines mental activity and physical relationships in polar interaction. The more sophisticated forms of conceptual activity emerge from primitive and rudimentary patterns of activity which pervade reality.

Not only is linguistic expression limited in respect to thought and experience, but the progressive development of language toward precise abstraction and highly general formulations increases the exclusiveness involved. This adds to the ever-present danger that a onesided view of reality may be taken as self-sufficient or exhaustive.

> The abstraction, inherent in the development of language, has its dangers. It leads away from the realities of the immediate world. Apart from a balanced emphasis, it ends in the triviality of quick-witted people.[73]

The contrast between spoken and written language is used by Whitehead to indicate how the increased abstraction, made possible by language, can be the cause of difficulty. The development of written language reflects the progressive exclusion of contextual factors which are always required for the interpretation of the written word.

Speech, as the original form of language, has a history that parallels that of humanity itself. Its written counterpart is a comparatively recent development. Like the steam engine, written language is "important, modern, and artificial."[74] The primary significance of speech is its use of symbols that indicate, by the very means of their presentation, important physical and emotional connections with concrete circumstances. Speech

72. *Sym*, pp. 19–20.
73. *MT*, p. 55.
74. *Ibid.*, p. 51.

maintains the organic connection between explicit detail and context, which is so important for definite communication. In its dependence on the production of sound, speech makes the environment an obviously important factor for consideration. Its demonstrative indications are thus more direct, and the perspectives for expression and interpretation are more readily correlated. As Whitehead understands it, speech is even more effective than signals and gestures in its capacity to give expression to the fundamental relationships on which definite meaning depends.

> Hands and arms constitute the more unnecessary parts of the body. We can do without them. They do not excite the intimacies of bodily existence. Whereas in the production of sound, the lungs and throat are brought into play. So that in speech, while a super-ficial, manageable expression is diffused, yet the sense of the vague intimacies of organic existence is also excited. Thus voice-produced sound is a natural symbol for the deep experiences of organic existence.[75]

Speech does better at indicating those factors in the environment which are to be the subjects of assertions. Such factors are indicated, not simply by the expression of ideas, but by a sense of importance which arouses feeling and emotion.[76] The demonstrative elements of a sentence do this by singling out those factors in experience which have special relevance for the particular linguistic expression. In this way, language is provided with contextual points of reference required for its interpretation. But these demonstrative elements are only par-tially effective. It is not enough to focus on the contextual factors which are explicitly indicated, but the circumstances which are taken for granted by the linguistic formulation must also be taken into account. Thus, Whitehead finds that "lan-guage is always elliptical, and depends for its meaning upon the circumstances of its publication."[77] Ultimately, all of its component symbols function demonstratively, appealing for a

75. *Ibid.*, p. 45.
76. *PR*, p. 403.
77. *Ibid.*, p. 397.

leap of imagination in order to understand its meaning in relation to a particular set of circumstances.[78]

Written language is designed to reduce the dependence of linguistic expression on a specific set of circumstances. By moving to higher and higher levels of abstraction, the powerful emotional and physical factors which accompany the spoken word are minimized. This increase in abstraction gives to language a flexibility and pragmatic sufficiency which comes from the "abstraction of its meanings from the presupposition of any particular environment."[79] The contrast between spoken and written expressions makes the extent of the abstraction involved in written language plain.

Spoken language is immersed in the immediacy of social intercourse. Written language lies hidden in a volume, to be opened and read at diverse times and in diverse places, in abstraction from insistent surroundings.[80]

Formal language, such as mathematics, algebra, and logic, carries the abstractive process further with special emphasis on broad, general features, which are largely taken for granted by other forms of language. Finally, Whitehead describes the language of algebra and logic as reducing the particulars of concrete experience to the "ghost-like character of the real variable."[81]

The importance of such formal language is its capacity for dealing with the connective patterns in experience. It inverts the abstractive emphasis of ordinary language. Instead of assuming a context of patterned connection in an emphasis on discriminated detail, formal language systematically neglects the particular character of factors in order to give explicit emphasis to patterns of wide generality. Whitehead is noted for his especially high regard for the usefulness of algebra and symbolic logic. Beyond their proven pragmatic value, these

78. *Ibid.*, p. 69, cf., *MT*, *p.* 20.
79. *MT*, p. 53.
80. *Ibid.*, p. 55.
81. *SP*, p. 138.

forms of language make plain the abstract character of all languages by giving emphasis to factors in experience which other languages neglect. In this sense, he understands algebraic method as the "greatest discovery for the partial remedy of defective language."[82] It is only a partial remedy because it, too, is a mode of abstraction and requires balance and qualification by other forms of emphasis.[83]

It is in this context that Whitehead's high expectations, in respect to the application of symbolic logic to problems of aesthetics, ethics, and theology, should be understood.[84] While symbolic logic may have a needed contribution to make in many areas of experience, it will continue to be a corrective mode of emphasis. The focus on patterns which can be disengaged from any particular set of circumstances will always be qualified by the reference of this mode of abstraction to the vague totality from which it has been derived. In this sense, the language of high-level abstraction can provide important correctives, but they cannot, by themselves, provide an exhaustive or final expression of experience.

The development of formal language can suggest that complete abstraction or generalization is a possibility. Whitehead, on occasion, gives explicit support to such a view. In *Science and the Modern World,* for instance, he describes mathematics as "complete abstraction from any particular instance of what it is talking about."[85] However, in other instances he asserts that complete abstraction is out of the question. Since his philosophy is based on the claim that "no entity can be conceived in complete abstraction from the system of the universe," it is proper to interpret his view as allowing for radical abstraction, which only approaches complete abstraction asymptotically.[86] This qualification would also seem to allow for the

82. *Ibid.*, p. 136.
83. *Ibid.*, p. 137.
84. *Ibid.*, p. 140.
85. *SMW*, p .27.
86. *PR*, p. 5.

corrective balancing of the abstractive formulations of symbolic logic in whatever field they are found effective.[87]

We have now explored the general outline of Whitehead's philosophy, including some features of his approach to language. It is an organic interpretation of reality in which living relationships are given precedence. Such interaction is evident in a reciprocal influence between man and his symbols. Words are tools that men use, but men are also affected by their use— their own and their predecessors. Language manifests in its own fabric the asymmetrical progression and rhythmic integration of organic reality. It is an instrument for dealing freely with present realities, at the same time as its stabilized forms contribute to the very environment in which decisions are made. It is both a *product* of experience and in the *process* of continuing development. This is a dialectical tension that is characteristic of the organic hypothesis. Becoming takes precedence over being, but never in such a way as to deny the significance of definite, emerging factors. With these general considerations in view, we can now give more specific attention to Whitehead's treatment of the relationship between language and metaphysics.

87. *SP*, p. 140.

3

LANGUAGE AND
METAPHYSICS

Whitehead's understanding of the role of abstraction in linguistic expression establishes an intimate relationship between all language and metaphysics. In his view, no expression has a completely definite meaning because of contextual considerations which, at some point, verge on the metaphysical. Any serious attempt to clarify the meaning of linguistic expressions thus requires a willingness to broach problems of broad generality.

Since metaphysical descriptions, themselves, must be articulated by means of language, Whitehead contends that such second-order expressions must make explicit their own qualifications by utilizing revised and carefully reinterpreted language forms. Only in this way can metaphysics express the evolutionary and expansive context which is involved in all linguistic expression.

The dependence of all linguistic meaning on metaphysical assumptions does not suggest that a full-blown metaphysical system must be developed before words and sentences can function. It does imply, however, that when words and sentences are used, certain types of relationships are assumed—like independent subjects—which require critical qualification, if they are not to be taken as ultimate characteristics of experience. Not every one who speaks is a metaphysician, in a technical sense, but the very use of language requires general assumptions about the nature of language and reality.

In most circumstances, such as those in which the spoken word prevails, generic assumptions are taken for granted because of physical proximity, shared interests, and common traditions. Whitehead's point is that when these spoken words are taken out of context, written down for posterity, and put forward as definite formulations of certain states of affairs, they require the articulation of a broader context so that their meaning may be clear and yet properly qualified. He therefore contends that all linguistic meaning requires some reference to a context of assumptions, which is finally described as metaphysical. Apart from some attempt to deal with such broad relationships, Whitehead understands all language as thoroughly indeterminate.[1] He agrees with Bertrand Russell in his claim that "complete metaphysical agnosticism is not compatible with the maintenance of linguistic propositions."[2]

If the metaphysical implications of language are consistently ignored, then Whitehead finds that the distinctions which are given explicit expression tend to assume metaphysical status by default. This can be seen most readily when the entire metaphysical enterprise is overtly rejected as meaningless, impossible, or unimportant. What this amounts to is the acceptance of the current language forms as our best clue to inclusive experience. Then the assumptions which have informed the language in the pursuit of specialized purposes will function as an implicit and uncriticized metaphysics.

This problem is evident in Whitehead's treatment of what many modern philosophers have called "ordinary language." Whitehead has a very high regard for this mode of expression. It enshrines a kind of cumulative common sense, and is extremely useful for many purposes. Properly understood, it is even an important source of evidence for metaphysics, but, taken in its common forms, with a focus on the apparent precision of expression, this type of language is not an indication of our best metaphysical intuitions. It was not developed

1. *PR*, p. 18.
2. Bertrand Russell, *An Inquiry into Meaning and Truth* (London: George Allen & Unwin, Ltd., 1940), p. 347.

for this purpose, but it was intended to serve in contexts where the broad features of experience could be taken for granted in the pursuit of limited interests. Of course, ordinary language gives some demonstrative indication of context, but its explicit forms do not need to indicate their own qualifications or partial character. There are non-linguistic factors which fulfill these tasks and establish a sufficiently exact meaning. In fact, as Whitehead understands it, it is precisely the generic and persistent features of experience that ordinary language is *not* designed to express. "Language has been evolved to express 'clearly and distinctly' the accidental aspect of accidental factors."[3] If such linguistic forms are allowed to assume metaphysical status by default, our most fundamental experience is inverted, and reality is understood on the basis of abstract and easily manipulated factors. As Whitehead has described it: "The essence of language is that it utilizes those elements in experience most easily abstracted for conscious entertainment, and most easily reproduced in experience."[4]

Whitehead's point is that apart from metaphysical description and criticism, the power and apparent precision of our language can deceive us. Ordinary language can lead us to interpret the fundamental character of reality in a manner that is not supported by our most concrete experience. Just those features of experience that are variable and contingent are given ontological precedence, without regard for the very continuities that allow us to discern changes in the first place.

Since the common forms of language do not readily provide expression for the more fundamental and persistent aspects of experience, Whitehead contends that the clarification of meaning by metaphysical inquiry requires the revision of these language forms. Other forms of available language also require revision, even the fundamental categories of the philosophical tradition. On many levels, language may enshrine metaphysical assumptions which are not warranted by our most dependable and inclusive experience. The explicit expressions of philos-

3. *SP*, p. 131.
4. *MT*, p. 48.

ophy are affected by changes in the climate of thought and experience, so that even metaphysical formulations that were adequate in their own context require revision, qualification, and reinterpretation. The literature of philosophy is inadequate for contemporary metaphysical description not because of a divergent purpose, but because of a change in context which requires a modification of formulation. Nevertheless, Whitehead also claims that many traditional philosophical approaches were in error. The mistake of the earlier philosophers was often just that they did not recognize the inadequacy of the given language as the key to metaphysics.

Language must be revised for metaphysical purposes because this is the only way connections with concrete experience and the one-sided character of linguistic forms can be brought to our attention. It is the task of metaphysics to express the relationship of relatively stable, and apparently definite, language forms to an evolutionary and interdependent context of experience. If this relationship is not to be distorted by the assumption that it reflects a precise and symmetrical correspondence between words and their referents, the language forms must be modified so that they point beyond themselves as provisional and approximate descriptions. The forms of language, which are only one factor in the linguistic situation, are not adequate just as they stand to give expression to their own relationship with concrete experience. "Thus philosophy redesigns language in the same way that, in a physical science, pre-existing appliances are redesigned."[5]

Whitehead's revision of language, for metaphysical purposes, takes two forms: one is the qualification of existing terms; and the other is the development of neologisms.

The first type of revision is illustrated by Whitehead's careful modification of the subject-object structure of experience. We ordinarily think and speak of subjects and objects as though they were totally independent of each other. Whitehead finds it necessary, for metaphysical purposes, to qualify that independence. By using the Quaker term "concern" he is able to

5. *PR*, p. 16.

express the interdependence and interaction that pertains between subject and object in concrete experience. It is the "concern" of the subject for the object that places the object as a component in the subject's experience with an "affective tone drawn from this object and directed towards it."[6] In this way, Whitehead expresses a dynamic give-and-take relationship, which qualifies the use of the terms, subject and object.

One neologism Whitehead develops is the term "subject-superject." This term indicates that a concrete reality is both what it is for-itself, in its own experience, and what it is as it contributes objective data for the experience of other actualities. In order to make both aspects of its reality evident, a new term is required that qualifies the common distinction between an experiencing subject and an object, merely given in experience. This need for the revision of language is illustrated by Whitehead when he refers to the significance of the decline and fall of the Roman Empire. While it is a fact that the Roman Empire perished, it also continues to influence the course of events in subsequent history. The Empire which perished continues as a stubborn factor in the universe. Things are affected *now* by the character of the Roman Empire *then*. In its fall, the Roman Empire has assumed a "new function in the process of generation."[7] The problem for metaphysics is how to describe both aspects of its existence. Whitehead cites Plato's difficulty with a similar notion, and refers to his statement in the *Sophist* that non-being is a form of being "at once an extreme instance of the breakdown of language, and the enunciation of a profound metaphysical truth."[8] The complexity of concrete experience requires continuing revision of language to express its subtleties adequately.

It is in this respect that Whitehead speaks of the weakness of language as a philosophical tool. "The great difficulty of philosophy is the failure of language."[9] The weakness is not

6. *AI*, p. 176.
7. *Ibid.*, p. 291.
8. *Ibid.*, p. 222.
9. *MT*, p. 67.

merely due to the present size of our vocabulary, or the state of syntactical development. It resides in man's tendency to take the explicitly expressed as the self-sufficient and final context of meaning. In this way, the apparent precision of language is a barrier to philosophical reflection. The usefully assumed exactness of language is an obstacle that obscures the fundamentally complex and dynamic character of experience. Language must be revised for metaphysical purposes, and any language resists revision.

The evolutionary context of meaning should make evident the need for such revision. The context in which man must articulate his descriptions of reality is never exactly duplicated. This suggests that while revision of the language is required to make the progressive character of experience evident, such revision can never be complete. If language is to make explicit, in its own forms, the evolutionary character of experience, those forms, themselves, must be in the process of continuous development. Based on the stabilizations of abstraction, all of our language, including that used for metaphysics, must be considered approximate and provisional.

There is one obvious problem here that should be faced, even if it cannot be entirely resolved. How are Whitehead's own formulations to be evaluated? Are they merely tentative and approximate? How about the very statements that indicate the provisional character of metaphysical descriptions? While there is the perennial danger of circularity at this point, Whitehead protects himself by claiming that the insights are valid but the formulations may need to be revised. Surely he is putting forward his own metaphysical scheme as expressive of sound insights into the nature of experience. Since those insights are purported to illuminate the most general and stable features of experience, they have a kind of dependability and permanence that does not have to be attributed to the formulations in which they are expressed. The formulations have to be revised because the concrete circumstances change. Knowledge changes. Experience penetrates further. Novel developments take place. These changes in the context of interpretation will mean that metaphysical descriptions cannot be put down once and for all. Their provisional character does not preclude their being more or less adequate; better or worse approximations of the generic features of experience.

Thus, while Whitehead insists that the development of metaphysical descriptions is necessary for increased clarification of linguistic expression, he does not suggest that metaphysics can ever escape the elliptical and one-sided character of language itself.

> Deficiencies of language stand in the way inexorably. Words and phrases must be stretched toward a generality foreign to their ordinary usage; and however such elements of language be stabilized as technicalities, they remain metaphors mutely appealing for an imaginative leap.[10]

On these grounds, any sentence or word is less precise in meaning than is often assumed. For the accuracy of the individual expression is dependent on the metaphysical commitments which inform its use. Those commitments may be vague and unrecognized, but they are implicit in the necessary reference of every abstraction to the totality of the universe. So, Whitehead can claim, "Language is thoroughly indeterminate, by reason of the fact that every occurrence presupposes some systematic type of environment."[11] The apparently precise indication of details always takes place in the polar and progressive interplay between focus and perspective. This dialectic limits the final accuracy of all explicit formulations.

Progress in understanding context and detail must then go hand-in-hand. The context determines the relevance of details, and the detail is a "weapon" for the further penetration and elaboration of the context. One does not begin, as is so often assumed, with completely dependable and precise statements about independent factors, and then proceed to ask questions about the mystery of the universe. The statements about the details are dependent on assumptions about the general char-

10. *PR*, p. 6.
11. *Ibid.*, p. 18.

acter of the universe, just as broad generalizations require a basis in discriminated factors and characteristics. There is thus a continuous interaction between the general and the particular aspects of experience in all knowledge and expression. Complete precision and dogmatic finality of expression are precluded by this persistent and pervasive tension. Human language is a multifaceted probe of experience which must, itself, be stretched and modified to give expression to those "flashes of insight beyond meanings already stabilized in etymology and grammar."[12] It is one purpose of metaphysics to make evident this provisional and progressive character of all language. By basing the definiteness of linguistic meaning on metaphysical generalizations, Whitehead calls attention to the evolutionary aspect of language, on all levels. Not only philosophy, but also literature and the special sciences are engaged in "finding linguistic expressions for meanings as yet unexpressed."[13] Thus, all language is in the process of development in which precision is sought but can never be assumed. "A precise language must await a completed metaphysical knowledge."[14]

It is the function of philosophy to keep this concern for correction and revision in touch with all man's specialized modes of inquiry and expression. While the urge toward abstract analysis is natural, necessary, and highly useful, philosophy reflects a corrective impetus which maintains an interest in inclusive experience. The concern for meaningful "wholes" Whitehead calls "rationalization," and he understands it as developing from the aesthetic impulse. It seeks the "essential connection within the apparent isolation of abstracted details."[15] It is limited to data that are available for conscious emphasis, but it is not limited to those factors that virtually leap into focus of attention. It inverts the abstractive process by corecting narrow forms of emphasis by their combination and comparison. In its fully developed stage, when all man's

12. *AI*, p. 227.
13. *Ibid.*, p. 227.
14. *PR*, p. 18.
15. *MT*, p. 170.

abstractions are taken into account, rationalization becomes metaphysics, the constructive criticism of limited forms of emphasis and expression in the broadest possible context.

> Philosophy is the critic of abstractions. Its function is the double one, first of harmonizing them by assigning to them their relative status as abstractions, and secondly of completing them by direct comparison with more concrete intuitions of the universe, and thereby promoting the formation of more complete schemes of thought.[16]

This dual function of philosophy can be seen in Whitehead's approach to language. It allows for the recognition of the power of language to deceive on the metaphysical level, at the same time as it permits language, properly understood, to function as a primary clue to the nature of concrete experience. On the one hand, Whitehead criticizes the failure to discern the abstract character of linguistic forms, and on the other hand, he sees these same forms, when kept in dynamic contact with the evolutionary context of extralinguistic reality, as fundamental evidence for the metaphysical enterprise.

The power of language to deceive is rooted in the same process of abstraction which gives language its high degree of utility. The very effectiveness of abstract language forms can lead to what Whitehead has called the "fallacy of misplaced concreteness." "This fallacy consists in neglecting the degree of abstraction involved when an actual entity is considered merely so far as it exemplifies certain categories of thought."[17] Such an error is not simply relevant to language, but language itself is one area of human experience in which it occurs. At the same time, it is Whitehead's view that the prevailing language forms tend to promote this fallacy by suggesting a greater precision and finality of expression than is, in fact, possible.

Whitehead criticizes linguistic "misplaced concreteness" on at least three levels. It takes place when particular words are understood to have a precise reference to independent entities.

16. *SMW*, p. 83.
17. *PR*, p. 11.

It is evident when single statements are taken by themselves as having a completely definite meaning. It occurs in an even more subtle way when it is assumed that the given structure and fundamental categories of a language system are the limits of thought or expression.

The problem of the precise reference of linguistic terms is clarified by noting Whitehead's primary example of the fallacy of misplaced concreteness, the doctrine of "simple location." This doctrine, as he understands it, dominated the development of Newtonian physics, and has also influenced many other areas of thought. Simple location is the notion that a body can be located precisely in space and time, without reference to other regions of space-time.[18] Because of its usefulness, this notion, which assumes the essential independence of entities, has tended to be treated as an ultimate description of concrete experience. Whitehead claims that, while simple location is obviously extremely useful for many purposes, it does not reflect man's most penetrating grasp of reality.

Only one mode of the occupancy of space is allowed for—namely, this bit of matter occupying this region at this durationless instant. This occupation of space is the final real fact, without reference to any other instant, or to any other piece of matter, or to any other region of space.[19]

Whitehead understands the misuse of the doctrine of simple location as promoted by the subject-predicate emphasis of our language, and the underlying sharp distinctions that inform Aristotelian logic. It leads to an inordinate emphasis on discrete factors in experience. As units of expression can be treated separately, so it is assumed that reality reflects similarly sharp distinctions.

Single words, each with its dictionary meanings, and single sentences, each bounded by full stops, suggest the possibility of complete abstraction from any environment. Thus the problem of

18. *SMW*, p. 51.
19. *MT*, p. 199.

philosophy is apt to be conceived as the understanding of the interconnections of things, each understandable, apart from reference to anything else.[20]

The treatment of such abstract factors as the final components of experience involves "misplaced" confidence in a particular mode of abstract expression. It becomes an implicit metaphysics which excludes organic connection and value from a fundamental role in experience. It is thus the source of so-called "scientific-materialism" and the ensuing dilemma between fact and value.

Whitehead pursues the criticism of linguistic expression by affirming the abstract character of the subject-predicate forms of language and by rejecting the precise reference of linguistic forms to extralinguistic realities. While expressions based on such sharp distinctions are extremely useful for many purposes, they are not the most adequate expression of concrete experience in its dynamic and pulsating continuity. It is a dangeous mistake to take the distinctions made explicit in language and treat them as ultimate. "We are left with the deceptive identity of the repeated word."[21]

A similar problem is involved when confidence in the independent meaning of a single statement is assumed. In this case, "misplaced concreteness" is attributed to a single expression as the carrier of a definite meaning. Whitehead calls this the "dogmatic fallacy" because of its arbitrary dismissal of inherent relations of interdependence and dynamic interaction. "The error consists in the persuasion that we are capable of producing notions which are adequately defined in respect to the complexity of relationship required for their illustration in the real world."[22] This fallacy takes place so easily, in many disciplines, that statements which are not intended to be metaphysical in scope are readily elevated to that status and effectively removed from critical analysis. Whitehead's concern is that the importance and usefulness of certain insights should

20. *Ibid.*, p. 90.   22. *AI*, p. 145.
21. *SP*, p. 136.

not be attributed to the exactness and finality of their formulation. To give ultimate weight to an explicit expression in any area of discourse is to turn a potentially helpful instrument into a dogmatic error. Whitehead is not opposed to the formulation of dogma, but to the uncritical elevation of formulations of limited validity to metaphysical status. Such dogmatic errors are widely recognized in the realm of religious conviction. Whitehead's concern is to indicate that the same type of errors are made in almost every discipline. Indeed, it is his judgment that scientific dogmas have been especially influential in modern culture in a manner that promotes over-confidence in their precision and finality. Insofar as they express important insights, such formulations are valid and useful but they do not and cannot stand alone as ultimate norms for experience and its interpretation. For Whitehead, "The important point is the way in which opinions are held, and the weight attached to particular modes of statement."[23]

When the entire language system is considered, Whitehead finds the deceptive influence of language even more subtle. If language, as it is given, is understood as adequate for the expression of any experience, Whitehead sees a misplaced confidence in the general structure of language, which is not warranted by concrete experience. In other words, the language structure itself, rather than a single word or statement, can be the occasion for the fallacy of misplaced concreteness. On this level, Whitehead speaks of the "fallacy of the perfect dictionary" to refer to the mistaken notion that language is adequate, as given, to express our most penetrating insights. The presupposition involved in this errror is that man has at hand all the fundamental notions and words that are required to express any element in his experience. Such a view of language suggests a deterministic and static view of the universe. Instead of the structure of language being involved in evolutionary development, it is conceived as reflecting the underlying basis for all experience and expression. The limits of experience

23. *Ibid.*, p. 106.

and expression are identified with what can be said. Whitehead understands this as the error which has led to the radical split between the critical and speculative schools of philosophy.

> The critical school confines itself to verbal analysis within the limits of the dictionary. The speculative school appeals to direct insight, and endeavours to indicate its meanings by further appeal to situations which promote such specific insights. It then enlarges the dictionary.[24]

In these ways, the apparent definiteness of linguistic forms contributes to a deceptive misinterpretation of the level of abstraction involved in words, sentences, and entire linguistic systems. It is a danger that is relevant to all kinds of expression and every type of specialized abstraction. It can affect the fundamental understanding of religious wisdom, scientific knowledge, educational procedures, and the moral or legal codes of society. Many of Whitehead's specific cultural criticisms can be understood as systematic attempts to correct this deceptive influence of language.

Whitehead's understanding of value as an intrinsic factor in all experience—in contrast to scientific materialism—is a primary example of his concern to correct the deceptive power of apparently precise expressions. The success of modern science in its emphasis on "bare" facts had promoted an implicit metaphysics, which excluded values. Linguistic formulations, in their scientific precision, were instrumental in establishing this materialistic point of view. Values were allowed to play a role in human life, but they were cut off from their reference to empirical data because facts could be described in an apparently definite way, without reference to value. Whitehead sees the correction of this error as partially dependent upon the proper understanding of language and its intimate connection with selective activity.

The development of relativity physics suggested that the materialistic hypothesis was based on scientific abstractions of

24. *MT*, p. 236.

a limited nature. Yet, the influence of scientific materialism remained, even after discoveries had indicated the limitations of a Newtonian understanding of matter in motion. The language, itself, enshrined notions which were easily interpreted in materialistic fashion. Whitehead attempted to call attention to the exclusive character of Newtonian scientific abstractions and thereby undercut the linguistic emphasis on bare facts with no reference to values. Basing his approach on the discoveries of relativity physics, Whitehead proposed an organic basis for understanding science, in which values could be seen as influential in the apprehension and interaction of physical realities. In this way, he attempted to call attention to the deceptive character of linguistic forms.[25]

Whitehead also sees language forms functioning deceptively in contexts where values receive the focus of attention. Religious expressions, for example, are susceptible to misinterpretation because of man's tendency to overemphasize that which is given explicit expression. In this sense, the acceptance of religious formulations as self-sufficient, precise, and final, works havoc because it turns expressions of penetrating insight into dead formulae which distort the very intuitions they were designed to express. Whitehead recognizes that the formulations are important, and that they may be extremely helpful; but if they are taken by themselves, they are merely "froth on the surface," and they can become stultifying and misleading. Religious formulations may be more or less adequate in a particular situation. They may be more or less stable in their capacity to elicit insight in a wide variety of circumstances. They are not self-authenticating or final. This is why Whitehead remarks: "Religions commit suicide when they find their inspirations in their dogmas. The inspiration of religion lies in the history of religion."[26]

Education, as one of the major areas of Whitehead's cultural interest, provides another important example of the dangerous results of too much confidence in the explicit distinctions of

25. *SMW*, p. 142.
26. *RM*, p. 138.

language. When distinctive modes of abstraction and expression are taken with too much confidence, they lead to a rigid compartmentalization of knowledge and narrow conceptions of its transmission. Learning becomes the isolated appropriation of information and methodology. Such pursuits are precise just because of their insulation from each other. The sense of creative discovery in a unified process of interaction is traded for the conventional manipulation of abstractions. Whitehead's interpretation of the power of language to deceive makes the definite modes of expression contributing factors in this distortion of the educational process. He is not opposed to pursuing narrow emphases, but he does contend that such considerations, and their definite results, should not be given ultimate status. Attitudes toward the distinctions that are made explicit in language require careful criticism or they contribute to cultural developments which impede progress. Whitehead's comments about the dangers involved in university education illustrate some of the consequences of misplaced confidence in language forms, as they affect this dimension of culture.

> Unless we are careful, we shall conventionalize knowledge. Our literary criticism will suppress initiative. Our historical criticism will conventionalize our ideas of the springs of human conduct. Our scientific systems will suppress all understanding of the ways of the universe which fall outside their abstractions. Our modes of testing ability will exclude all the youth whose ways of thought lie outside our conventions of learning. In such ways the universities, with their scheme of orthodoxies, will stifle the progress of the race, unless by some fortunate stirring of humanity they are in time remodeled or swept away.[27]

The effect of misunderstood linguistic forms is even clearer in Whitehead's critique of moral codes. If these are taken as completely definite and final, they are accepted as principles which apply in any situation, regardless of mitigating circumstances or changes in the interpretation of underlying concepts. Whitehead sees no problem with the codification of moral insight, but he sees real difficulty in the view that such formula-

27. *SP*, p. 33.

tions can be applied without a good measure of common sense. The insights expressed cannot be too closely tied to the explicit form of their expression. Moral codifications are "useful, and indeed essential, for civilization. But we only weaken their influence by exaggerating their status."[28] They must be construed as abstract expressions which depend on their relationship to concrete circumstances for productive utilization. This may well mean reformulation and re-interpretation in terms of the new context. The meaning of terms shifts as circumstances change, so that the codifications cannot be applied without a continuous appeal to supplementary intuitions.[29] If moral codes are taken in a dogmatic way, they become barriers to moral progress. "The result is that the world is shocked, or amused, by the sight of saintly old people hindering in the name of morality the removal of obvious brutalities from a legal system."[30]

By this type of criticism in a metaphysical context, Whitehead attempts to put linguistic expressions, and the special interests which inform them, in their proper relative position with respect to concrete experience. The potentially deceptive character of language is recognized by elucidating components of experience which transcend the language forms.

Whitehead also utilizes a broad range of linguistic evidence in the development of his own metaphysical scheme. When language is understood as one contributing factor in a context which transcends its explicit forms, then language is a primary source of metaphysical insight, a productive clue to the nature of reality. When experience, in its most inclusive dimensions, is the subject of inquiry, man's use of language is an illuminating source of evidence. "The main sources of evidence respecting this width of human experience are language, social institutions, and action, including thereby the fusion of the three which is language interpreting action and social institutions."[31]

When Whitehead uses language as evidence for metaphysical descriptions, his primary concern is that limited types of discourse or selected components of expression not be given exclu-

28. *MT*, p. 19.
29. *Ibid.*, pp. 290–291.
30. *AI*, p. 290.
31. *Ibid.*, p. 226.

sive attention. His interest is in inclusive experience, and only as language is treated in *all* of its aspects can it be expected to provide a guide for metaphysical interpretation. Whitehead suggests three basic levels on which linguistic evidence must be sought. "Language delivers its evidence in three chapters, one on the meaning of words, another on the meanings enshrined in grammatical forms, and the third on meanings beyond individual words and beyond grammatical forms, meanings miraculously revealed in great literature."[32] His criticism of those who have utilized language as evidence in metaphysical inquiry centers on those who have limited themselves to one or two of these chapters, and even pursued narrow emphases on a single level. All three must be considered, and in no case can their content be limited to those expressions which are easy to handle and apparently precise in their reference. The need for inclusiveness is of special importance with respect to the language of literature. This has been an easy chapter to ignore, but Whitehead feels that it is of special importance in the evaluation of linguistic evidence. Its primary virtue is that it makes the fragmentary and evolutionary character of language evident.

It is here that Whitehead's interest in the language of poetry is important. Given the success of scientific modes of abstraction, such literary expressions have often been taken as superfluous in the quest for understanding man's concrete experience. Whitehead, however, finds in poetic expressions powerful insights which make evident the abstract and partial character of the scientific mode of emphasis, undercutting the materialistic and mechanistic interpretations of ultimate reality derived from it. For instance, Wordsworth's phrase, "We murder to dissect," is used by Whitehead to support his citicism of scientific absorption in limited modes of abstraction.[33] The poet's insight is that important aspects of concrete experience have eluded the scientific net. Whitehead thus utilizes the poetic expression of experience to correct the scientific exclusion of values. Such

32. *Ibid.*, p. 226.
33. *SMW*, p. 79.

poetic language gives evidence of values which transcend the precision of our formulations. As Whitehead describes it: "Remembering the poetic rendering of our concrete experience, we see at once that the element of value, of being valuable, of having value, of being an end in itself, of being something which is for its own sake, must not be omitted in any account of an event as the most concrete actual something."[34]

In a similar way, language drawn from religious literature is useful in the metaphysical task. Whitehead's own use of the words of the well-known hymn, "Abide with me, fast falls the eventide," to articulate the fundamental problem of metaphysics is an illustration of the importance of religious expressions as evidence for metaphysics.[35] Whitehead sees the exclusion of just this kind of literary evidence as one of the reasons for the dilemmas of modern philosophy.

> The best rendering of integral experience, expressing its general form divested of irrelevant details, is often to be found in the utterances of religious aspiration. One of the reasons of the thinness of so much modern metaphysics is its neglect of this wealth of expression of ultimate feeling.[36]

It is not just the language of literature that Whitehead finds indicating factors in experience which transcend and qualify the definite language forms. All language, for example, bears persuasive witness to the impact of purpose, anticipation and value on its own utility. The symbols are derived and stabilized in a perspective of interest. They are used with particular intentions in mind. They are interpreted in the light of another person's sense of relative importance. Of course, if attention is strictly limited to the forms themselves, such extralinguistic factors are not likely to be noticed. But, if language is understood in relation to concrete experience as it actually develops and is utilized, the evidence of the influence of purpose and value is highly significant. Whitehead puts it this way:

34. *Ibid.*, p. 89.
35. *PR*, p. 318.
36. *Ibid.*, p. 318.

The conduct of human affairs is entirely dominated by our recognition of foresight determining purpose, and purpose issuing in conduct. Almost every sentence we utter and every judgment we form, presuppose our unfailing experience of this element in life. The evidence is so overwhelming, the belief so unquestioning, the evidence of language so decisive that it is difficult to know where to begin in demonstrating it.[37]

For Whitehead, language not only gives evidence of purposes that transcend its definite forms, but it also bears witness to the relatively stable aspects of experience, which can be referred to repeatedly. The effective use of language is evidence for the reality of factors which transcend, not only the linguistic forms, but also the single occasion of experience. These factors have a reality which is relatively stable, and can therefore provide the identities which are the basis for knowledge and prediction. Whitehead recognizes the dependence of effective language on the practical identities which can be discerned, symbolized, and expressed on different occasions. Language depends upon abstraction, but the factors emphasized have a reality that is not exhausted by the particular occasion of experience and expression. This suggests that while our abstractions are partial and one-sided, they do give us an authentic grasp of the factors that constitute our environment. In spite of their selective origins and partial character, abstractions can be expected to be useful in their illumination of a real world beyond the apparent limits of experience.[38]

> To speak of the same thing twice is to demonstrate that the being of that thing is independent of either singular act of speech. . . . If we cannot speak of the same thing twice, knowledge vanishes taking philosophy with it. Thus, since speech can be repeated, things spoken of have a determined being in abstraction from the occasion of experience which includes that act of speech.[39]

One of the most important identities which language assumes is that of the person who expresses himself in linguistic forms. Whitehead claims that language gives evidence for the per-

37. *FR*, p. 13.
38. *AI*, pp. 223–224.
39. *Ibid*., p. 224.

sistent reality of the factors expressed, and also for the individual who refers to those factors. Both kinds of identity have been somewhat problematic in modern philosophy. Whitehead contends that the use of language assumes such identities and thus gives persuasive evidence for their contribution to our concrete experience.

Whitehead describes the evidence of language for personal identity as decisive. "We cannot dismiss Personal Identity without dismissing the whole of human thought as expressed in every language."[40] More concretely, he takes a single word and shows how it implies the persistent identity of the one who uses it. When a word of many syllables such as the term "overwhelming" is used, in order for the language to function it must be assumed by both the speaker and his audience that the same person articulates all of the syllables.

> Of course the person who said 'over' was identical with the person who said 'ing.' But there was a fraction of a second between the two occasions. And yet the speaker enjoyed his self-identity during the pronunciation of the word, and the listeners never doubted the self-identity of the speaker.[41]

Whitehead also understands this continuity of linguistic expression as a clear indication of the importance of derivation and anticipation as fundamental features of our concrete experience. Language functions because the present is understood as derived from the immediate past, with a large degree of conformity. It also requires the assumption that the future can be anticipated with some dependability. Again, the word "overwhelming" articulated by a single individual illustrates the dependence of language on these features of experience. "Throughout this period of saying that word everyone, including the speaker, was expecting him to finish the sentence in the immediate future beyond the present; and the sentence had commenced in the more distant past."[42]

40. *SP*, p. 94.
41. *Ibid.*, p. 93.
42. *Ibid.*

The significance of this progression in the background of linguistic expression is that it qualifies the definite symbols by reference to the ongoing process in its complex combination of stability and change. Language is evidence that practical identities can be maintained, but there is a movement from past to future that is inexorable and which qualifies every linguistic expression. Language cannot be understood in complete abstraction from the ongoing process. Its definite distinctions are important and useful, but they are always partial. Language gives evidence of significant distinctions and relatively stable patterns in experience, but it also indicates its own dependence on a process in which changes are taking place and in which the future, in its broad ramifications, cannot be expected to be exactly like the past.

In these different ways, Whitehead finds language giving evidence for continuities in concrete experience which transcend the explicit language forms. Experience, in this sense, provides a context for the interpretation of all linguistic expression. The discrete words and sentences must be understood against a qualifying background of continuous development. Even though words and the factors in experience to which they refer can be treated as relatively independent, the use of language gives compelling evidence that places both words and things in a flux of interdependence.

Whitehead also finds that some philosophers who have taken linguistic evidence into account have missed the continuities required by language use because of their preoccupation with certain types of words. By stressing substantives and adjectives, these thinkers have arbitrarily focused on those symbols that most readily suggest the independence of factors in experience. By excluding the consideration of the connective words—such as conjunctions and prepositions—language has been used to give support to interpretations of experience that are essentially nominalistic. The problem here, as Whitehead sees it, is that substantives and adjectives reflect the basic structure of the subject-predicate language and tend to give more weight to the independence of subjects and their qualifications than is actually warranted by concrete experience. The connective words, on the other hand, involve basic ambiguities which qualify the precise distinctions of nouns and adjectives. When the connectives are considered in their relationship to concrete experience, the abstract character of linguistic expression becomes evident. While a noun can be given a fairly precise one-to-one correspondence with some factor in reality, a conjunction indicates the very structure of continuity in which relative independence must be understood. By attending to words expressive of conjunction, it becomes evident that the subject-predicate form of language is one-sided and partial. It is the connective words that indicate the dependence of apparently precise expressions on the concrete context of meaning. Unless these words are seen in respect to their relationship to experience, language can be taken to be far more precise than is actually the case. Words like "and" or "together" are highly ambiguous, and only rarely subject to careful analysis. "Such words are the death-traps for accuracy of reasoning. Unfortunately, they occur abundantly in sentences."[43]

The concern of Whitehead for the ambiguity of connectives is reflected in his interpretation of statements that might be understood as tautologies or merely analytic statements. He finds that the manner in which the terms are connected linguistically affects the meaning of the terms themselves. The symbols do not stand alone as precise in their meaning; they are affected by the purposes which inform their use, and these purposes determine the way in which the connectives are to be understood. That is to say, the consideration of the ambiguities of the connective words can give a clear indication of the dependence of the entire statement on a concrete context which qualifies its meaning.

For example, Whitehead remarks that the man who refused to admit that two and two make four until he had some indication of the use to which that premise was to be applied had some justification for refusing. Of course, on a very abstract

43. MT, p. 74.

level of thought, the meaning of such a statement is precise, but Whitehead will not allow such abstract precision to be used as a self-sufficient context of meaning. In other words, within the mathematical mode of abstraction, the statement is absolutely true, but that mode of abstraction does not function in complete independence from connection with concrete experience. As soon as the statement is applied in ways that transcend the mathematical level of abstraction, fundamental transformations of meaning take place that qualify its truth and its precise interpretation. "In 'two and two make four,' the words 'and' and 'make' entirely depend for their meaning upon the application which you are giving to the statement."[44]

In a similar fashion, Whitehead qualifies the apparent precision of a mathematical equation involving multiplication. Again, it is the connectives that reveal the concrete perspective which ties this apparently tautologous statement to the process in which exact distinctions are problematic. Whitehead puts it this way:

> I am contradicting a widespread belief. A prevalent modern doctrine is that the phrase 'twice-three is six' is a tautology. This means that 'twice-three' says the same thing as 'six'; so that no new truth is arrived at in the sentence. My contention is that the sentence considers a process and its issue.[45]

This tautology is not simply true by definition, without reference to the general character of experience. It is a statement that reflects in its use of the connective "is" or "equals" that its meaning is directly dependent on the concrete context of experience in which those connectives can have quite different meanings. In the concrete situation where such a statement must be put to work, the process of multiplication is not exactly equivalent to the result of multiplication, which is the datum for further manipulation. Indeed, Whitehead even contends that the statement "six equals six" need not be taken as a mere tautology. "It can be taken to mean that six as dominat-

44. *RM*, p. 75.
45. *MT*, p .125.

ing a special form of combination issues in six as a character of a datum for further process."[46]

Whitehead's emphasis on the reference of connective words to concrete experience is in effect a challenge to the radical distinction between analytic and synthetic statements. As he sees it, all linguistic units of meaning are dependent on extra-linguistic factors. There is no way of treating language in a completely abstract way, so that its definite meaning is strictly dependent on the structure of language and not on some reference to the vague and ongoing aspects of concrete experience. Precision is possible on the mathematical or analytical level because factors that resist such precision have been intentionally excluded. Thus, when the definiteness of tautologies is in question, the qualification of the exclusions involved is always a relevant consideration. It is not simply a question of the equivalence of statements, but also the recognition that precise equivalence is only possible if factors that resist such precision are intentionally left out of consideration. That is to say, while they can be left out of the focus of attention, they continue to be relevant when the definite meaning of the statement is considered.

What can be seen in all of the ways that Whitehead utilizes language as metaphysical evidence is his recognition that definite forms of language are not self-explanatory. In every instance, language makes evident its own partial character by pointing beyond itself to extralinguistic factors that contribute to its meaning. The linguistic factors in an occasion of expression will not permit their isolation from non-linguistic factors in experience. For all the apparent clarity of its own symbols, language is not intelligible apart from the process in which its symbols are developed and utilized. That process resists reduction to definite and independent factors. It is heavy with emotional connections. It reflects the wide coordination required by value. While remaining vague with respect to many details, it reveals pervasive interdependence and a persistent thrust toward the future. This process is assumed by every language

46. *Ibid.*, p. 127.

use. It qualifies every linguistic expression by some reference to the vague totality of things as viewed from a particular perspective. Whitehead sums up his interpretation of language as metaphysical evidence when he describes the ultimate reference of linguistic symbols to the process of events that underlies the definite and distinguishable patterns of sense-perception.

> When we examine the content of language, that is to say, the experiences which it symbolizes, it is remarkable how largely it points away from the abstractions of high grade sensa. Its meaning presupposes the concrete relations of real events happening and issuing from each other.[47]

So, language not only points beyond its own definite symbols, but it requires continuities which transcend even the apparently discrete factors of sense experience. It is fundamental evidence that on the metaphysical level reality cannot be understood merely as an aggregate of disparate and independent factors.

The key to Whitehead's understanding of language is his unwillingness to separate definite and stable factors from the process in which they are generated and to which they make their own contribution. Being cannot be separated or understood apart from becoming. Distinctions cannot be maintained apart from the purposes which make them relative to the entire process. By the same token, the apparently definite features of linguistic expression must be understood in relation to selective activity, intentional exclusion, and some metaphysical grasp of experience. The word, the phrase, the sentence, and the language system are not to be treated as self-sufficient instruments of meaning, but they must be seen in polar dependence on the extralinguistic factors involved in their development and use.

One can compare Whitehead's theory of language to the contemporary identification of meaning with "use," which draws on the later philosophy of Wittgenstein.[48] While Whitehead does not reduce the meaning of language to a simple dependence

47. *Ibid.*, pp. 46–47.
48. Ludwig Wittgenstein, *Philosophical Investigations*, trans. by G. E. M. Anscombe (New York: The Macmillan Co., 1953), p. 20.

on the purposes of those who use it, he does indicate that the meaning of linguistic expression cannot be given maximum clarification apart from consideration of purpose and intention. Whitehead also, like the later Wittgenstein, insists that language must be considered at work and not merely in an idle state.[49] The product of the process must not be divorced from the flux of experience in which discrimination and novel synthesis take place.

Underlying this polarity of language is a view of experience and reality in which exclusive abstraction is the fundamental means of relationship and mutual influence. Entities are related to each other in the organic process in such a way that they include each other in their own identities, but only in a partial manner. Abstraction does not mean separation but, rather, partial inclusion. It can never be complete because the perspectives which are involved in the selective process are themselves firmly rooted in the fabric of concrete relationships. Thus abstractions, for Whitehead, allow the manipulation of important empirical factors but always with a reference to purpose, perspective, and context which qualifies every distinction. The crucial point here is a revised notion of transcendence, which follows from such a relativistic view of abstraction. For Whitehead, transcendence does not normally imply absolute separation. "To be abstract is to transcend particular concrete occasions of actual happening. But to transcend an actual occasion does not mean being disconnected from it."[50] This qualification of abstraction, and the concomitant revision of the nature of transcendence is a key insight. It keeps being in touch with becoming. It makes the definiteness of language important, without being self-sufficient. It keeps knowledge from being either unattainable or exhaustive. With the exception of our own subjectivity, everything we experience, know, or speak about is available only in a partial manner. This means that in no instance can apparently definite facts and symbols be taken as independent of the values which inform their emergence and

49. *Ibid.*, p. 51.
50. *SMW*, p. 143.

their potential utilization in the process. The partial character of these abstractions is taken as powerful evidence that our experience is dependable and yet not exhaustive with respect to transcendent realities. This is one type of evidence for Whitehead's realistic epistemology, and it contributes directly to his metaphysical generalization of affective experience. Abstraction without separation is understood, not only as the basis for language, but as the fundamental relationship between actual entities.

> Each experient enjoys a perspective apprehension of the world, and equally is an element in the world by reason of this very prehension, which anchors him to a world transcending his own experience. For, it belongs to the nature of this perspective derivation, that the world thus disclosed proclaims its own transcendence of that disclosure. To every shield, there is another side, hidden.[51]

It is the polarity of abstraction that permits Whitehead to understand the very foundation of experience as emotional and affective interaction. A radical separation between intellectual and physical aspects of experience cannot be maintained if abstraction is the basis for conceptual and linguistic stabilization of concrete relationships. Abstraction, for Whitehead, thus characterizes physical as well as conceptual experience. As Whitehead puts it: "Abstraction expresses nature's mode of interaction and is not merely mental."[52] Relativity is universal. "There is no self-contained abstraction."[53] Definite entities, concepts, and expressions all refer beyond themselves in such a way as to qualify their own character.

Such relativity, however, does not deny transcendence or novel identity. Every entity transcends the process in some respects and is thus unique. In its own experience, each entity grasps the universe from a peculiar perspective. In that respect, at least, every entity transcends the universe. Whitehead even understands the transcendence of God in this manner.

51. *AI*, p. 228.   53. *SP*, p. 88.
52. *Sym*, p .26.

> The notion of God . . . is that of an actual entity immanent in the actual world, but transcending any finite cosmic epoch—a being at once actual, eternal, immanent, and transcendent. The transcendence of God is not peculiar to him. Every actual entity, in virtue of its novelty, transcends its universe, God included.[54]

The understanding of language, which Whitehead bases on this view of abstraction and transcendence, presents a metaphysical alternative in which language and extralinguistic reality are seen in polar interdependence and interaction. Thus, Whitehead's approach is distinguished by the dual assessment of language it involves. Language deserves both confidence and criticism. It is both a potentially deceptive instrument and an important clue to the nature of reality.

In contrast to this polar view of language, many modern philosophers have suggested that language must be either the key to reality or an essentially deceptive structure which does not reflect distinctions of ontological significance. These sharply contrasted options can be identified with important schools of modern thought. The influence of critical idealism is to be seen in the alternative which would affirm the essential identity of fundamental conceptual and linguistic categories with the very structure of experience. On the other side, both the intuitive approach of Bergson and the empiricism of David Hume are prime examples of the rejection of linguistic structures as a key to reality. Bergson sees linguistic abstractions as a distortion of immediate participation in reality.[55] The empiricists who follow in Hume's footsteps tend to separate linguistic structures from the data of sense-experience so radically that they make language merely expressive of mental conventions. In both of these cases, the linguistic structures do not provide a reliable clue to the character of our most fundamental experience.

Wilbur Urban, an important critic of Whitehead's approach to language, raises these mutually exclusive options, in the sharpest possible way, as a framework for criticizing White-

54. *PR*, p. 143.
55. Henri Bergson, *Introduction to Metaphysics*, trans. by Mabelle L. Andison (New York: Philosophical Library, 1961), p. 8.

head. Recognizing that language is a human creation, Urban sees the crucial issue as whether or not language is "moulded on reality."[56] As Urban describes it, language is either the key to the very structure of our experience, or it is a distortive creation which tends to obscure the fundamental character of reality. As he puts it: "The only real problem is whether our creations have taken us to reality or away from it, whether they have become a veil to be torn away, or are, after all, when properly understood, the only road we have to reality."[57]

Whitehead's polar alternative rejects these mutually exclusive options and affirms both the illuminating and potentially deceptive character of language in respect to metaphysical inquiry. It is an alternative that presses beyond such sharp dichotomies to the organic unity of the process in which all distinctions arise. Language reflects man's experience, but in a partial and provisional manner. It utilizes abstractive techniques that parallel patterns of interaction and influence on the physical level of experience. In this way, its structures are in productive continuity with extralinguistic reality. At the same time, since in Whitehead's organic philosophy continuity does not preclude novelty, language is also an instrument which man can use in deceptive and creative ways.

Surely, as Wilbur Urban and others have described it, Whitehead's theory of language is naturalistic.[58] It is not, however, a naturalistic view which downgrades the potential of language or denies it the capacity to serve noble ideals. For Whitehead, language, like other aspects of man's inheritance, is not merely a given structure to which he must conform, but it is also an instrument of freedom. It is both a system which contributes to man's experience and a tool which man must evaluate and revise.

Without attempting to do justice to Whitehead's critics, it is useful to indicate some of the crucial problems created by

56. Wilbur M. Urban, *Language and Reality* (London: George Allen & Unwin, Ltd., 1939), p. 51.
57. *Ibid.*, p. 50.
58. Wilbur M. Urban, "Whitehead's Philosophy of Language and its Relation to his Metaphysics," *The Philosophy of Alfred North Whitehead*, p. 305.

Whitehead's point of view. There are two primary difficulties that arise using Whitehead's theory of language. The first centers on the availability of experience which transcends the forms of language, providing some criterion for their evaluation. The other has to do with the fundamental polarity of Whitehead's approach, which raises questions concerning the consistency and intelligibility of his claims.

Urban, for example, has insisted that there is no experience against which the fundamental subject-predicate categories of our language can be tested. He criticizes Whitehead for claiming access to experience which does not conform to the basic structure of language, and describes Whitehead's alternative as one in which language is viewed as essentially deceptive. Urban contends that man simply has no cognitive vantage point from which he can criticize his linguistic structures. For him, language, itself, is a condition of experience and therefore a practical boundary for empirical penetration and interpretation.[59]

A similar criticism is raised, from a different perspective, by Richard Rorty. In an article that is essentially sympathetic to Whitehead's realistic conclusions, he argues that the appeal to feelings which transcend the expressions of ordinary language is mistaken. Rorty's point is that clarification is better achieved in philosophy by referring to unproblematic expressions than by an appeal to experience that is even more fundamental. In his perspective, too, the question is whether we do, in fact, know more than we are able to express in available forms.[60]

In both of these examples, the problem turns on the kind of boundaries that impede man's empirical and expressive efforts. Are these boundaries to be understood as final or, virtually, determined? Or are they somewhat flexible, due to the progression of history and the capacity of man to vary his modes of attention and interest? The point of Whitehead's organic philosophy is that such boundaries, the limits of certain modes

59. *Ibid.*, pp. 307–309.
60. Richard M. Rorty, "The Subjectivist Principle and the Linguistic Turn," in George L. Kline, ed., *Alfred North Whitehead: Essays on His Philosophy* (Englewood Cliffs, N.J., Prentice-Hall, 1963), pp. 146–47, 152.

of abstraction, are not permanent boundaries. They are changed by the creative movement, itself, and by man's exercise of his own freedom. Man's advantage is that he can multiply perspectives and thus gain more penetrating insight into his developing environment. This is not to say that he can know anything exhaustively, or everything at once. It is to say that he can know more than he did, and, indeed, that in a developing universe his option is between deeper penetration and the loss of concreteness in barren abstractions. Thus, man either attempts to correct his modes of expression, or he settles for determinate formulations that are out of touch with the reality that matters. Urban is right that there is no completely neutral or objective vantage point, but Whitehead would contend that there are ways of increasing the effectiveness and inclusiveness of our abstractions and their interpretations.

Some modern discussions in the field of linguistics suggest that while language does influence the fundamental shape of our experience, it is possible to transcend one such language and assess its structure and adequacy in respect to concrete experience. Thus, one may not have to accept Urban's claim that the subject-predicate forms are beyond radical revision.

Benjamin Whorf discovered in a study of the Hopi Indian language that it enshrines a different metaphysics than languages of a standard European origin. Indeed, the metaphysics underlying the Hopi language has many features that are similar to Whitehead's organic metaphysics. Events with subjective and objective aspects are the final realities, and in order to describe them in English a radical revision of that language is required.[61] Evidently, Whorf was able to vary his perspective enough to transcend the forms of his own language. He should then have been able to make some estimate of the comparative adequacy of these two languages in respect to concrete experience. Whorf could not deny his own place in a culture which was informed by standard, average European languages, but he could discover a way to transcend the limits of his own linguistic categories.

61. Benjamin Lee Whorf, *Language, Thought, and Reality*, ed. by John B. Carroll (Cambridge, Mass.: M.I.T. Press, 1966), p. 147.

His description of the problems involved in bridging the linguistic gap between the two cultures suggests that Whitehead may well have been correct in claiming that language can be revised for metaphysical purposes. Whorf writes in respect to the metaphysics enshrined in the Hopi language: "Monistic, holistic, and relativistic views of reality appeal to philosophers and some scientists, but they are badly handicapped in appealing to the 'common sense' of the Western average man—not because nature herself refutes them . . . but because they must be talked about in what amounts to a new language."[62]

The problem of deciding what is and what is not included in man's experience leads to the question of consistency. Given Whitehead's combination of confidence in linguistic abstractions, with a call for their persistent criticism, the question of the reality of empirical distinctions emphasized in language is raised. Are these distinctions based in the actual character of our environment or are they arbitrarily introduced? Whitehead seems to want it both ways. Nathaniel Lawrence puts this type of criticism concisely. "Whitehead in one passage seems to maintain that the boundaries between events are *there* to be discerned; in another passage, when the continuity of nature is at stake, he admits that the demarcation of an event is arbitrary."[63]

This type of criticism can be made more relevant to linguistic expression when one considers Whitehead's contention that the Aristotelian laws of logic and their influence on the subject-predicate forms of language are not applicable in a precise way to concrete experience. For this reason, Whitehead's alternative may seem to be self-contradictory. What should be understood is that Whitehead is pressing to the very foundations of logic, and there he claims that contradictions and identities can only be discerned against a background of continuity. When this is considered, Whitehead's polar attitude toward language and the distinctions it expresses looks somewhat different.

Logic applies to determinate realities. In a world where

62. *Ibid.*, p. 152.
63. Lawrence, *op. cit.*, p. 45.

process is pervasive, and in which novelty emerges, the classical laws of logic have only partial relevance. At the same time, in respect to determinate realities, logic seems to require the discernment of broad similarities even as radical distinctions are noticed. Morris Cohen describes the assumptions behind classical logic in a way that clarifies Whitehead's alternative. Cohen writes: "The kind of world which logic assumes is that of propositions denoting states of affairs which are connected by threads of identity, so that we have unity in diversity."[64]

Cohen also suggests a principle of rational inquiry that illuminates Whitehead's approach and goes behind the sharp distinctions of logic and language. This is the "principle of polarity," an instrument of intellectual search that takes into account the factors in experience which are the result of contrasting or opposing influences.[65] This principle is utilized just at the point where sharp distinctions, such as those of classical logic, seem to break down. It allows for the consideration of contrasting alternatives as though they were not mutually exclusive. In physics, it leads to the consideration of both action and reaction in a single context. In biology, it brings us to reflect on both life and death as relevant factors. In ethics, it allows for both self-sacifice and self-satisfaction as important aspects of motivation in the same act. "Philosophically it may be generalized as the principle, not of the identity, but of the necessary copresence and mutual dependence of opposite determinations."[66] The appreciation of this principle illuminates what may seem to be inconsistencies in Whitehead's theory of language. With polarity in mind, it is possible to see the distinctions expressed in language as both real and yet influenced by attention and emphasis. The neat identities of logic and language, while useful for so many purposes, may be seen to rest on a fabric of concrete relationships which will not allow such precise distinctions without qualification.

64. Morris R. Cohen, *A Preface to Logic* (New York: Meridian Books, Inc., 1956), p. 192.
65. *Ibid.*, pp. 87–88.
66. *Ibid.*, p. 88.

The references to critical comments here or the suggested responses to such criticism are not intended to be exhaustive. Instead, what has been shown is that, while there are important problems with Whitehead's alternative, they are not so difficult as to exclude a constructive appreciation of his thought. With that in mind, we are in a position to consider some of the implications of his views on language for the problem of religious discourse.

4

SOME IMPLICATIONS FOR
RELIGIOUS DISCOURSE

What bearing does Whitehead's organic philosophy have on the problem of religious discourse? What implications for religious language can be derived from his general interpretation of language? It should be understood that the answers to these questions are primarily inferences based on Whitehead's thought. The conclusions are intended to be interpretive rather than expository. Later in this study, we will deal more directly with Whitehead's own treatment of religion and its utilization of language.

As we have seen, the key to Whitehead's understanding of language is his expansion of the scope of abstraction, so that the most fundamental relationships are constituted by this process. Also important is his insistence that the products of abstraction cannot be separated from the purposes, activity, and context which inform their development. This amounts to a qualification of every definite expression and the recognition that no linguistic formulation can be fully understood apart from extralinguistic factors or in separation from other modes of abstraction and expression.

Language, in its own dependence on extralinguistic factors, reflects the fundamental polarities of concrete experience. It is complex abstract evidence for dynamic realities that are even more complex. When understood as a derivative and abstract expression of experience, language indicates, both by its emphasis and its exclusion, something about the more concrete levels of experience, which it symbolizes. In other words, language will lead us beyond its own structures, if we do not arbitrarily disregard its abstractive character. It can point to the realities which underlie expression. It can indicate its dependence on the circumstances of a concrete situation. It can suggest the need for metaphysical assumptions as a basis for its own use and interpretation. In all of these instances, language gives evidence that what is obvious and explicit is not self-explanatory. Language points beyond itself, and in doing so, it gives a clue to the nature of reality and suggests how all evidence should be handled. It makes clear that the most dangerous mistake in evaluating any data is the assumption that the focus of attention is a self-sufficient context of meaning. This view of language has direct implications for the specific problems that are involved in religious assertions.

In the first place, Whitehead's understanding of language radically reduces the power of those criticisms of religious discourse that are based chiefly on its metaphysical features. His recognition of the ultimate dependence of every linguistic expression on assumptions of maximum generality challenges the view that religious discourse is problematic because of its intimate connection with metaphysics. The fact that religious discourse does involve assertions of the broadest possible scope does not imply that this mode of expression is either "meaningless" or without cognitive content. The problems inherent in metaphysical generalization are shared by all uses of language, including those which make knowledge and expression seem ultimately simple and precise. Such problems cannot be used to mark a distinctive flaw in any mode of discourse, without also rendering all other uses of language problematic. In this perspective, the necessity of metaphysical commitments binds all uses of language together into an organic unity. It indicates a continuity in which no linguistic expression can be separated from the difficulties involved in statements of universal scope.

Instead of being the avenue whereby religious assertions may be discredited or separated from other forms of discourse, the metaphysical dimension of religious discourse actually contributes to the clarification of language, both religious and secular. The articulation of claims which are, in fact, the basis for linguistic expression can lead to a more adequate understanding of language, even in its apparently precise modes. Religious language, by its persistent and deeply personal expression of generic features of human experience, can thus be an important influence toward linguistic clarity, rather than the misleading formulation of virtually "empty" convictions and pseudo-propositions. It points to the assumptions and purposes that underlie the more definite and precise modes of expression that have so often been used as self-authenticating norms for the criticism of religious discourse.

Conversely, Whitehead's view of language also questions those attempts to insulate religious assertions from secular criticism by denying their metaphysical character. That is to say, the continuities that are described by assertions of metaphysical scope qualify the easy criticisms of religious discourse and also demand that religious language be kept in critical contact with other uses of language. They make possible the recognition of metaphysical assumptions in empirical or logical norms, qualifying the precision and finality of such standards of meaning and intelligibility. At the same time, these metaphysical continuities require that the religious use of language be critically compared with other types of discourse and understood in relation to them. The very significance and relevance of religious assertions are dependent upon these relationships which reach beyond the distinctively religious realm.

If every linguistic expression requires some decision about the nature of man's most general experience, then the attempt to isolate religious insight and expression in some esoteric, non-metaphysical compartment is self-defeating. Such a tactic is not a defense of the significance of religious claims; it is a subtle attack on the content, intelligibility, and importance of religious assertions. It is a gambit which purports to sacrifice metaphysical connections for the sake of preserving religious meaning. In fact, this move leads to a situation in which the major goal cannot possibly be accomplished. If immunity from criticism for a set of favored assertions is gained by isolation from mundane experience and language, what is abandoned is the meaning and relevance of such symbolic formulations. Divorced from the continuities which make criticism possible, religious language can hardly be considered language at all. Similarly, the religious power to integrate all of life also seems diminished to the point of no return. At the very least, if religious assertions cannot be positively related to other uses of language, then their only possible religious content would seem to be radical renunciation of this world and finite existence. Thus it would seem that if Whitehead's view of language is valid, then the insulation of any kind of language by the denial of its metaphysical implications is the quickest way to reduce such discourse to gibberish. To make the criticism or defense of religious discourse turn on the distinction between metaphysical and non-metaphysical language is to exclude, from the very outset, those considerations which are at the heart of the matter.

The importance of Whitehead's view is that it transforms the context in which questions about the meaning of religious language are often raised. To accept the old framework means to lose the battle by default. Whitehead offers an alternative which, in calling the old assumptions into question, makes the appreciation of religious discourse, as a significant and influential mode of expression, possible. By asserting the interdependence of language and metaphysics, Whitehead changes the ground rules for the controversy. He thus makes possible an intelligible defense of religious language in the context of man's total experience and competence.

In this revised framework, the general and particular aspects of reality are accepted as thoroughly interdependent. Thought and expression always reflect a similar polar relationship of mutual influence, even though one or the other aspect may be largely taken for granted. A difference in emphasis is not excluded, but the radical separation which would suggest the virtual independence of either component is eliminated. Ultimately, the general and particular are rooted in the same complex of concrete experience. Therefore, no contrast between them can be pressed to the point of separation without a consequent loss of concrete reality. To set the general against the particular is to settle for abstraction.

As far as language is concerned, it is the challenge that Whitehead offers to the radical opposition of generalizations and statements about particulars which is decisive. One does not begin with the assumption that the basis for generalization is an activity of the mind entirely alien to the input of specific physical encounters with sense impressions, objects, or other discrete empirical data. These are two levels of abstraction based on the same data and derived by selective activity which differ in their dominant purpose. They are modes of expression, then, which are ultimately interdependent, even though limited interests may be served by ignoring that connection. When the very meaning of language is at stake, it is just this fundamental interdependence that must be recognized. The particular and the general require each other in experience, thought, and expression. Language reflects this relationship in its own one-sided and partial character.

Consider the preoccupation with the sentence as the unit of meaning in linguistic analysis. The intent is to clarify language in a piece-meal fashion, but the hidden presupposition is the radical opposition of the general and the particular. If a single sentence can be given a definite meaning apart from the consideration of generic relationships, what is in fact put forward is a kind of implicit nominalism in which only the particulars are real. Without the recognition of the metaphysical implications of this method, the connections between empirical particulars and between linguistic expressions are ignored in an arbitrary fashion. It is not surprising that on such grounds, language about a God who coordinates value and existence is in difficulty. The premises involved in the method, which set the general and the particular against each other, have been decisive from the outset.

It is just this kind of error that Whitehead's approach makes apparent. As a consequence, the meaning of an assertion about

God does not have to be assessed on the same level as statements about tables, chairs, and other objects. Yet, by being obviously on a different level, religious statements do not automatically lose their empirical roots or relevance. The contention is that man must grasp generic relationships in order to deal with particulars. Therefore, the expression of such broad empirical traits is not based on mere rational speculation. Neither are expressions referring to particular factors merely based on definite, specifiable physical encounters with virtually independent empirical components. Metaphysics never reaches the complete generality associated with logical necessity, nor is it strictly empty of empirical content. On the other hand, the factors often considered as the empirical input for thought and expression are not strictly independent, definite, and self-authenticating apart from apprehension of the generic traits of experience. Therefore, religious assertions, with their close relationship to metaphysics, are not faced with the radical option between conceptual necessity and empirical reference. General descriptions, even of a metaphysical nature, are more than perpetual antagonists in a battle for linguistic supremacy against statements about particulars. To accept such a conflict as the framework in which the meaning of any language is scrutinized is to accept arbitrary incoherence and promote persistent dilemmas. On the basis of man's most fundamental experience, Whitehead suggests that significant language, or cognitive language for that matter, cannot be limited to the expression of discrete empirical factors or to some combination of linguistic components which can be ultimately traced back to such simple foundations. Neither can diverse "language games" be compartmentalized. Expressions that refer to various grades of generality must also be allowed, and the influence of the patterns thus expressed on the grasp of detail recognized. The nature of language, itself, requires such a polar concern in which the mutual influence of general relationships and particular factors is acknowledged. Whether or not to generalize is not the vital question. It is the validity and utility of our generalizations which is decisive. This is especially true on the metaphysical level, where, in Whitehead's view, some posture towards the broadest patterns of experience is always necessary.

In this framework, religious assertions are not problematic or insignificant merely because of their metaphysical aspects. Neither are they without influence and intelligible relationship in respect to our most precise and mundane expressions. They cannot be isolated from some "cognitive" mode of discourse that only refers to particular facts and objects, or which is restricted to one facet of human experience. Instead, religious assertions in their universal thrust make explicit the kind of assumptions which are ultimately implied in all discourse. In this way, the recognition of the metaphysical scope of religious discourse is a potential means of clarifying other modes of discourse which do not make their metaphysical premises explicit. By calling attention to the partial and provisional character of all definite formulations, religious discourse can contribute to the illumination of all uses of language. It suggests, by its obvious dependence on persons, communities, and universalized convictions, that no language can be definitely understood without considering the human values and selective activity which underlie all expression. Thus, challenged by the precision and practicality of certain modes of expression, religious language, understood in Whitehead's framework, transforms that challenge by laying bare the assumptions and exclusions, which are the very basis of any mode of precision. If metaphysical assumptions are involved in every significant expression, then there is no use for language which can ultimately escape from the vagaries of personal decision and purposive activity. Metaphysical risk is pervasive in linguistic activity. Indeed, insofar as all linguistic meaning is dependent on the assumptions, purposes, and values of persons, every expression is in touch with the dimension of experience which is the distinctive concern of religion.

A second implication may be seen as the forceful challenge to the neat rules of evidence and narrow interpretations of the empirical data which have been so important in raising questions about religious discourse. Not only is religious language potentially meaningful in Whitehead's scheme, but the criteria which have been put forward as dependable and final are called into question. The complex reality to which language refers does not present definite self-authenticating norms for meaning or validity. Whatever authentication it does allow is in the midst of selective interaction and dynamic development, not in separation from it.

When language itself indicates more than the obvious, the dependence of any system of argument or demonstration on decisions reaching beyond those systems becomes evident. The rules of logic or evidence can more readily be seen as somewhat arbitrary and intentional. The method is not established by its own procedures. The relevance of evidence is not determined by the same principles which provide for the handling of that evidence. The laws of logic are not, themselves, established altogether by logic. In this way, Whitehead's understanding of language brings the complexity of empirical evidence and rational argument to light.

It is not only the precise linguistic formulations of rules of evidence and empirical criteria which are qualified by Whitehead's point of view. His understanding of language also implies that the simplistic interpretation of the empirical data which is often enshrined in these norms is partial and one-sided. His position undercuts any critical perspective, which would ultimately reduce experience to simple and discrete components. Whether these empirical components are described as sense-data, objects, or occasions of experience makes little difference. Whitehead's argument is with the ready acceptance of radical discontinuity on the most fundamental level of experience. His contention that our grasp of definite factors depends on selectivity makes all distinctions relative so that they cannot be pressed to complete disjunction. The apparently separable and and independent components of experience are understood as the products of intentional emphasis and exclusion. In this way, every approach to empirical evidence which treats the easily distinguishable data as self-explanatory is called into question.

Such a qualification of the manner in which the data and

rules of evidence are understood has direct consequences for the problem of religious discourse. It is just these definite rules of evidence and narrow interpretations of the perceptual data which have cut off religious assertions from any intelligible relationship with concrete experience. Given the ready acceptance of such views, the only avenue for the defense of religious assertions has appeared to be some retreat to an esoteric realm. If the rules of evidence are themselves qualified by exclusive intentions, then religious assertions are not suspect just because they do not conform to standards that were designed for other purposes—like the scientific investigation of severely limited aspects of human experience or the fulfillment of physical needs. If it is assumed that the empirical data are exhaustively constituted by independent and separable components, then religious assertions have to refer to discrete sense impressions or specific objects in order to have any empirical reference at all. The possibility that man's most fundamental experience includes relationships which are broad enough to warrant even metaphysical assertions, makes a crucial difference. Of course, there is no way of grasping empirical relationships that are purely general. But then, there are no simple particulars to be grasped either. If the data of experience are finally enmeshed in a fabric of generic relationships, even the notion of God as a factor related to all value and existence is not cut off automatically from all empirical reference. As language implies more than the explicit, so the empirical data are not exhausted by the definite and obvious. A wide variety of factors can be traced to perception, rather than limiting this empirical input to discrete data.

It should be obvious that if the rules of evidence and the definite aspects of experience are taken at face value as exact and final then any religious assertions are going to be in difficulty. If one has to judge them by the norms applicable to scientific measurements, common-sense prediction, or even limited theories, religious assertions are going to seem like poor substitutes for significant expression. Evaluated in this fashion, what can they be but misleading pseudo-propositions which look like assertions, but actually are cognitively "empty."

Whitehead presents an approach to language in which it is just these neat criteria of cognition and significance which are recognized as partial and one-sided. The consequence is that religious assertions may be understood as based on an empirical grasp of broad patterns, and therefore actually contribute to the development and accumulation of knowledge. They may not be cognitive in the sense that they can be dealt with in apparent isolation from human values and commitments, but they do express a dimension of experience that is involved in every precise mode of cognition, and which has some influence on the apprehension and articulation of definite details. Insofar as religious assertions express claims about values and the universal context of valuation, they illuminate more limited forms of knowledge claims.

This different approach to the most fundamental evidence, the data of perception, affects the very basis of all thought and conviction. Every use of language is influenced by the assumptions one makes about the data, and the dependence of Whitehead's view on what is actually given in experience should be recognized. He does not present rigorous logical proofs for his conclusions about language or experience. Here Whitehead is existential. He points all of us to our own experience and asks if we do not find the same organic, purposive, and dynamic complex that he has tried to describe. Language, in its practical efficacy, is one kind of evidence that leads to this understanding of the empirical data. Indeed, religious language contributes to this type of evidence. But when an organic understanding of the data is adopted, it also puts religious discourse on a new foundation. It allows it to refer to both God and the world, to express the broadest patterns of coordination and yet not lose contact with specific and limited segments of experience.

A third implication follows from Whitehead's recognition of the fundamental polarity of language and experience. The status of analogical discourse in relation to the more literal uses of language is radically revised. Analogy is understood as playing a very fundamental role in all understanding and expression. As a direct consequence, the obviously analogical character of religious assertions does not reduce their significance or isolate their "meaning" from cognitive and apparently univocal modes of discourse. Instead, the explicit polarity of religious expressions is one indication of the very complex character of concrete experience. Religious assertions, by making their own dependence on analogy apparent, suggest the ultimate dependence of the most literal expression on apprehensions, which can only be articulated by resorting to overt analogy, myth and metaphor. When this pervasive influence of analogy is recognized, religious assertions must be criticized in terms of the adequacy and validity of their metaphors, not simply on the grounds that they depart from literal modes of expression.

Usually, only poetic, imaginative, and elusive uses of language have been allowed the dual reference of analogy. These forms of language call attention to more than one factor, utilizing the comparison as a mode of partial illumination. Ultimately, such dual reference depends on a polar contrast between the definitely discriminated detail and a more vaguely delineated context of relevant relationships. In the last analysis, every analogy depends on man's capacity to grasp the nature of the relationships that bind different entities together in a single perspective. The dual reference of a simple metaphor leads to a dialectic concern for detail and context—the particular and the universal. Finally, one is led to the fundamental analogies of metaphysics that illuminate all of experience, and the religious metaphors that are capable of integrating human activity around a central purpose.

What Whitehead indicates is that the apparently literal modes of expression also involve the dual reference of analogy in a truncated form. We speak of "things" as if the language were completely precise, and fail to recognize the analogies hidden by shared assumptions and limited purpose. No matter what is said, assumptions about generic relationships are required, and these fundamental commitments will only allow the partial and qualified articulation of analogy. Because these underlying analogies can so often be taken for granted, the unqualified precision of univocal modes of expression is quite easily taken as the ground of all expression. The purported advantage of language based on a literal foundation is that the indication of a single referent suggests a certainty on which more complex and venturesome uses of language can be developed. While Whitehead's approach to language does not deny the practical utility of so-called literal usage, it does warn against the acceptance of this one form of expression as the norm of meaning and dependability. Understood with complete disregard for the influence of analogy, such univocal discourse can lead to dangerous over-simplification. It suggests the independence of significant linguistic expression and metaphysical assumptions. It tends to compartmentalize human experience so that connections which are essential for the understanding of language are obscured. It makes the explicit articulation of metaphysics impossible, and effectively removes all assumptions about language and meaning from the power of criticism. Since religious language is concerned with the integration of human life based on some discernment of the broad context of relationships, the precedence of literal uses of language relegates the assertions of religious commitment to an esoteric and peripheral status, where their very meaning and relevance is in doubt.

Given Whitehead's point of view, the accuracy and utility of certain selected linguistic formulations do not warrant the general conclusion that analogical language is a second-rate mode of expression, strictly dependent upon univocal assertions. It is true that the apparently literal uses of language are often modified to produce metaphor and analogy. Such projective creations gain in flexibility, but lose a degree of accuracy. But, we should also note that the development of literal forms of language also depends on analogy. These forms become literal symbols because of an intentional neglect of analogies discerned in experience and taken for granted by the more precise and detailed modes of expression. A word that emerged as an obvious metaphor becomes common parlance with a very precise meaning. A sentence that depends on analogies shrouded in its connective components, is taken as literal and precise because certain commonly accepted analogies can be taken for granted. The language system, itself, because of its slow rate of change in respect to fundamental structure, obscures the assumptions and fundamental models which inform its central categories and syntax. In this manner, Whitehead's general understanding of language makes the problems associated with analogy complicate and qualify every use of language. It is not just those forms of discourse which obviously resort to metaphor and imaginative symbol that lack precision and finality. But all the uses of language reflect the influence of an experience that demands metaphor and analogy for its articulation.

While the relationship of the analogical and the literal uses of language continues to be complex in Whitehead's thought, the dependence of these two forms of language is made reciprocal. In this way, the significance and dependability of analogical language is increased, even as the precision of more literal uses is qualified and limited. The dependence of apparently literal expressions on general assumptions about experience makes the dual reference of analogy a far more fundamental feature than is usually recognized. It is this that allows for the influence of metaphor, myth, and metaphysics on man's entire process of understanding and expression. The relationship of the univocal and the analogical becomes a rhythmic and polar interdependence in the pulsating advance of human experience. Commitments as to the nature of reality, the availability of that reality in our experience, the dependability of abstractive discrimination and repetition, and the relative importance of various factors are involved in every apparently literal expression. Since these assumptions can only be articulated in language that is analogical and explicitly qualified in some respects, literal and precise assertions must be seen as dependent on the kind of dual reference that is usually associated with more elusive types of language. The difference is only that the univocal modes of expression disguise and neglect these qualifications for the sake of some practical and limited efficacy. In the grasp of concrete circumstances, such precision is highly useful.

For the sake of the maximum comprehension, which is desired in the general evaluation of language and meaning, the underlying complexity and qualification must be brought to the surface.

Analogical expression thus contributes to a different kind of precision. It indicates the fundamental polarities of experience, which are the basis for all significant expression, and seeks to characterize them in an obviously partial and provisional manner. Whereas literal predication develops the distinctions given in experience to the point of sharp separation, analogical discourse attempts to trace the broader similarities which must ultimately provide the very context for distinctions. They are not really two types of discourse that can be separated with accuracy. They reflect two aspects of language which themselves are noticed by divergent interest and emphasis. Even the question of "which is more fundamental" seems out of order in this context. In one sense, the literal is more fundamental because it allows the increase of detailed precision. In another sense, the analogical is more basic because it expresses a level of abstraction closer to our most concrete experience. Whitehead does not suggest that such a choice is necessary between two productive partners in the enterprise of understanding and expression. Only because of the danger of oversimplification is it necessary to reassert the pervasive influence and importance of the analogical. In its explicit expression of the polarity between the definitely discriminated and the context of discrimination, analogical discourse points to the interrelation and active development of realities which defy literal symbols. With its enunciation of parabolic features of experience, it keeps the literal modes of discourse from contributing to a linguistic and cognitive imperialism. At the very least, Whitehead's approach to language makes it difficult to consider analogical language as inferior to that which appears to be univocal and precise. Literal uses arise from the apprehension of analogies, and they give way to metaphorical expression whenever man seeks to deal with the generic, novel, and progressive aspects of experience. The two modes of discourse are not to be weighed against each other; they must be used together in a never-ending attempt to express the intricacies of experience.

The importance of this for religious discourse is that it enhances the significance of this patently analogical form of expression. The fact that analogy in religious discourse is so obvious and irreducible does not destroy the significance of these expressions or deny them a cognitive role. Instead, it indicates, in a profound way, the difficult and provisional character of all human attempts to gain dependable knowledge and precise symbolic formulations. It points to the qualified character of all expression. By speaking of mystery, it suggests that no human effort toward understanding or clear expression can be final. It shifts the model from that which is complete to an active, partial penetration. The alternatives are not exhausted by knowing and not knowing, or by the expressible and the inexpressible. What remains is the full range of partial achievement as the appropriate way to deal with a world of process.

Insofar as religious language is analogical, Whitehead's general view of language puts it on a new footing. Both the critic and the defender of religious assertions are forced to recognize their own implicit analogies and deal with them as alternative interpretations of experience. The issue becomes one of comparing models and metaphors in a context that ultimately allows no neutrality. Some analogical discourse is required in order to understand any use of language with maximum definiteness. By the same token, the proponent of religious expression cannot hide in the sheer ambiguity of his analogies. He must face the power of increased definiteness as it is expressed in rigorously formulated details and clearly recognized metaphysical models. Thus, Whitehead protects the importance and significance of religious language. He does so by maintaining its intelligible contact with the univocal, not by some arbitrary isolation. Analogical and univocal modes of discourse are to be understood together, not in separation.

Finally, Whitehead's view of language calls attention to the relative character of all distinctions used in the analysis of language. Understood as abstraction, language does not permit any simplistic analysis that would separate the linguistic structure from concrete extralinguistic reality or utilize sharp distinctions within a language system as a means of compartmentalizing modes of expression. This organic view of language maintains the contact and mutual influence between assertions of religious import and every type of "secular" discourse. Of special importance is the intimate relationship of fact and value in expression that this implies. None of the distinctions suggested by neat classifications of types of linguistic meaning can be pressed to the point where statements about facts can be completely divorced from assertions of personal decision and valuation. As a consequence, religious discourse with its focus on value can be understood as partially dependent on factual assertions, at the same time as the most objective statement of fact carries with it some valuation and the influence of that dimension of experience, which is the province of religion.

Language, itself, does not permit any precise or final analysis into discrete or separable components. It has its own organic and dynamic character that makes it a complex and integral phenomenon. Its components are so interdependent that the analysis of language must always be characterized by partial penetration and approximation. As it cannot be broken down into simple and independent components, so it cannot be understood when attention is limited to linguistic factors or to selected linguistic components. Language is best understood when it refers to the total context of experience which includes many linguistic and non-linguistic factors. Some of these non-linguistic components which must be considered are: the persons who use the language, the communities in which the language has developed and in which it is interpreted, the intentions which inform its structure and specific use, the conceptual and physical contexts which provide effective definitions, and the imaginative and affective influences involved in actual communication. Language suggests that many other factors are involved in expression other than the clear and distinct linguistic forms which readily seize the focus of attention.

Of fundamental significance for religious discourse is the

close relationship and interaction between fact and value that is involved in all expression. In the face of sharp distinctions which would isolate the realms of fact and value, Whitehead's approach to language makes these two aspects of experience and expression strictly interdependent. Statements of personal valuation and propositional content are not separable in any final fashion. Just as fact and value are reciprocal and correlative aspects of all reality in the organic metaphysics, so in the understanding of language, expression of personal commitment and definite descriptions are intertwined in mutual dependence.

Of course, one can distinguish between the propositional content of a statement and the personal intentions of those who use it. The same statement can be used to accomplish different goals, to perform different tasks. Still, since the statement cannot function apart from some personal intention, its meaning is never strictly reducible to its propositional content. Nor is its significance solely dependent on the purposes for which it is used. The relative distinction between the objective and subjective aspects of linguistic significance cannot be pressed to the point of absolute separation.

It is possible, on this basis, to insist that any use of language, no matter how esoteric it may appear to be, shall allow some discrimination of its positive relationship to other more mundane forms of language. No linguistic formulation can be considered language without some traceable connections which allow its partial translation into other types of language. Language that has no discernible connection with the common parlance, or which cannot be related to the common structures of experience, will be meaningless. Some assertions may have a more objective content than others, but none can be treated as strictly objective. At the same time, no assertion can be divorced from the prevailing assumptions and common experience of a community without ceasing to be language at all.

There is, then, no impenetrable barrier between statements of fact and assertions of valuation. Religious assertions must face the rigor of criticism which is based on man's best apprehension of the facts, but it is not necessary to accept the pretension that they are scrutinized from a value-free perspective. The removal of the barrier between these two modes of expression indicates that statements of fact are likely to be misunderstood if the values which influence their development are not recognized. At the same time, the mutual influence that pertains between factual judgments and valuation suggests that any valuation expressed with a disregard for the fabric of facts is trivial. Thus, religious language which focuses on the coordination of values is defended as a relevant, significant, and influential mode of expression. But it gains this status at the price of maintaining and articulating its relationship to man's best secular knowledge of the facts, no matter what abstractive method was involved in their discernment.

The language of the laboratory provides an example of the way in which statements of fact are related to expressions of valuation. It would appear that this type of discourse is notably objective and free from affective influence. It was designed just for that purpose. It is reducible to a propositional content that seems to have little residue of the influence of personal decision and valuation. Such language purports to express measurements that are standard and reliable, without regard for subjective evaluation. When the thermometer reads 70°, we can all agree about that, the questions of value seem to be excluded.

Problems arise, however, when value is strictly excluded from consideration. One can accept the language of laboratory measurement as one form of limited obectivity, without denying the influence of decision, valuation, and purpose on the entire scientific enterprise. Attention is given to a certain kind of detail because it is considered important for one reason or another. Many individual and corporate choices have gone into the development of science as it now exists, and they play a role in determining the relevance of data, the comparative influence of various theories, and the vigor with which scientific research is pursued. The language of the laboratory is not used apart from valuation, but with the intentional exclusion of values, to the degree that this is possible. This results in only a relative distinction between the language of the laboratory and other types of discourse that give greater emphasis to valuation. An appreciation of the abstractive character of language allows this kind of scientific discourse to be very precise and dependable in a certain context, without making it either the norm for all wisdom, or separating it from other forms of discourse, abstractive emphases, and empirical factors. The ultimate dependence of the laboratory scheme of abstraction and expression on the qualification of purpose and theory, which give relevance to the evidence in that perspective, provides a bond of continuity with other aspects of experience and other modes of expression which cannot be broken.

It is just at the point where fact and value, the propositional and the expressive, are often separated that Whitehead's philosophy provides a new departure. If the abstractive character of language is taken into account, the various types of language and the distinctions by which they are classified are so relative that the different modes become complementary and supplementary—rather than mutually exclusive—in their contributions. Instead of being alternatives which call for radical choice, discursive classification, and isolation, these different abstractive emphases are understood as interdependent, compatible, and mutually corrective. What is eliminated from one abstractive scheme is not thereby unimportant when other factors or purposes are involved. The fact that religious aspiration is not relevant to the taking of a reading of temperature and reporting it in a simple sentence, does not mean that there is no connection whatsoever between the two. There is a connection between the value judgment that makes the temperature reading important and the articulation of the coordination of values which culminates in God, or the "good". It is when the absence of connection is assumed that such simple and apparently definite expressions usurp a kind of ontological, cognitive, and linguistic precedence. Problems, then, become serious for religious assertions because the choice involved in giving precedence to one mode of language is not recognized. A single type of abstraction, such as the scientific concern for precise measurement, becomes normative in a dogmatic and arbitrary manner.

Not only are empirical factors ignored, but the very act of exclusion, and the purposes which inform that act, are hidden from criticism. Whitehead's description of the danger of the scientific focus on facts makes the dogmatic problems involved in the expression of such facts evident. "Matter-of-fact is an abstraction, arrived at by confining thought to purely formal relations which then masquerade as the final reality."[1] The recognition of the abstraction involved in such apparently precise and obective uses of language will not automatically deny them precedence or normative status. It will make clear that some choice in a broader perspective has been involved, and that there are important empirical connections that qualify every use of language. Any language that is set up as a norm will have to be justified in relation to a broader context, not by arbitrary isolation from it.

In this way, Whitehead's understanding of language puts religious discourse in creative and critical contact with those modes of discourse that are more readily accepted as cognitive, important, and intelligible. All the distinctions that have been used to isolate or denigrate religious uses of language are thus called into question—they are relative and provisional distinctions. This is the way language is effective in an organic and dynamic universe. This is also the way it must be understood. The analytic and synthetic contrast is not finally decisive. The cognitive-emotive dichotomy does not stand as the definitive classification of linguistic meaning. The performative and propositional distinction is not absolute. Even the distinction between the descriptive and the prescriptive uses of language is carefully qualified. These distinctions remain useful tools for the clarification of language, if they are not absolutized as virtually independent compartments of significance. They cannot be used in a dogmatic way to insulate or destroy religious assertions. Even the multiple distinctions allowed by moderate linguistic analysis is qualified by Whitehead's contention that such distinctions are relative. Given many language games, the "family

1. *MT*, p. 25.

resemblances" must be allowed to carry more weight, so that some translation from one language to another is possible. Whitehead's approach to language will not allow this apparently pluralistic understanding of linguistic significance to be used in a subtle way to promote the more precise forms of language as cognitive and linguistic norms, or to segregate religious discourse. Every attempt to discriminate a completely independent use of language, or for that matter, the independence of language, itself, is challenged. As a consequence, the language of religion can be seen in a new and positive light. Once again it is not a question of the meaningful and the meaningless, but of the particular content and adequacy of the various religious options. The attempts of religious discourse to articulate the essential connection of all human experience in which both fact and value find their place are not excluded from significance or influence by some arbitrary emphasis on absolute distinctions.

These implications, drawn from Whitehead's philosophy of language, are both highly general and interdependent. They reflect the overlapping character of the various facets of the problem of religious discourse, as earlier delineated. They also indicate that Whitehead's fundamental approach to language is only relevant to a very general conception of religious discourse. On this level, Whitehead's philosophy does have bearing on the crucial issues involved in the appreciation of religious assertions as both meaningful and important. It does not present a defense for a single type of religious assertion, or a particular religious alternative. It does suggest that the specific interpretations of life expressed in religious discourse can be understood in both their content and reference, even though the basis for their adoption cannot be expressed exhaustively.

Having given extensive consideration to Whitehead's treatment of language, it is now appropriate to turn to other aspects of his thought. It is clear that the very nature of perception is a crucial issue in Whitehead's understanding of language, even as it was seen to be one facet of the problem of religious discourse. We can proceed, then, by giving careful attention to Whitehead's interpretation of perception and its data.

5

THE DATA OF
PERCEPTION

Whitehead's understanding of the data of perception is of crucial significance for his philosophy of language and for the application of that philosophical approach to the problem of religious discourse. It is Whitehead's realistic interpretation of perception that makes it possible for him to put forward an empirical metaphysics, providing reference and meaning for discourse about God. This chapter intends to explore Whitehead's approach to perception in order to clarify the relevance of his philosophy for religious language.

The understanding of perception has been profoundly influenced by a concern for clarity and certainty. Since the emergence of the Cartesian method, philosophy has been characterized by a rigorous effort to establish itself on precise and dependable foundations. This concern has had a powerful impact, not only on the aims and methods of philosophy, but also on the manner in which the empirical data have been understood. Preoccupation with those factors in experience that could be clearly discriminated and manipulated with precision has led to assumptions about the very data of perception, which have given its discrete and separable components precedence.

In the linguistic phase of modern philosophy, a similar concern for the clarification of language and meaning has been widespread. It has given support to the view that clarity in language is to be attained as the result of analytic procedures that break down the apparently complex into constituent and relatively simple components. The goal has often been to reduce language to a combination of discrete expressions that could be referred to corresponding simple factors given as the data of perception. It is in the light of this analytic search for clarity that the assertions of metaphysics and theology have come under careful and critical scrutiny. The very significance of these assertions has seemed to depend on the possibility of distinguishing simple empirical factors as a reliable basis for constructions of such wide generality. When analysis has not been able to produce clarity in this manner, statements of metaphysical and theological import have often been relegated to a kind of linguistic limbo, somewhere between neglect and oblivion. At the very least, the result of the linguistic quest for clarity and precision has been that radical limitations and skeptical qualifications have been attached to these uses of language just because their foundation in the clear and distinct factors in experience has been difficult to establish.

The concern for analytic clarity as the goal and basis of philosophical achievement has not gone unchallenged. The point has been made that "clarity is not enough."[1] Both the expectations and the empirical assumptions of the "analytic" concern for clarity have been challenged.[2] It is in respect to this challenge that Whitehead's philosophical alternative is relevant. He, too, would modify the commitments and the procedures that have dominated the analytic quest for clarity. While he does not repudiate the search for clarification as an appropriate and crucial aspect of the philosophical task, he will not allow clarity and precision to be used as the only criterion in philosophical reflection.[3] Nor will he permit a clarity that is solely dependent on the analysis and simplification of the complex to dictate the description of the most ultimate factors of experience. It is his view that clarity attained by analysis is

1. H. D. Lewis, ed., *Clarity Is Not Enough* (London: George Allen & Unwin, 1963).
2. H. H. Price, "Clarity Is Not Enough," *Ibid.*, suggests that analytic clarity needs the balance of synoptic clarity and that, even then, clarification must be seen as a tentative and partial achievement, pp. 39–41.
3. *PR*, p. 12.

always qualified by the purposes and the point of view that inform the inquiry. For Whitehead, "Clarity always means 'clear enough'."[4] It must be sought and understood within the limitations of specific perspectives. The interest pursued affects the degree and type of clarity achieved.

Whitehead makes a major point of denying the assumption that the clear and distinct features in experience are the most fundamental. He insists that those things that are obvious and easily grasped must be understood in relation to the context, which makes possible the discrimination and assessment of details. Philosophy must seek a clarity that does justice to a broad range of experience, even if that means that precise distinctions must always be qualified and tentative. Such clarification is not to be found by the direct pursuit of simplicity to its isolated and independent origins. It is to be found by an inclusive and critical appropriation of all the data of experience, including the most general relationships which will not submit to analytic separation and manipulation. Clarification is the result of pushing our understanding to its limits.[5] It is not attained by limiting our understanding to that which is simple, clear, and precise. Both focus on detail and the qualification of perspective are important in this kind of approach to clarification.

> We enjoy the detail as a weapon for the further discrimination of the penumbral totality. In our experience there is always the dim background from which we derive and to which we return. We are not enjoying a limited dolls' house of clear and distinct things, secluded from all ambiguity. In the darkness beyond there ever looms the vague mass which is the universe begetting us.
> . . . We can never disengage our measure of clarity from a pragmatic sufficiency within occasions of ill-defined limitations.[6]

Whitehead understands the overemphasis on the clear and distinct in philosophical reflection as the result of numerous factors in the history of Western thought. It has obvious roots

4. *SP*, p. 132.
5. *PR*, p. 232.
6. *SP*, p. 132.

in the philosophical stance of Descartes. Whitehead also attributes a great deal of influence, in this regard, to the logic of Aristotle and the success of Newtonian science. The logic of Aristotle exhibits a powerful preference for differences in kind and the classification which they allow. In Newtonian science, precise distinctions in terms of location and measurement are made so productive that their fundamental significance is difficult to dispute. Whitehead sees this emphasis on distinction and difference as having a profound effect on the very forms of language and thought in the Western world. The facility of language for dealing with distinctions that are apparently precise contributes to the preference for that which can be singled out from the flux of experience and treated as if it were independent of other factors. Whitehead therefore insists that a corrective is in order. The neat distinctions based on qualitative differences must be taken with less absoluteness.

> There is no clear division among genera; there is no clear division among species; there are no clear divisions anywhere. That is to say, there are no clear divisions when you push your observations beyond the presuppositions on which they rest.[7]

Philosophy must therefore consider the presuppositions on which clarity is based as it determines the status which can be given to the distinctions that are made under a particular perspective or with a specific purpose in mind.

In his qualification of the concern for clarity, Whitehead's respect for Plato's approach to philosophy can be noted.[8] Plato was sensitive to the need for structured continuities within which details could be understood. Even though such general characteristics of experience tended to blur and qualify the clear-cut and useful distinctions, Plato found it necessary to take them into account in his systematic reflection. He saw the need for myths to adumbrate these fundamental truths in spite of the lack of precision inherent in such forms of expression. Whitehead respects this concern of Plato's and understands the

7. *MT*, p. 21.
8. *PR*, p. 63.

attempt to give partial and tentative description of the broad continuities in experience as an essential part of any adequate philosophical interpretation.[9]

For Whitehead, perception itself presents a similar problem: the emphasis on the clear and distinct can lead us to accept these criteria as normative for experience as well as understanding. The question then must be raised: Is perception actually and exclusively constituted by clear and distinct factors? It is Whitehead's contention that it is not. At this point, the problem of clarity in language and knowledge is directly related to the problem of perception. Modern philosophers have not maintained their emphasis on the clear and distinct, without the support of specific doctrines of perception. It is necessary, then, if Whitehead is to provide a viable alternative or corrective, that he present a different approach to perception as a basis for his qualification of the quest for clarification. It must be shown how it is possible for the data of perception to include more than the easily discriminated and discrete data that have undergirded an analytic approach to the clarification of thought and language.

Whitehead's approach to perception may be understood best as a critique of modern philosophy. This critique centers on three misconceptions: the substance-quality doctrine of actuality, the sensationalist doctrine of perception, and the Kantian doctrine of the objective world as a construct from subjective experience.[10]

In dealing with these misconceptions, Whitehead fulfills his announced intention to bring philosophy back to pre-Kantian modes of thought.[11] He is not proposing any wholesale adoption of all the commitments of the philosophers who preceded Kant. As Wilbur Urban has pointed out, it is just these philosophers who were largely responsible for the very errors Whitehead seeks to correct.[12] Whitehead is simply asking that the

9. *MT*, p. 14.
10. *PR*, p. 237.
11. *Ibid.*, p. vi.
12. Wilbur M. Urban, "Whitehead's Philosophy of Language," *The Philosophy of Alfred North Whitehead*, p. 307.

problems to which Kant's philosophy was addressed be re-opened for further consideration. Specifically, it is not always noted that the great Kantian synthesis of the empirical and rationalist traditions rests on crucial assumptions about what is given in perception. These assumptions were inherited in large part from David Hume, and they have been reinforced by his persistent influence in linguistic forms of empiricism. Their acceptance has shaped the framework in which much modern discussion has taken place.

Both Kant and Hume have been given such status in con-temporary philosophy that the various attempts to understand language tend to be dependent on one or the other of these thinkers. It is their initial assumptions that Whitehead chal-lenges. The nature of perception is at issue, and Whitehead's view is that both Hume and Kant made serious errors in their analysis of the concrete data. His challenge to their views is explicit and direct. He writes: "It will be evident to you that I am here controverting the most cherished tradition of modern philosophy, shared alike by the school of empiricists which derives from Hume, and the school of transcendental idealists which derives from Kant."[13] He is not calling for a return to older systems of philosophy, but for a new departure in which the full range of alternatives can be considered.

In dealing with modern philosophy, Whitehead discerns both helpful and misleading insights. He appeals to the great philosophers as authorities, but not in the usual sense.[14] Their inconsistencies are as important to him as their systematic achievements. He wants to uncover the actual problems with which they wrestled. If he can show that even philosophers who developed positions quite different from his own recog-nized elements in the perceptual data which would not fit into their systematic formulations, his case for an alternative ap-proach to the same problems is appreciably advanced. In this sense, Whitehead's appeal to the philosophical tradition is an

13. *Sym*, p. 31.
14. *PR*, p. 63.

historical extension of his attempt to recover concrete experience as the basis for philosophical interpretation.

Whitehead begins his critique of modern philosophy by focusing on Descartes and the substance-quality doctrine. He affirms the subjective bias which Descartes is said to have introduced into modern thought. Subective experience is the primary datum with which philosophy must begin.[15] However, Whitehead understands this subjective bias as requiring radical reformation, if it is not to be misleading. It should not be arbitrarily construed in terms of substance-quality categories.[16] Like the subject-predicate forms of language, these categories isolate factors whose attributes are then treated as in no way dependent on relationships. This is seen to be the Cartesian error; it leads Descartes to treat independence as fundamental and to limit subjective experience to one kind of actuality. Such a restriction of immediate experience to "thinking subjects" Whitehead finds unwarranted. He would extend the term "experience" so that it applies to all actualities. The standard of actuality is no longer the Cartesian independent substance, but subjects who are constituted by their experience of each other. In this way, Whitehead's "reformed subjective principle" maintains the precedence of immediate experience but bases it on radical relativity rather than independence. To be actual is to be an experiencing subject, constituted by the objectification of other subjects. "Apart from the experiences of subjects there is nothing, nothing, nothing, bare nothingness."[17]

Descartes' problems, as Whitehead sees them, can be traced to the acceptance of the given linguistic structure. "Descartes allowed the subject-predicate form of proposition, and the philosophical tradition derived from it, to dictate his subsequent metaphysical development."[18] Experience was not allowed to give evidence that would challenge the available categories as the most adequate instruments for metaphysical description. According to Whitehead, the discontinuities en-

15. *Ibid.*, p. 243.   17. *Ibid.*, p. 254.
16. *Ibid.*, pp. 241–243.   18. *Ibid.*, p. 219.

shrined in the language have led Descartes to misinterpret experience. Useful distinctions are pressed to the point of absolute separation. But this is not only a problem that affects the Cartesian philosophy, it is also a difficulty that permeates modern thought, resulting in persistent dilemmas and vicious dualisms.

> The difficulties of all schools of modern philosophy lie in the fact that, having accepted the subjectivist principle, they continue to use philosophical categories derived from another point of view. These categories are not wrong, but they deal with abstractions unsuitable for metaphysical use.[19]

Whitehead describes the difficulties arising from the unreformed subjective principle as the notion of "vacuous actuality," and the conception of quality as a universal inherent in a substance. Vacuous actuality suggests an unchanging substratum underlying accidental variations. The other notion leads to an interpretation of experience in which the only data are universal characteristics, without any given reference to particulars. Together they isolate independent actualities from each other and from the network of relationships and interaction that are necessary for any meaningful experience. They make experience primarily an intellectual matter that can only be understood by moving toward solipsism or introducing the deity as an epistemological guarantee. The crucial issue is the weight to be given to conceptual and linguistic distinctions. Without careful qualification, Whitehead sees the distinctions of the subject-quality categories leading to an interpretation of perception itself in which discontinuity is decisive. That which is clear and distinct becomes normative. Differences between entities, sensations, and occasions of experience are so sharply drawn, that any understanding of experience is problematic. If independence or discontinuity is taken as the key to reality, vicious dualisms like that reflected in the modern mind-body problem are unavoidable. There is simply no way to under-

19. *Ibid.*, p. 253.

stand relationships because they have become "metaphysical nuisances."[20]

It should be carefully noted that Whitehead is not opposed to the useful distinctions inherent in the substance-quality categories. Even dualism presents a problem for Whitehead only if it amounts to a radical bifurcation of reality. Indeed, the reformed subjective principle requires a kind of dualism based on the relativity of the subject-object distinction. "The universe is dual because each occasion unites its formal immediacy with objective otherness."[21]

The reformed subjective principle is, in effect, a different way of construing the subject-object relationship. In this reformed view, "subject and object are relative terms. An occasion is a subject in respect to its special activity concerning an object; and anything is an object in respect to its provocation of some special activity within a subject."[22] It is this fundamental polarity that informs the alternative view of perception Whitehead presents. In his view of the most fundamental empirical data, continuity and discontinuity belong together. Differences are distinguished against a common background of interaction and interrelationship.

In this way, the reformation of Descartes' subjective principle avoids the disjunction of the "components of subjective experience from the community of the external world."[23] The data of perception cannot be understood apart from the dynamic encounter in which they arise. They do provide significant contact with other actualities. Thus, existence is not characterized by independence, nor are the factors discernible in perception given, apart from some transcendent reference and mutual coordination.[24] Whitehead describes the difference clearly.

The organic philosophy interprets experience as meaning the 'self-enjoyment of being one among many, and of being one arising out

20. *Ibid.*, p. 208.
21. *AI*, p. 190.
22. *PR*, p. 208.
23. *PR*, p. 288.
24. *SP*, p. 91.

of the composition of many.' Descartes interprets experience as meaning the self-enjoyment, by an individual substance, of its qualification by ideas.[25]

Whitehead has been criticized just at this point. For example, Arthur O. Lovejoy, in his celebrated *Revolt Against Dualism*, claims that Whitehead falls into an epistemological dualism so like those he attacks as to undercut his correction.[26] He finds Whitehead only reenunciating the same dualism in novel terminology.[27] Whitehead accepts the claim that his approach to epistemology is an alternate form of dualism. He maintains, however, that the qualified dualism he represents is quite different in its substitution of productive contrasts for radical separation.[28] The universe is both *one* and *many,* and exhibits both continuity and discontinuity.

> There is thus a dualism in this contrast between the unity and multiplicity. Throughout the universe there reigns the union of opposites which is the ground of dualism.[29]

Whitehead proceeds to compare the organic philosophy with the work of the classical British empiricists, Locke and Hume. In this comparison, the sensationalist doctrine of perception receives the focus of attention. Let us first consider Whitehead's relationship to the philosophy of John Locke.

Locke's interest was epistemology. His empiricism, his willingness to deal with the raw material of experience, commands Whitehead's respect. In contrast, Locke's successors are much more apt to make experience conform to their own preconceived theories.[30]

Whitehead distinguishes between the earlier and later books of Locke's *Essay Concerning Human Understanding*. This distinction enables him to commend Locke for comprehensiveness

---

25. *PR*, p. 220.
26. Arthur O. Lovejoy, *Revolt Against Dualism* (LaSalle, Ill.: Open Court Publishing Co., 1930), pp. 193–234.
27. *Ibid.*, p. 223.   29. *Ibid.*
28. *AI*, p. 190.   30. *Ibid.*

at the same time as inconsistencies are noted that can be used in support of the organic philosophy. The earlier books tend toward the sensationalist error, while the later books suggest a more inclusive view of the data of perception.

Sensationalism reduces the content of experience to the deliverances of the five senses. It combines with the neat distinctions of the substance-quality categories to make the experience of other individuals, or the relationships between individuals, problematic. The data of the various modes of sensation do not, by themselves, provide more than repeatable and recognizable qualities. So, in the first two books of Locke's *Essay*, the primary components of experience are characterized as universals, leaving the problem of the reality of particulars and their interaction unresolved. The end result of this sensationalist error is that experience is deprived of any objective content.

In the third book of the *Essay*, there is, according to Whitehead, a different understanding of the perceptual data—"the primary data are explicitly said to be ideas of particular existents."[31] Universals are grasped by a process of comparison and analysis. They are derived from the primary data rather than identified with them. In this second doctrine, Whitehead finds Locke endorsing a realistic and relativistic view of experience not unlike his own. Experience includes direct *causal* contact between particulars. The "powers" belonging to particular existents influence and condition each other. Thus Locke suggests that the fundamental description of particular realities should exhibit their capacity to affect one another. The universals involved in such descriptions must have a relational function that does not preclude the reality of diverse individuals.[32]

Whitehead believes that Locke, by his undeveloped and unsystematized insights, is suggesting the need for an organic metaphysics. The crucial issue is the content of perception, and the later Locke is enlisted by Whitehead in the support of interdependence as a fundamental feature of concrete experience.

31. *PR*, p. 230.   32. *Ibid.*, p. 222.

Perception gives direct access to actualities in a network of relationships, not a collection of discrete impressions or ideas. As Whitehead describes it, "Locke's principle amounts to this· That there are many actual existents, and that in some sense one actual existent repeats itself in another actual existent, so that in the analysis of the latter existent a component 'determined to' the former existent is discoverable."[33] The experience of any actuality is constituted by its relationships to other actualities. On the most concrete level of man's physical encounter with his environment, relationships, connections, and diverse actualities are in some manner "given" for partial and effective appropriation.

Intimations of the organic philosophy are found by Whitehead even further back in the empirical tradition. In a reference to Francis Bacon, Whitehead points to that empiricist's recognition of the influences that bodies have on each other, even at a distance.[34] Bacon suggests, and Whitehead agrees, that selectivity plays a role long before thought, consciousness, or even sense-perception have entered the picture. Such references are important to Whitehead because they indicate instances in which important philosophers have found more in experience than they could justify within their explicit systems. In the case of John Locke, it makes his *Essay* the "invaluable storehouse for those who wish to confront their metaphysical constructions by a recourse to the facts."[35]

It is in dealing with the philosophy of David Hume that Whitehead brings his criticisms of sensationalism to their ultimate conclusion. Hume developed Locke's earlier sensationalist doctrine with a consistency that Whitehead finds admirable. The consequence of Hume's rigorous development of sensationalism is a *reductio ad absurdum* against the doctrine.[36] Hume so stresses the clear and distinct aspects of perception that all continuity and structure seem to collapse. The continuities required

33. *Ibid.*, p. 211.
34. *SMW*, pp. 43–44.
35. *PR*, pp. 220–221.
36. *Ibid.*, p. 223.

for the interpretation of experience are left without empirical or rational foundation. Even causality and the inductive method are deprived of any intelligible basis in experience.

Whitehead agrees with Hume that nothing should be accepted into philosophy which is not discoverable as an element in subjective experience.[37] He also praises Hume for his insight into the "composite" character of mental activity.[38] It is with Hume's narrow interpretation of the content of experience that Whitehead argues. Hume's over-emphasis on the deliverances of the five senses tends to reduce experience to the discernment of universals, which can then be manipulated mentally to produce complex notions and emotional responses. In this way, Hume makes emotions and feelings derivative from mental activity, rather than the other way around.[39] As Whitehead understands it, such a view of perception excludes the recognition of the body in its functional support of the senses. It restricts the data of perception to the point where the influence of the body on the production of the sense data cannot be taken into account. It is this narrowing of perception to "sense-perception" which elicits Whitehead's criticism of Hume and other proponents of sensationalism. He rejects the doctrine of "mere sensation" and the claim that the "primary activity in the act of experience is the bare subjective entertainment of the datum, devoid of any subjective form of reception."[40]

Whitehead's criticism of Hume is based on the claim that in perception we have a direct intuition of inheritance which expands the informative capacity of the data.[41] "Each moment of experience confesses itself to be a transition between two worlds, the immediate past and the immediate future."[42] As a result, the data of sensation are connected with the functioning body which receives the impulses of interaction from the external world. Thus, the "living organ of experience is the living

37. *Ibid.*, p. 253.
38. *Ibid.*, p. 229.
39. *Ibid.*, p. 214.
40. *Ibid.*, p. 239.
41. *Ibid.*, p. 253.
42. *AI*, p. 192.

body as a whole."[43] Perception includes more than the deliverances of the senses in the form of disembodied universal characteristics. It also includes the modes of "sense-reception" and the emotional interchange in which definite characteristics are derived.

> Our perception is not confined to universal characters; we do not perceive disembodied color or disembodied extensiveness; we perceive the wall's color and extensiveness. The experienced fact is 'color away on the wall for us.'[44]

In this manner, Whitehead sees a more careful examination of concrete experience transforming the problems with which Hume wrestled. Hume could not find impressions of relationships on which to base ideas of causality or connection. Nor could he find anything in experience that could give information about the origin of sense-impressions, or their relationship to an external world. Whitehead's argument is that such impressions as would have been helpful were excluded from the very beginning. The only kind of connection that Hume would allow was mere succession or repetition. This initial limitation on what can be given in the data isolates sense impressions from any intelligible or ontological relationships. What Hume does not notice is that even the notion of serial order seems to require some corresponding impression. "Hume seems to have overlooked the difficulty that 'repetition' stands with regard to 'impressions' in exactly the same position as does 'cause and effect.' "[45] Whitehead also notes that the derivation of ideas from impressions is without a corresponding impression. "There is a relation of 'derivation' of 'ideas' from 'impressions' which he is always citing and never discussing. . . . It constitutes an exception to the individual independence of successive 'perceptions.' "[46]

Whitehead thus claims that Hume's own philosophy contradicts his explicit claims about perception. Hume's failure to

43. *Ibid.*, p. 225.   45. *PR*, p. 204.
44. *Sym*, p. 15.   46. *Ibid.*, p. 208.

criticize "habit" and "practice" in the same rigorous manner as "causality" gives an indication of the use of continuities and connections which are not themselves supported by Hume's doctrine of experience.

> The truth is that Hume retained an obstinate belief in an external world which his principles forbade him to confess in his philosophical constructions. He reserved that belief for his daily life, and for his historical and sociological writings, and for his *Dialogues Concerning Natural Religion.*[47]

Hume's problems are attributed, by Whitehead, to his combination of the unreformed subjective principle with a sensationalist doctrine of perception. The subjective principle, interpreted in the unqualified subject-predicate framework, makes the occasion of experience an isolated, private, and ultimately empty affair. Reinforced by a sensationalist view of perception which excludes the forms of "sense-reception," the subjective principle in its unreformed state deprives experience of all pattern and connection.[48] First, one does not experience other actualities but only the data of sensation. Secondly, those data include no indication of origin that could facilitate their own interpretation. Whitehead sees no escape in this perspective from "solipsist subjectivism."[49]

Whitehead is not simply critical of Hume at this point. He sees Hume as facing up to the problems raised by his philosophy in an honest and persistent manner, which differed from the great majority of his followers.[50] Hume's rigor makes his critique of causality, from the sensationalist point of view, an important piece of evidence for Whitehead's argument. Hume proves that his own doctrine of perception must be mistaken. Perception has to involve more than Hume would allow. A more inclusive approach to the data of perception will surely include continuities which enable us to relate critically and con-

47. *Ibid.*, p. 213.
48. *Ibid.*, 231.
49. *Ibid.*
50. *Ibid.*, p. 206.

structively to our environment. "This conclusion that pure sense-perception does not provide the data for its own interpretation was the great discovery embodied in Hume's philosophy. This discovery is the reason why Hume's Treatise will remain as the irrefutable basis for all subsequent philosophic thought."[51] The sensationalist doctrine of perception has to be wrong because it excludes any rational interpretation of experience—including its own.

In the place of Hume's focus on discrete impressions, Whitehead suggests that the data of perception yields other factors which do provide a basis for the appropriation of pattern and connection. Perception does not simply present clear and distinct universals with no tale to tell of their particular exemplification or origin. The distinct factors in perception are given, together with evidence of duration and derivation. As Whitehead puts it: "The crude aboriginal character of direct perception is inheritance. What is inherited is feeling-tone with evidence of its origin."[52] An important, indeed the most fundamental aspect of perception, is the feeling of interaction and continuity.

It is the philosophy of Immanuel Kant that Whitehead attacks for its phenomenalism—the reduction of the ordered world of experience to mere appearance. As a realist, it is necessary for Whitehead to challenge the radical separation of the phenomenal and noumenal worlds as it is put forward in Kant's work.

> The philosophy of organism is the inversion of Kant's philosophy. *The Critique of Pure Reason* describes the process by which subjective data pass into the appearance of an objective world. The philosophy of organism seeks to describe how objective data pass into subjective satisfaction, and how order in the objective data provides intensity in the subjective satisfaction. For Kant, the world emerges from the subject; for the philosophy of organism, the subject emerges from the world."[53]

Whitehead sees the problem in Kant's philosophy as his acceptance of an interpretation of the perceptual data that is

51. *MT*, p. 182.
52. *PR*, p. 182.
53. *Ibid.*, pp. 135, 136.

even narrower than the one adopted by David Hume.[54] All patterns and relationships are excluded from the data so that order must be contributed by the experiencing subject.[55] The result is the "degradation of the world into 'mere appearance'."[56] A dependable order is attained as a basis for experience and knowledge, but the achievement is a costly one. All cognitive contact with reality is cut off, and the distinction between phenomena and noumena tends to become absolute.

Kant's phenomenalism offered a promising way out of the skepticism which seemed to result from the interpretation of perception adopted by Hume and inherited by Kant. Even though no order is given in man's intuitions of other actualities, a dependable and necessary structure is provided by the forms of intuition and the categories of thought. Problematic claims about reality are given up for dependable assertions about phenomena. Whitehead describes it this way: "Thus the phenomenal world, as in consciousness, is a complex of coherent judgments, framed according to fixed categories of thought, and with a content constituted by given data organized according to fixed forms of intuition."[57] By giving the phenomenal world a universal structure based on the conditions of experience, the Kantian philosophy was able to provide an impressive rationale for Newtonian science, and still leave room for the claims of faith and morality. The radical distinction between the knowable (phenomena) and the unknowable (noumena) gave to the distinctions of science a high degree of dependability, without making them normative in other realms of interest. The confidence in distinctions could be extrapolated to delineate bounda-

54. *AI*, p. 224.
55. Kant makes all order in experience, including spatial relations, temporal arrangement, and causal connections, dependent on the contribution of the percipient. Thus, any claims about the thing in-itself are out of the question. The order given in experience is not simply subjective in any "private" sense because it reflects the universal conditions required for human experience. As John E. Smith has commented: "If . . . we describe the Kantian idealism as a subjective philosophy, it becomes necessary to add that the subject in question has a structure which is universal; in other language, Kant's subject is not 'subjective.'" (John E. Smith, *Reason and God* [New Haven: Yale Univ. Press, 1961], p. 8).
56. *PR*, p. 78.
57. *Sym*, p. 38.

ries between different kinds of experience and their appropriate methodologies. In this sense, as John H. Randall, Jr., has described him, Kant was the great liberator, who set limits on scientific knowledge, drew boundaries between different uses of reason, and "parceled out fields for different methods."[58]

In a world where both science and other important interests are challenging such neat boundaries and the consequent compartmentalization of culture, the price of imprisonment in phenomenal structures seems a bit high. Whitehead suggests that it need not be paid. For, as he sees it, our experience does give us a partial grasp of actualities and relationships which transcend our experience. The appropriation of the data of perception is also the concomitant grasping of the order and pattern given in the data. The ordered world does not emerge from the experiencing subject's structuring of chaotic intuitions or discrete sense impressions. Rather, the subject appropriates, in a partial manner, the ordered relationships in which he participates.

However, Whitehead is appreciative of Kant's treatment of space and time, in that the order given by these forms of intuition gives pre-intellectual experience, or feeling, precedence in the cognitive process.[59] Yet, even here, the contrast is between an order imposed and discrete sensations. Thus, in Whitehead's view, the precedence properly given to feeling is warped by the assumption that no structure can be attributed to the fundamental data. This sets the stage for a view of all empirical structure that emphasizes the more sophisticated modes of human functioning and the schematization of thought. Whitehead would reverse that emphasis, making feeling and its appropriation of given patterns and particulars the basis for all consciousness and intellectual organization. "In the organic philosophy Kant's 'Transcendental Aesthetic' becomes a distorted fragment of what should have been his main topic."[60] Continuity and con-

58. John Herman Randall, Jr., *The Role of Knowledge in Western Religion* (Boston: Starr King Press, 1958), p. 77.

59. *PR*, pp. 172–173.

60. *Ibid.*, p. 173.

nection are not to be sought only in the forms of intuition or conceptual structures. "The datum includes its own interconnections."[61]

Whitehead's criticism of the Kantian view of conceptual structure is really the crux of the matter. Are these categories the virtual limits of our experience, or are they the provisional and partial appropriation of an order that extends beyond them, awaiting appropriation? It is Whitehead's view that there is no reason to identify the limits of our concepts with the boundaries of relevant experience.

The important difference between Whitehead and Kant can be understood to rest on the use they make of distinctions, and the resulting difference in their treatment of limits and boundaries. For Kant, the distinctions given in experience are taken as much more definite and final than Whitehead finds necessary. In the place of a radical distinction between phenomena and noumena, Whitehead sees a relative distinction between objects and subjects. Subjects are inaccessible in their formal immediacy, but they are not completely beyond our grasp since they are given in a partial form as objects. In this way, experience and knowledge are productive and have real content, even though they are never exhaustive. The result is that we have a partial and limited access to the actualities and their relationships, and that data can be emphasized in various selective abstractions to provide different kinds of accuracy and utility. At some point, and with certain specific purposes in mind, it results in knowledge as an especially productive level of simplification and emphasis. However, in no instance can the distinctions involved be taken to imply separation or independence. The distinctions, for Whitehead, are always relative to the purposes and perspectives which have been involved in their discrimination. They always refer to more inclusive levels of experience which they simplify by emphasis and exclusion. Dichotomies give way to contrasts and polarities. Distinctions are made to function against a background of continuity and connection.

61. *Ibid.*

It is worthwhile to note two significant points where Whitehead is in agreement with Kant, so that his disagreement will
stand out more sharply. First, Whitehead accepts the active contribution of the percipient in experience. Perception is not a
passive affair in which "objective" data are appropriated with
no influence exerted by the percipient. Perception is always
affected by the purposes and perspective of the experiencing
subject. Secondly, Whitehead agrees with Kant that concepts
are necessary for knowledge. Categories allow the organization
of facts and information so that we can assert the claim of
cognition. The divergence of Whitehead's views from those
of Kant comes when the question is raised: "What does the
percipient contribute?" Whitehead's point is that the contribution is not order—but the sensitive capacity to appropriate
order by selective intensification of feeling. Thus forms are not
merely applied to disorganized data, but the forms, themselves,
are initially derived from the data.

Whitehead adopts the Kantian relativism, but extends it
beyond the limitation of a single, given set of conceptual categories. Thus the separation of noumenal things in-themselves
from phenomenal experience is radically modified. All things
are constituted by their relationships and can be known in a
partial manner. Our experience is always limited, but not by
our conceptual forms. It is limited by the absence of exhaustive
access to other centers of experience. But this lack of total
knowledge does not eliminate the validity of our partial and
abstract grasp of other actualities. The patterns that we do
grasp and emphasize are given in the data and reflect the constitution of other actualities in a partial but dependable way.
And, there are ways of increasing this knowledge provided by
the movement of the process, and by our capacity to vary our
abstractive emphasis within it. Without complete knowledge or
exhaustive experience of other actualities, we learn to appropriate and appreciate the type of knowledge that is available in a
world of dynamic transition. We cannot get outside the exclusiveness of our abstractions, but that does not vitiate their
capacity to give us helpful indications of relatively stable pat-

terns in our experience. The actualities and relationships which constitute that experience are apprehended in a context of relativity which is ultimately rooted in physical relationships. The integrity of our experience and knowledge does not rest on a conceptual unification of disparate components. It is not the creation of an esoteric human experience in which its conditions do not include reference to realities which have some transcendence of our symbol systems. It is the partial appropriation and selective intensification of the relationships which constitute reality.

The basic outlines of Whitehead's doctrine of perception have already been intimated. Its most radical and fundamental claim is that perception is metaphysical in scope so that all actualities are related by prehensions or "experience" of each other. Perception is not based on thought or consciousness, but it precedes both of these "special" characteristics of higher organisms. It has to do with the way in which every actuality takes the rest of the universe into account. It is perception understood as involving more than sense-perception or sense-data.

Sense-perception is understood by Whitehead as an essentially high-grade abstraction which is only important in higher organisms. It is a derivation from the more fundamental mode of perception which the higher organisms share with all other actualities. "Sense-perception is the triumph of abstraction in animal experience. Such abstraction arises from the growth of selective emphasis. It endows human life with three gifts, namely, an approach to accuracy, a sense of the qualitative differentiation of external activities, a neglect of essential connections."[62] The features of perception in human experience which are most readily subject to conceptualization and accurate discrimination are seen as a special development from the more basic interchange of feeling which is the metaphysical mode of perception. In the higher organisms, perception becomes a dialectical process of interaction between two modes—pre-

62. MT, pp. 100–101.

sentational immediacy and causal efficacy.

Presentational immediacy is what classical empiricism has termed "sense-perception" and it provides data that illustrate definite spatial relationships and qualitative characteristics. The extension of this mode of perception is such that it invites the division and rearrangement of its content. However, presentational immediacy taken by itself isolates the contemporary cross-section of experience from its roots in the past and from its connections with the concrete actualities which its data apparently illustrate. Presentational immediacy gives data that are easily discriminated and manipulated in various ways, but it achieves this flexibility by the exclusion of fundamental continuities.

Causal efficacy, the second mode of perception, is the more fundamental and metaphysical mode. It provides a different kind of data—the vague feelings of continuity and conformity with actualities encountered in interaction and mutual influence. It is rooted in the intimate feeling of the body as a functioning organism and organ of perception. It does not give data that are easily distinguished or treated with accuracy. Its data do provide a sense of rapport with the external world and feelings of continuity with the ongoing process. Whitehead describes these two modes, and their contrasting data, with vivid comparison.

> One part of our experience is handy, and definite in our consciousness; also it is easy to reproduce at will. The other type of experience, however insistent, is vague, haunting, unmanageable.
> The former type, for all its decorative sense-experience, is barren. It displays a world concealed under an adventitious show, a show of our own bodily production. The latter type is heavy with the contact of the things gone by, which lay their grip on our immediate selves.[63]

Presentational immediacy is the mode of perception which had been made the exclusive content of perception in the sensationalist error of Hume and Kant. What is significant in

63. *Sym*, pp. 43–44.

Whitehead's own doctrine of perception is the secondary and less exclusive place given to this mode of perception. There are two modes of perception and they provide different types of content. Presentational immediacy gives vivid illustration of the manner in which contemporary entities have relevance for each other without sacrificing their momentary independence.[64] Indeed, in the illustrated contemporary aspect of perception, causal independence is apparent in a way that invites the distinguishing of specific factors, and suggests their possible combination and comparison in ways that are not limited by their location or connections. Presentational immediacy is the mode of perception in which there is "clear, distinct consciousness of the 'extensive' relations of the world."[65] In it, the contemporary world is objectified as a continuum of potentiality readily subject to discrimination, division, and manipulation, but without definite relations to the actualities which it illustrates.[66]

Presentational immediacy provides data that are characterized by precision, qualitative distinctions, clarity of spatial relationships, and the apparent absence of necessary connection with the past or with particular actualities other than the percipient. These data invite analysis and classification. If they are taken as the exclusive data of perception, they suggest that definite distinctions are the fundamental metaphysical clue and they lead to many different points of view in which differences in kind are given ultimate status. The absence of connection with the past is of special importance to Whitehead because he sees it leading to an understanding of duration as mere temporal succession. The instantaneous cross-sections of experiences are taken as the fundamental constituents of reality.[67] Then, the very structure of experience becomes a problem that can only be resolved by retreating to habit or imposed patterns. In other words, giving sense-perception priority in experience leads to

64. *Ibid.*, p. 16.
65. *PR*, p. 95.
66. *Ibid.*, p. 188.
67. *Sym*, p. 40.

radical emphases on discontinuity in other areas of understanding. This is the way Whitehead sees sensationalism as a primary source of problems for modern thought. It is the basis for the doctrine of simple location, and an instance of the fallacy of misplaced concreteness. It changes the question "What do we know?" into the persistent query "What can we know?" Then it provides a dogmatic answer to that question by assuming that all knowledge must begin with the space-time order of sense-data.[68] In contrast to this, Whitehead proposes a different basis for both knowledge and sense perception in the network of causal efficacy. In this mode of perception, derivation, inheritance, and continuity play the fundamental roles. The very foundation of philosophical reflection is established in "given" continuities and patterns. Instead of a rigorous focus on the clear and distinct, Whitehead claims, "The study of human knowledge should start with a survey of the vague variety, discernible in the transitions of human experience."[69]

In order to show the availability of the causal mode of perception, Whitehead points to the exclusions which make the accuracy and precision of presentational immediacy possible. The barren character of mere sense-perception indicates that the practical application of its data depends on other resources. By itself, presentational immediacy does not provide for the direct connection of the "qualitative presentations of other things with any intrinsic characters of those things."[70] That is to say, the things we want to know are not given in this mode of perception in any direct manner. What is given are characteristics that may or may not apply to the real world. The deficiency of this mode of perception indicates that perception does provide us with a broader range of data. There must be more to perception than sensations or the very utility of the definite data is unintelligible.[71]

When presentational immediacy is not treated as self-sufficient and final, its dependence on bodily functions becomes

68. *MT*, p. 102, cf., *AI*, p. 224.
69. *AI*, p. 224.
70. *Sym*, p. 24.   71. *Ibid.*

obvious. It is recognized as derivative from emotional and bodily interaction. There is a more fundamental mode of perception that connects the data of sense-perception with the world of actualities. It gives direct contact with reality. The sense-data derived from the causal mode of perception reveal the functioning of bodily organs interacting with an external world. Whitehead's own words express this polarity in perception concretely: "We see the picture, and we see it with our eyes; we touch the wood, and we touch it with our hands; we smell the rose, and we smell it with our nose; we hear the bell, and we hear it with our ears; we taste the sugar, and we taste it with our palate."[72]

Not only is this experience of derivation available to us directly, but it is here that the inconsistencies of such philosophers as Locke and Hume are useful evidence. Thus, Whitehead can claim that Hume presupposes the perception of causality, even as his system is designed to deny it. "Hume with the clarity of genius states the fundamental point, that sense-data functioning in an act of experience demonstrate that they are given *by* the causal efficacy of actual bodily organs."[73]

Whitehead is well aware of the difficulty of discerning the operation of the second mode of perception. He attributes this difficulty to the general tendency to take the body's normal functions for granted. The body only gets attention when a malfunction calls a halt to normal activity.

> The animal consciousness does not easily discriminate its dependence on detailed bodily functioning. Such discrimination is usually a sign of illness. When we observe the functionings of our viscera, something has gone wrong. We take the infinite complexity of our bodies for granted.[74]

Causal efficacy provides the vector quality of experience in contrast to the scalar qualities evident in the mode of presentational immediacy. It gives us data that are vague, powerful,

72. *Ibid.*, p. 50.
73. *Ibid.*, p. 51.
74. *MT*, p. 41.

and emotional. It includes persistent indications of the derivation of the present from the past and the thrust of the present
toward the future. In the awareness of the present moment, it
gives the sense of derivation and conformity which is the basis
for all causal inference. "Each step in such reasoning depends
on the primary presupposition of the immediate present moment conforming itself to the settled environment of the immediate past."[75] This sense of continuity and transmission is more
prominent in the behavior of low-grade organisms which do not
have the highly developed use of sense-perception.[76] But in the
case of every organism, there is some conformity to the past and
some anticipation of the immediate future.

Causal efficacy is the connective network of interaction which
spreads throughout the universe. It is the emotional and energetic interchange whereby actualities are influenced by each
other. It is best characterized by Whitehead's use of the term
"enjoyment" to indicate the way in which actualities synthesize
all the components of the universe in some grade of relevance.
Whitehead puts it this way: the "self-enjoyment of an occasion
of experience is initiated by an enjoyment of the past as alive in
itself and is terminated by an enjoyment of itself as alive in the
future."[77] The emotional basis of perception provides feelings
of identification with the past and a sense of anticipation with
respect to the future. Just as presentational immediacy excludes
the past and future from attention, so the effect of causal efficacy
is to neglect the present for the sake of the transition from the
past toward the future. This not only introduces the patterns of
causality and conformity into the data of perception, but it
makes it possible to claim that "value" is grasped, along with
definite facts and sensations. The thrust from past to future
makes relevance to a particular subject an inherent dimension
of our most concrete experience. Such an existential experience
of value can then be traced to the various levels of organic coordination which are partially given in perception. Causal effi-

75. *Sym*, p. 41.
76. *Ibid.*
77. *AI*, p. 193.

cacy enables us to perceive things in their mutual relationships, and thereby to grasp their value for each other as well as their structural interdependence.

Causal efficacy and presentational immediacy can be distinguished as the two fundamental modes of perception, but this distinction cannot be pressed to the point of separation or independence. Presentational immediacy is empty without some reference to causal efficacy. Causal efficacy is blind and does not provide the distinctions needed for sophisticated mental activity, without the intermediate derivation of presentational immediacy. In perception on the human level, these two modes function together in a complex interplay which Whitehead calls "symbolic reference." Presentational immediacy contributes accuracy and precision in the apprehension of qualities and spatial relations in such a way that seizes the focus of attention. Causal efficacy gives vague feelings of continuity and importance transmitted directly from the encounter with the world of actualities, but we are only conscious of this mode of perception with difficulty. Normally, it escapes notice in the productive emphasis on the clear and distinct data of presentational immediacy. However, our bodies do provide a basis for interaction between these two modes of perception, allowing their integration into satisfying and practical correlations. Thus, the body is given a decisive role in the integration and testing of perception. As the fundamental mode of perception, causal efficacy is based on physical interaction and feeling, so the body has a primary role as the point of intersection and reference for the two modes.[78]

In the mode of causal efficacy, exact discrimination of actualities and their characteristics is extremely difficult. Distinctions between actualities, and of position from position, are so vague as to be of negligible significance. The only exception is that the

78. W. Russell Brain, *Mind, Perception and Science* (Oxford: Blackwell, 1951) praises Whitehead for his attention to the role of the body in perception. As a neurologist, Brain finds even the modern realist philosophers neglecting the part played by the body in the perception of the external world. At the time he wrote, Whitehead seemed to be the only philosopher who gave due weight to this crucial consideration. (p. 12.)

body, itself, is more clearly given than the world beyond it. So, even in the mode of causal efficacy, there is one fairly clear distinction which can be made. "There is still vagueness in comparison with the accurate definition of immediate presentation; although the locality of various bodily organs which are efficacious in the regulation of the sense-data, and of the feelings, are fairly well-defined in the pure perceptive mode of causal efficacy."[79] Causal efficacy approaches clear definition and location in the body of the percipient, just as presentational immediacy reveals its derivation from vague origins in the functioning bodily organs.

Whitehead's claim about perception is that it has a peculiar dual character from the very outset. It does not provide man with simple and discrete data to function as building blocks for manipulation, without the concomitant recognition of qualifying continuities and patterned connections. Perception gives the organic interaction of wholes and parts, not an atomic or subatomic aggregate of irreducible and discrete data for molecular combination and mental constructions. This dual character is partly irrelevant to the body (presentational immediacy) and partly dependent on the body (causal efficacy).[80] But the body has a primary role in perception because it is the locus of the interaction (symbolic reference) of these two modes and the point of reference for practical application. This role of the body makes perception a direct encounter with the external world so that the discriminations of both perception and thought can have productive reference to actualities and their relationships.

Without completing the exposition of Whitehead's view of perception by the analysis of symbolic reference, it is still possible to pause for a brief assessment of his introduction of causal efficacy with respect to the understanding of religious discourse. Such an assessment is not an attempt to muster compelling evidence or decisive arguments for the adoption of Whitehead's view. Perception is an extremely complicated subject with a

79. *Sym*, pp. 55, 56.
80. *MT*, p. 209.

long history of scientific and philosophical discussion behind it.[81] The nature of the problems involved illusion, hallucinations, relative perspectives, and the causal transmission of the perceptual data is such that modern scholarship, in a broad range of disciplines, is relevant and would have to be included in any attempt to establish Whitehead's option. Psychology, anthropology, sociology, and physiology would have to be taken into account in a manner that goes well beyond the scope of this study. The concern here is to explore the shape of Whitehead's alternative and the implications that follow from it in order to understand the religious use of language. While this may be a partial argument for his views, it is not intended to establish Whitehead's doctrine as the option which solves all the persistent problems, or which takes into account the many discoveries of all the relevant disciplines.[82]

There are, of course, reasons for believing that the option that Whitehead presents is feasible. Here, one can note the growing recognition of the importance of pre-conscious experience, and the many attempts—exemplified by Gestalt psychology—to trace structure to the perceptual data.[83] Also, the most promising attempts to deal philosophically with the problem of perception parallel Whitehead's approach at significant points, even though total agreement cannot be claimed. For example, a number of critical realists have been highly appreciative of Whitehead's interpretation, and constructive approaches like the dual-aspect theory are not far removed from Whitehead's theory of the subject-object relationship.[84]

A primary implication of Whitehead's approach for the understanding of religious language is the focus of critical attention which it brings to the fundamental data provided in man's

81. R. J. Hirst, *The Problems of Perception* (London: George Allen & Unwin, 1959.)

82. For a discussion of some of these contributions, see Paul Henle, ed., *Language, Thought, and Culture* (Ann Arbor, Mich.: Univ. of Mich. Press, 1966.)

83. Floyd H. Allport, *Theories of Perception and the Concept of Structure* (New York: John Wiley and Sons, 1955.)

84. For supportive comments by a critical realist see Roy Wood Sellars, "Philosophy of Organism and Physical Realism," *The Philosophy of Alfred North Whitehead*, pp. 405–433. For the dual-aspect theory, see Hirst, *op. cit.*, pp. 189–202.

physical encounter with the environment. Whitehead's view makes it evident that there are alternative interpretations on this basic level. His articulation of a novel interpretation of the perceptual data calls attention to assumptions about the data which affect decisively any ensuing analysis or evaluation of language. This is of particular importance for religious discourse, since its expressions of generic coordination can quite easily be cut off from the empirical data by any radical emphasis on discontinuity in the raw perceptual input. Whitehead's doctrine of perception thus amounts to a direct challenge to assumptions that have often informed the criticism of religious assertions. Specifically, it questions the understanding of perception implicit in the quest for precise empirical verification, and in those treatments of language which draw on the idealist identification of structures with mental activity. It is in this way that the historical articulation of Whitehead's doctrine of perception is significant. The influences which he challenges on the contemporary scene can be traced to Hume and Kant. Therefore, the manner in which he sets his doctrine of perception against these two men is especially relevant.

It is in a framework heavily dependent on both Hume and Kant that religious assertions have been criticized most powerfully and, all too often, defended less convincingly. Whitehead shifts attention to assumptions about the perceptual data and by doing this he makes a more effective defense of religious language possible. One is not forced to defend the assertions of religion in a framework that is simply given, like that shaped by the sharp distinction between analytic and synthetic statements, but it is just the choice of fundamental assumptions that is the decisive question.

The influence of Hume is generally recognized as a dominant factor in the demand for linguistic verification. What is not so often admitted is that Hume's emphasis on discontinuity in the perceptual data is also evident in the "falsification" and "use" criteria. These apparently moderate norms of linguistic significance can be utilized in a manner that is not so far removed from the old use of the verification principle. None other than

A. J. Ayer makes the point that the identification of the meaning of an expression with its use is sustained by the verification principle.[85] Specifying with precision the circumstances that make a particular use of language appropriate can be only a more subtle way of asking for some exact and final determination of meaning—"to specify the use of a sentence, in this sense, is to describe the situations to which it is applied; in other words, to describe the situations, the states of affairs, by which the statement it expresses would be verified."[86]

The insistence on precise meaning is what is crucial here. Such a demand always depends on treating experience as fundamentally discontinuous so that, like language, it reflects sharp distinctions of inclusion and exclusion. Some neat correspondence between a linguistic formulation and its empirical referent is anticipated. Or, if that is too much to ask, then some clear-cut instance of incompatibility is sought. Finally, one can look for those distinguishable circumstances in which the use of certain words is appropriate or inappropriate. This is not to say that these tests are useless, it is only to point out how in seeking precision they can also assume it. Whenever concrete experience is treated as neatly divisible into sensations, objects, discrete periods of time or virtually independent contexts of significance, it is possible to see the influence of Hume. The consequence is always the inability to make a reliable transition from these segments of experience to generalizations of broader scope. With respect to religious discourse, one cannot move from concrete experience to assertions about the ground and goal of all experience.

In a similar way, the influence of Kant is obvious in idealistic and critical approaches to philosophy, but the same emphasis on the imposition of conceptual order on diverse perceptual intuitions is at work whenever the coordination of broad theories or metaphysical schemes is attributed primarily to mental activity. Whenever form is seen as fundamentally a mental or interpretive contribution to experience, assumptions

85. A. J. Ayer, "Philosophy and Language," *Clarity Is Not Enough*, pp. 401–428.
86. *Ibid.*, p. 418.

like those of Kant are involved. For example, when Frederick
Ferré recognizes metaphysical "facts" but makes them much
more dependent on mental activity than the discriminated
details, a Kantian bias is evident.[87] The details are dependable
contributions of experience, while the forms of coordination
are more speculative interpretations somehow imposed on the
perceptual data. As a direct consequence of this Kantian perspective, any existential inference from the necessities of
thought and language is precluded. Natural theology founders
on the Kantian critique, and the generic reference of religious
terms is cut off from man's common experience. Thus it is
possible to see the persistent influence of both Hume and Kant
on the interpretive and critical frameworks within which
religious language has often been treated. Both emphases give
distinctions more finality than may be warranted. Discontinuity
is given an ultimate significance, which shows up in the disjunction of deductive and inductive methods, the divorce of
conceptual and physical aspects of experience. This is expressed
in many ways, all equally detrimental to the positive interpretation of religious and metaphysical discourse, i.e., the
analytic-synthetic dichotomy, the separation of linguistic and
extralinguistic questions, the radical contrast between *a priori*
and *a posteriori* elements in experience, or the sharp distinction
between form and content. Hume's influence makes the move
from experience to broad generalizations problematic, while
Kant's influence is such that necessity is strictly a phenomenal
and conceptual reality.

The effect of Whitehead's innovative approach to perception
can be seen in relation to both these methods as they have
bearing on the problem of religious discourse. It can be illus-

---

87. Frederick Ferré in *Language, Logic and God* (New York: Harper & Broth-
ers, 1961) does not deal directly with the perceptual data and as a consequence
his identification of metaphysical "facts" with key "concepts" is not given any
empirical warrant; the " 'facts' of metaphysics are supremely dependent on the
conceptual activity of mind." (p. 161.) Ferré is led to an extreme relativism in
respect to metaphysics which does not resolve the problems inherent in the relationship of assertions of generic scope to the concrete data. (James A. Martin, Jr.,
The New Dialogue Between Philosophy and Theology [New York: The Seabury
Press, 1966], pp. 171–173.)

trated with respect to the falsification criterion on the one hand, and with respect to the problem of "necessary existence" on the other.

Antony Flew clearly expresses the relevance of falsification for religious convictions. "What would have to occur or to have occurred to constitute for you a disproof of the love of, or of the existence of, God?"[88] With respect to religious assertions, this amounts to a modification of the verification principle. If no confirming instances can be specified, then at least some incompatible circumstances should be conceivable. This recognizes the fact that religious assertions are more like broad scientific theories than like simple observation statements. Therefore, the request is put forward for them to be evaluated on terms comparable with those that seem applicable to the justification of scientific theories.[89] Nevertheless, there is still the obvious concern that a single instance, a specific sequence of events, or a discrete set of circumstances should give conclusive evidence of the exclusive significance of a formulation. When religious assertions cannot be provided with even such a falsifying possibility, then cognitive meaning and empirical reference is in doubt. They appear to express only conceptual and linguistic necessities or subjective states.

Whitehead's understanding of the data of perception points out the subtle effect of assumptions concerning concrete experience on this sort of argument. When the falsification criterion is used, a radical emphasis on discontinuity can be taken for granted in the attempt to justify the more general by comparison with some discrete segment of experience. It does not matter much if the discontinuity emphasized is between sensations, objects, occasions, or experience or definite periods of time. Even one human life, with an abrupt beginning and end, can carry with it a stress on definite boundaries circumscribing the empirical data. In this sense, falsification may give the same kind of precedence to discontinuity as the concern for precise

88. Flew, *op. cit.*, p. 99.
89. Karl Popper, *The Logic of Scientific Discovery* (New York: Basic Books, 1959), pp. 40–42.

verification. In both cases, a small sample of experience, which in principle is cut off from the rest of reality, is set up as the basis for a final judgment on extrapolations of much broader scope. When these generalizations approach metaphysical import, they include so much that precise and final confirmation is out of the question. They become conceptual networks projected toward the future, with a pragmatic adequacy that is always provisional. They are subject to continued testing, but it is the total impact that counts, not a few instances of congruence or one occasion of apparent incompatibility. The broadest interpretations of experience cannot rest on any assemblage of discrete particulars, nor can they be falsified by a single isolated instance of incongruence.

Statements of broad generality cannot be established in experience if at any point the contrast between the general and the particular, or between particulars is made an absolute disjunction. The confirming connection in both its supporting and qualifying power is missing. Once that has happened, the conclusion is determined. Religious assertions cannot be based on perceptual data, nor do they tell us anything about it. If the discontinuities are decisive, no language of highly general scope can be rooted in experience. Whatever can be verified by an aggregate of instances, falsified by a single instance, or restricted to an esoteric classification of significance is not a statement about God, or a formulation that has the universal import required by religious assertions. On this level, the only completely falsifying experience would be no experience whatsoever. If God is the coordinating factor in reality, pervasive chaos might work to falsify the claim that he exists, but who would carry out the test? The love of God might be falsified by the absence of all significance from my life, but then what interest would motivate me to live and ask questions about falsification? To assume that any definite occasion or limited period of experience could disprove God's existence or love is, in fact, to assume the empirical irrelevance of assertions about God from the very outset. If discontinuity is the primary characteristic of the empirical input, all attempts to express maximum generality are doomed from the start. It is this fact that Whitehead calls to our attention by his critique of modern philosophy, and by his articulation of an alternative doctrine of perception.

In providing an approach which can be used to challenge the acceptance of falsification as the final basis for cognitive meaning and empirical relevance, Whitehead gets some support from developments in the history of science and contemporary philosophy. It is now frequently admitted that deduction and induction are not mutually exclusive methodologies. They do not function in complete separation in any significant inquiry, let alone the illuminating "discoveries" of science. Thus "unity" or "form" does not have to be attributed to mental activity while the perceptual input is characterized by pluralistic diversity. In some fashion, "pattern statements" are empirical even though they are notably resistant to both verification and falsification.[90] It turns out that falsification is not the ready-made key to empirical relevance or cognitive meaning that some have thought. Scientific theories, like religious convictions are often held in spite of evidence, as well as because of it. Thomas Kuhn puts the case against falsification strongly: "If any and every failure to fit were ground for theory rejection, all theories ought to be rejected at all times."[91]

In a similar way, contemporary philosophy reveals a growing recognition that the pairs, analytic-synthetic or *a priori-a posteriori,* veil somewhat arbitrary commitments that need to be re-analyzed.[92] It is these distinctions which are intimately involved in the concern for precise confirmation, the very notion of analytic being defined by the irrelevance of empirical evidence.[93] Thus, verification and falsification seem to stand and fall together, and there are many voices raised to indicate problems

---

90. Norwood Russell Hanson, *Patterns of Discovery* (London: Cambridge Univ. Press, 1958), pp. 87–88.

91. Thomas S. Kuhn, *The Structure of Scientific Revolutions* (Chicago: The University of Chicago Press, 1964), p. 145.

92. For an extensive study of the problem see Arthur Pap, *Semantics and Necessary Truth* (New Haven and London: Yale Univ. Press, 1958).

93. W. V. O. Quine, "Two Dogmas of Empiricism," *Clarity Is Not Enough,* p. 128.

involved in both precise confirmation and the notion of analyticity. Willard Van Orman Quine's comment is representative, even if it does put the matter in polemic form. "A boundary between analytic and synthetic statements has not been drawn. That there is such a distinction to be drawn at all is an unempirical dogma of empiricists, a metaphysical article of faith."[94] If this is the case, then neither verification or falsification provides an independent or precise criterion of empirical significance. Analyticity, itself, is something of a problem and is not a completely dependable instrument for clarifying or resolving problems.[95]

Assumptions about the perceptual data can also be seen as important factors in the discussion of "necessary existence." This, of course, involves the classical ontological argument and its widely accepted refutation by Immanuel Kant. In respect to religious language, a similar problem is involved in the formulation of statements asserting God's existence in such a way as to make that peculiar existence seem logically necessary. Is it possible to entertain a concept that strictly implies the existence of its referent? Or, is it possible to formulate the assertion of God's existence so that it cannot be false?

It is the Kantian arguments against inferring existence from a concept which are considered decisive in most discussions of necessary existence. What is not usually dealt with, and which is brought to light by Whitehead's discussion of causal efficacy, is the degree to which Kant's arguments rest on his assumptions about the perceptual data. If order is imposed on disparate intuitions by given forms and categories, is it not already established that patterns of coordination cannot have existential reference? At best, only those that refer to objects in space and time could be said to indicate contingent existences. Necessary existence is strictly precluded. This makes intelligible Kant's comparison of God's existence with the obviously contingent existence of "triangles" and "dollars." Existence is so tied to contingent and

94. *Ibid.*, p. 124.
95. A J. Ayer, "Philosophy and Language," *Clarity Is Not Enough*, p. 416, and Morton White, *Toward Reunion in Philosophy* (New York: Atheneum, 1963), p. 19.

distinguishable intuitions that the empirical apprehension or the inference of necessary existence is out of the question. Kant's emphasis on discontinuity in the data is further indicated by his confident use of the notions of "containment" and "addition" in his discussion of existence as a predicate. Inclusion and exclusion are taken as fundamental and, more importantly, as precise and final in the distinctions they establish. The grasp of pervasive order with existential implications is vitiated by initial assumptions about the relation of form and content, the contribution of the percipient, and the input of sensation. It is just on this basis that Kant's arguments against all natural theology are established, and it would seem that they can carry no more weight than his interpretation of perception.

However, on the contemporary scene, the ontological approach to necessary existence is generally rejected. As J. N. Findlay has described the situation: "The proofs based on the necessities of thought are universally regarded as fallacious: it is not thought possible to build bridges between mere abstractions and concrete existence."[96] While the ontological argument still fascinates philosophers, there are not too many who will defend it as a convincing proof. Fortunately, the nature of proof itself on that level is problematic so that the ontological approach can be appreciated for reasons which transcend the canons of logic.[97] And, there are those, like Charles Hartshorne and Schubert Ogden, who persist in defending the logical force of the argument.[98] It is in this context that Whitehead's doctrine of perception suggests a subtle difference in the approach to necessary existence.

Whitehead is as skeptical of the ontological approach as Kant, if it is simply a question of moving from *mere* concepts or linguistic formulations to existence. If the ontological type of

---

96. J. N. Findlay, "Can God's Existence Be Disproved," *New Essays in Philosophical Theology*, p. 47.

97. Cyril C. Richardson, "The Strange Fascination of the Ontological Argument," *Union Seminary Quarterly Review*, Vol. XVIII, No. 1, (November, 1952), pp. 1–21.

98. Charles Hartshorne, *The Logic of Perfection and other Essays in Neoclassical Metaphysics* (LaSalle, Ill.: Open Court Publishing Company, 1962), Schubert Ogden, *The Reality of God* (New York: Harper & Row, 1966).

approach requires such a leap, then Whitehead offers little support for it.[99] But, the subtle difference is that Whitehead's doctrine of causal efficacy allows for a necessity that is not *merely* conceptual or logical. Order is derived from concrete experience and not simply imposed upon it. With respect to dollars, islands, and other particular existences this does not make too much difference, but when it comes to the widest possible mode of coordination, contingency gives way to necessity. At the point where the broadest patterns of experience are grasped, necessity becomes an empirical intuition. The apprehension of maximum generality, even as it is implied in ordinary experience, carries with it a conformal power approaching necessity. Thus, the idea of God, and the assertion of his existence as the factor in experience that contributes the very order which makes any experience possible, carry with them a necessary reference to existence.

It is Whitehead's interpretation of the perceptual data as providing organic, hierarchical patterns of various grades of generality, which is the basis for the revised notion of necessity. Every experienced factor, every occasion of experience, depends on a relatively stable order of such scope that its reality must be taken for granted. This necessity precedes conceptualization and logical development. It depends on Whitehead's introduction of causal efficacy as the fundamental mode of perception.[100] Whitehead thus presents grounds for an argument from empirical necessity, not one based on sheer logical contradiction or inconceivability. The experience of relative stability provides a reference for various characterizations of this aspect of reality.

This shift in the meaning of necessity provides a new point of departure for the interpretation of natural theology. It insures that expressions about God always have denotation, even if their connotations are tentative, vague, and indeterminate. Like classical natural theology, Whitehead's approach is of more help with respect to God's existence than in filling out the details of

99. *RM*, pp. 68–69.
100. While Hartshorne, *op. cit.*, and Ogden, *op. cit.*, both draw on Whitehead's insights, they put such emphasis on the logical force of the argument that Whitehead's subtle innovation in respect to necessity may be obscured.

his character. *That* God exists is necessary, but *what* he is discerned to be depends on specific intuitions which run the risk of serious error.

The largely negative character of necessary existence is the culmination of Whitehead's view that consciousness is grounded in the negative type of prehension. It is based on the discernment of contrasts and the partial grasp of entities in their relationships. This suggests that concepts, as well, are less definite with respect to what they contain than with respect to the contrasts that distinguish them. As Whitehead has described the process of understanding empirical data which transcend the boundaries of thought, "A partially understood pattern is more definite as to what it excludes than as to what its completion would include."[101] Man's grasp of realities thus always leaves room for mystery and further penetration. On the level of the broadest possible pattern, what is definitely excluded is non-existence. The rest is open to inquiry.

The recognition of necessity in the perceptual data gives to the tautological relationships of both thought and language a residual empirical content. They are not strictly empty merely because they reflect patterns of the widest generality. The necessities that are evident in conceptual and symbolic structures are, for Whitehead, abstract derivations from concrete experience. Since man can focus his attention on the very general contours of experience, abstract formulations expressing necessity can be referred to the perceptual data. In this way, the concept of God as the one necessary existent, or the assertion of that unique mode of existence, can indicate and illuminate what is ultimately an empirical intuition. Fundamental religious assertions are not simply weighed in the balance between formal necessity and concrete possibility, with no mediating alternatives. They can express the connections between the necessary and the contingent aspects of human experience.

Whitehead's attribution of conceptual and linguistic necessity to an empirical intuition can be compared with Martin Heideg-

101. *MT*, p. 72.

ger's understanding of language. Heidegger's view has also been seen as providing a new departure for the understanding of statements concerning necessary existence.[102] As Arthur McGill describes it: "Words, according to Martin Heidegger, are not primarily the tools by which men express what is already in their heads. Rather they are the *instrument of reality itself,* the medium through which being discloses itself, using man's voice as its spokesman. Language is not about reality, it is reality in the state of unveiledness, and in every statement it is the subject matter—not the subjectivity of the author—which addresses man's thought.[103]

In this more positive sense, Whitehead's doctrine of causal efficacy enriches the perceptual data so that the meaning of religious assertions is elucidated by mundane experience as well as by the special intuitions, scriptures, and history of the religious perspective. The reference of religious expressions can be found by attending to ordinary, average, human experience, rather than by exclusive interest in the narrowly religious appropriation of special connotative intuitions. Whitehead offers an option for the interpretation of religious language in which the ultimate reference of all religious discourse can be discerned in *any* occasion of experience. Whitehead's philosophy suggests that the most productive starting point for reflection on patterns of wide generality is not the clear and certain discrimation of distinct and discrete factors. In a similar way, religious assertions are not clarified merely by focusing upon the obviously religious intuitions they express. Instead, even the most esoteric religious claims require some reference to man's common experience, which is only available if such experience offers more than objects or sensations.

The richness of the perceptual data is insured by the connections and conformation grasped in the mode of causal efficacy. By insisting that continuities are given in the empirical data, Whitehead provides a basis for understanding religious

---

102. Arthur C. McGill, "Recent Discussions of Anselm's Argument," *The Many-faced Argument,* ed. by John H. Hick and Arthur C. McGill (New York: The Macmillan Co., 1967), pp. 109–110.
103. *Ibid.,* p. 110.

language that does not preclude reference to a mode of coordination which is universal in its relevance to both facts and values. The apparently clear-cut and highly useful distinctions are not allowed to develop into insoluble and unsatisfying dilemmas. Instead, they are important as they are relative to a context of integrated relationships given in perception.

This underlying continuity allows man's fundamental physical experience to include a wide range of diverse factors. There are encountered actualities—particular and unique in their own right. They are given in a concrete process of abstraction, through the direct interchange of emotion which is the fabric of experience. These particulars cannot be singled out from their relationships without selective emphasis. They are not given as independent entities, even though they can be treated that way. They enter experience as distinguishable factors in a complex of relationships. These relationships can also be the basis for other forms of abstraction and expression. Causal derivation is such a relationship. Other coordinating patterns of various grades of generality are relationships available for emphasis. Even the crucial influence of valuation is given in the data. There simply are no naked facts which do not reflect the selective activity involved in their generation, apprehension, and emphasis.

It is this common experience of value that shapes the religious dimension of experience and which provides generic reference for the term "God." Value implies order, diverse possibilities, and stability. The "timeless co-ordination of the infinitude of possibility for realization."[104] Values require alternatives arranged in some relative order, with some basis for comparison and contrast. Arising out of the past, they point to antecedent valuation whereby some arrangement of alternatives is established.[105] As they perish, they contribute to the significance of the universe in a manner that suggests some conservation of attainment. God is identified by Whitehead with this

104. *SP*, p. 99.
105. This is the argument used by Whitehead to establish the metaphysical necessity of a principle of concretion in *Science and The Modern World*, pp. 160–161.

"reservoir of potentiality" and "coordination of achieve-ment."[106] Pursued either in respect to the physical enjoyment of definiteness or the intellectual entertainment of possibilities, value experience points beyond itself to the transcendent and permanent. "As physical feelings are haunted by the vague insistence of causality, so the higher intellectual feelings are haunted by the vague insistence of another order, where there is no unrest, no travel, no shipwreck."[107]

Perception offers a wealth of data integrated initially in a single occasion of experience. Physical feelings of a multitude of temporal actual entities contribute their massive and insis-tent data. Conceptual feelings abstract forms of definiteness as a distinctive type of data. Other conceptual feelings are given which have only a secondary relationship to the objectified data derived from the impact of temporal actualities. Such con-ceptual feelings introduce the proximate alternatives which are the basis for novelty and diversity. They are the product of conceptual reversion (if God is not considered) and they pro-vide data which are partially identical with, and partially derived from, that given by physical rapport with temporal realities. Their status is clarified when Whitehead claims that God, the one non-temporal actual entity, is their origin and the initiator of their relevance for each organism. In other words, a physical feeling of God's conceptual vision of a range of possi-bilities is a fundamental component of the perceptual complex. God provides the initial subjective aim and a structure of pos-sibility which is the basis for the contrast between the actual and the potential, the ground of consciousness and freedom. Hume made such ordered possibilities as that implied in the color spectrum an insignificant exception to his doctrine of independent impressions. Whitehead makes them fundamental to perception, whether attributed to conceptual reversion or the vision of God.[108]

Whitehead sees values as leading beyond themselves because

106. *MT*, p. 128.
107. *PR*, p. 516.
108. *Ibid.*, p. 377.

of their relative independence of temporal consideration. "No heroic deed, and no unworthy act, depends for its heroism, or disgust, upon the exact second of time at which it occurs."[109] Or, for example, the enjoyable taste of a delicious apple tart implies a coordination of values that transcends a single time sequence.[110] What is enjoyed *now* leads to the consideration of what might be enjoyed at some other time and in a different set of circumstances. In this way, all value experience suggests significance in respect to the totality of the universe. The experience of value, in a very mundane way, involves both the coordination of possibility and some conservation of significance.[111]

Value experience depends on selection and exclusion, maintenance and disregard. Beginning on the physical level, all experience is "accompanied by an appetite for, or against, its continuance."[112] Thus it tends to differentiate into a sense of multiple values in a context of coordination. "There is the feeling of the ego, the others, the totality."[113] When these feelings are conceptualized, the generic basis of religion becomes evident. Grasped in one moment of consciousness, the value of the individual for itself, the value of the diverse individuals for each other, and the value of the derivative totality combine to give empirical reference to special religious claims.[114]

The ordinary experiences of value, if their implications are heeded, lead to a general formulation of the religious problem, an open question about the character of the universal coordination of fact and value. Does the temporal perishing of actualities contribute to an order in which "novelty does not mean loss?"[115] This does not preclude the empirical grasp of unique and illuminating special religious intuitions. Instead, it is the fabric in which they are discerned, providing the connections so they can shed light on the broadest dimensions of human

109. *SP*, p. 88.
110. *Ibid.*, p. 89.
111. *MT*, pp. 149–152.
112. *PR*, p. 48.
113. *MT*, p. 151.
114. *RM*, p. 58.
115. *PR*, p. 517.

experience. The general characteristics of religious experience are given along with novel insights, not in separation from them. All experience is partial disclosure of the unanticipated. Such revelatory experiences provide the specific content of concrete experience. The particulars experienced and the relationships discerned are in some respects unique. In this sense, Whitehead's emphasis on the generic reference of religious assertions does not restrict the elucidation of special insights. Indeed, there could be no significance in special religious claims, if the universe itself did not reflect some primordial order of importance and a concrete appropriation of every achievement. What is important and what is conserved are then the relevant questions.

Thus, Whitehead's view of perception permits religious assertions to be based on the pervasive experience of value. There is no special religious sense, separate and insulated from the normal channels of discovery.[116] Intuitions of holiness, the sacred, or an absoluteness in the nature of things, which are the foundations of all religion, can be traced to common values—enjoyed or imagined. The sweet taste of a lump of sugar or the beauty of a primeval flower are clues to a transcendent initiation and sharing of value. Through them, as well as through our own specifically religious intuitions, "our sense of the value of the details for the totality dawns upon our consciousness."[117] Or, on the cultural level of experience, the limited loyalties and obligations of our social structures point beyond themselves to a universal structure of opportunity and responsibility. Beyond the ruling Caesar, the economic system, or a specific religious community "there stretches the array of aspirations whose coordinating principle is termed God."[118]

This is the way in which Whitehead gives empirical anchorage to the term "God." Its meaning is not to be sought in logical or conceptual relationships alone, nor is it a linguistic symbol that it merely instrumental in the integration of our

116. RM, pp. 119–120.
117. MT, p. 164.
118. SP, pp. 73–74.

understanding. Instead, the term refers initially to man's physical encounter with his environment and the perceptual data that it provides. In principle, the term "God" refers to a factor involved in every occasion of experience, without which "every activity is merely a passing whiff of insignificance."[119] Religion is founded on stability and valuation discerned in the process, apart from which nothing else could be significantly apprehended.[120] The reference of religious assertions is not to be found by turning away from concrete realities and physical interaction, but by looking more closely at what is involved in our feelings of rapport with the on-going process, and our selective grasp of "objects" and "facts" given in perception. Single out a tree in the midst of a pastoral scene, or a definite pattern in scientific observations, and the selective enjoyment involved offers an empirical key to the ultimate reference of any religious assertion.

This amounts to a radical modification of the persistent demand for linguistic clarification in its usual forms. When causal efficacy is taken into account as a mode of perception, it qualifies the use of any one definite type of precision as the norm of clarity and cognition. There are different kinds of clarity and different types of empirical reference, depending on the intentions involved and the scope of the experience included. Clarification of experience and expression can be attained on various levels of generality without the complete loss of concrete connections. It can be achieved by emphasizing the manner in which "things" are together, as well as the ways in which they can be treated as independent and separable. Clarity does not automatically require the pursuit of reductive analysis in which the complex and general must always be seen as a secondary construction.

The fact that clarity seems somewhat more difficult to attain when we focus on patterns of general scope does not justify the narrowing of the empirical data to that which can be handled with relative ease and precision. In Whitehead's view,

119. *Ibid.*, p. 102.
120. *RM*, p. 8.

clarity is always qualified, tentative, and partial. Exactness pursued in one perspective is achieved by excluding other important factors in experience. When achieved, it gives a certainty which is provisional and a confidence that does not exclude either qualification or the risk of partiality. But such clarity functions to provide useful points of reference by its holding some features of experience in abeyance. Some factors given in the perceptual data are treated as constants, so that other factors can be explored in relationship to them. What is discovered is what Dorothy Emmet calls "systematic concomitant variation."[121] Such clarity as is given is relative and partial. Things are clear enough for the moment .They are clear enough for specific purposes. They are clear enough to provide one contribution to an inclusive interpretation of experience which involves all the modes of abstraction available. We move from tentative and partial clarity toward new investigations of our environment in the continually expanding search for an increased understanding which will take as much of our experience as possible into account.

The significance of this doctrine of the perceptual data for religious language is that assertions about God and the meaning of life do not have to be seen as totally divorced from scientific or common sense expressions of empirical observations. Whitehead makes room for language about God which is firmly based in the mundane and fundamental experience of every organism. Such language refers to perceptual data, even though it utilizes such data by extension and extrapolation that is metaphysical in scope. Such extension of given data beyond its origin is patterned after the activity involved in the mixed mode of perception which Whitehead calls "symbolic reference." That activity must now receive the focus of our attention.

121. Dorothy M. Emmet, *The Nature of Metaphysical Thinking,* uses this term to correct what she sees as a too precise isomorphism between the perceptual data and transcendent actualities in Whitehead's thought. It would seem that "systematic concomitant variation" is a type of isomorphism, and, in fact, just the kind that is available in a world of process and interaction. (p. 62.)

6

SYMBOLIC

INTERPRETATION

The purpose of this chapter is to provide a more direct examination of the pervasive symbolic activity which, in Whitehead's system, underlies sense-perception and all linguistic expression. Such symbolic activity is relevant to the problem of religious language because it establishes continuity between discourse that is apparently precise and the obviously analogical expressions of religion. If a common pattern of selection and projection is the basis for all language, then *any* expression of cognition is qualified, and no form of language can be isolated from the cognitive process merely because of its highly symbolic character. Thus, Whitehead's doctrine of symbolic reference gives further support to the general thesis that the assertions of religion may have both cognitive and affective import.

Whitehead understands symbolism as the movement from one element in experience to another. One factor calls attention to the other and thus functions as a symbol for it.[1] This is what Whitehead terms "symbolic reference." As the transition which relates any symbol to its meaning, this activity is the "interpretive element in human experience."[2]

Whitehead distinguishes between fundamental forms of symbolism and those which are relatively superficial. Some modes of symbolism are easily adopted and readily discarded. Medieval

1. *Sym*, pp. 7–8.
2. *PR*, p. 263.

heraldry, architecture, and ceremony are illustrations of superficial types of symbolism. Highly significant in their own time,
they were purged by the Reformation with relative ease in an
attempt to return to a more direct apprehension of ultimate
facts. Such a reduction in their importance did not radically
change the fundamental character of man's existence.[3]

Language, on the other hand, is a much more fundamental
type of symbolism. It is difficult to conceive of man as truly
human without it. As a fundamental form of symbolism, language provides a ready example of the nature of symbolic
activity. Words, for instance, indicate the characteristic pattern of the symbol-meaning relationship. "The word is a
symbol, and its meaning is constituted by the ideas, images, and
emotions, which it raises in the mind of the hearer."[4]

Whitehead claims there is an even more basic symbolic
activity involved in perception. This symbolism is not limited to
man, but is shared by all the higher organisms in which the
sense-organs and sense-perception have developed. This mode
of symbolic activity is the interpretive transition whereby the
experiencing subject refers the definite and ordered appearances of presentational immediacy to the vaguely and dimly
discerned actualities perceived in the mode of causal efficacy.
It transforms the barren deliverances of sense-perception into
useful clues to the actualities in the environment. This symbolic activity is not normally noticed. It takes place without
conscious effort, and without reflection. It is a condition involved in the development of sophisticated mental activity, and
is not the result of what could be considered judgment or
inference. It is required by the nature of sense-perception and
the abstract presentation of reality given by this mode of perception. The consequence of this fundamental form of symbolic
activity is the ability to recognize and identify objects for practical utilization. It enables us, from the very beginning of
experience, to refer our definite perceptions to those actualities
that are important in respect to our decisions and actions. It

3. *Sym*, p. 1.
4. *Ibid.*, p. 2.

also provides a basis for the development of other levels of symbolism and their continued application to concrete reality. As Whitehead describes it: "Symbolism from sense-presentation to physical bodies is the most natural and widespread of all symbolic modes."[5] It is interpretive activity, not because it is consciously contrived or based on reflective inference, but because it relates two factors given in experience in a synthetic fashion that is not entirely required by the given relationship or content of the components. This form of symbolism is essential to the higher organisms because it makes both serious error and the satisfaction of productive interpretation possible. "It plays a dominant part in the way in which all higher organisms conduct their lives. It is the cause of progress, and the cause of error."[6] It has great potential and commensurate risk. It enables the higher organisms to give some accurate definition to those factors in their immediate world, which partially determine their future adventures and existence.

Symbolic reference, in its most fundamental role, seems to utilize the less concrete component of experience as a symbol for that which is more concrete and more complex. It is, therefore, quite natural for the data given in presentational immediacy to function as symbols for the data given in causal efficacy. The direction of symbolic movement, however, is not necessarily from the more abstract to the more concrete. Symbolic reference can also function in the opposite direction. There is nothing in the components, themselves, that conclusively determines which one will be symbol or meaning.[7]

Symbolic activity does require some basis for the transition from symbol to meaning. There must be something that the two components have in common to provide a partial ground for the movement from the one to the other. In respect to the two basic modes of perception, the functioning body provides such a common ground. The body gives an identical point of

5. *Ibid.*, p. 4.
6. *Ibid.*, p. 59.
7. *Ibid.*, p. 10.

reference for the data given in both presentational immediacy and causal efficacy. The illustrated, contemporary world and the transition from the settled past to anticipated future intersect in the one body.

> In this way, the animal body is the great central ground underlying all symbolic reference. In respect to bodily perceptions the two modes achieve the maximum of symbolic reference, and pool their feelings referent to identical regions.[8]

An example Whitehead uses to illuminate the point of intersection is that of the eye as perceived in both modes. The eye is perceived in the mode of causal efficacy as functioning prior to the present moment and the fleeting impression of eye strain is included in the data of presentational immediacy. Because of this intersection in a functioning organ of the body, an identification can be made in respect to the two modes which provides some basis for further correlation in more complex symbolic reference.[9]

Whitehead also refers to this ground of symbolic reference as the presented locus. This is the field of contemporary data as it intersects with the transition from past to future as given in causal efficacy. It is that contemporary cross-section of actuality which indicates the complementary nature of the two modes by its exclusion of past and future. What is left out in the one mode is given in the other. The presented locus is defined negatively by causal efficacy and positively by presentational immediacy. This intersection of the two modes occurs in the body and allows the two to be productively related.[10] Like two interlocking pieces in a jigsaw puzzle, the two modes of perception indicate their compatibility and interdependence.

A second ground for symbolic reference is provided by the forms of definiteness which qualify both the experiencing subject and the actuality perceived.[11] These forms of definiteness

8. *PR*, p. 258.
9. *Ibid.*
10. *Ibid.*, p. 257.
11. *Sym*, p. 15.

are what Whitehead has termed "eternal objects." They are similar to the traditional universals, those repeatable and recognizable characteristics which have been understood as both ideas and sense-impressions. The crucial feature of these forms is their capacity for abstract consideration apart from their particular exemplification. They can be detached from the actuality which they characterize and entertained in their general potential for determining definiteness. But, in Whitehead's view, this abstraction can never be complete. It is always a matter of degree, and at some point the origin of the partially detached forms must be taken into account. It is this kind of abstraction that takes place in both causal efficacy and presentational immediacy. Forms of definiteness are perceived in causal efficacy in the most concrete manner. The same forms are grasped more definitely in the second mode of perception.

Since the forms are the same in the two modes of perception, a second ground is given for matching up the two types of empirical data.[12] The characteristics which are given distinctly in presentational immediacy are simplified and enhanced abstractions of the same forms which are appropriated through the mode of causal efficacy. Moving further, those same forms actually qualify both the actuality perceived and the percipient. They can therefore be the basis for symbolic reference between the two modes and also the foundation for realistic claims about actualities. The perception of these forms in the actual encounter of the percipient with other realities produces a partial re-enactment of the same forms in the two modes of perception.

Whitehead thus modifies the more traditional understanding of universals much in the same way as he relativized the subject-object distinction. Universals and particulars are two different aspects of the same actualities. "Every so-called 'universal' is particular in the sense of being just what it is, diverse from everything else; and every so-called 'particular' is universal in the sense of entering into the constitutions of other

12. *PR*, p. 259.

actual entities."[13] One cannot, in Whitehead's view, make a precise and absolute distinction between a universal and a particular. To do so would be to commit the fallacy of misplaced concreteness, taking a distinction that holds on a high level of abstraction and attributing it to concrete reality. There is a productive distinction to be made between the forms of definiteness and their particular exemplifications, but this distinction is achieved by abstraction from our most concrete levels of experience in which universals and particulars are inextricably enmeshed in the interdependence of process. The universals functioning relationally are constitutive factors in the particular actualities, and the qualification of a particular actuality is the only basis on which a universal has the power to function at all. The primary data given in perception are always actual entities which are particulars mediated by universals.[14] They are not perceived except as they are "absorbed into feeling in virtue of certain universals shared alike by the objectified actuality and the experient subject."[15] This is but another way of saying that the content of our experience applies to a real world of actualities which are characterized by the qualities and relationships perceived.

While the two grounds of symbolic reference do provide some basis on which the two modes of perception can be correlated, they do not by themselves determine the resulting combination. Symbolic reference always involves some flexibility of interpretation so that various degrees of success and failure are possible in the attempt to relate the two modes of perception productively. The common elements do not by themselves necessitate symbolic reference, nor do they give an immunity from error and disaster for the percipient.[16] The datum is the same for both modes of perception, but it is treated so differently and presented in such diverse ways that

13. *Ibid.*, p. 76.
14. *PR*, p .230.
15. *Ibid.*, p. 78.
16. *Sym*, p. 8.

mistakes can easily be made.[17] Even on the most fundamental level of symbolic reference errors occur as a result of the incomplete intersection of the two basic modes.

The initial errors in perception are not seen as the result of the inadequacy of either mode of perception or as the consequence of conceptual analysis. Rather, error is introduced by the faulty combination of the two modes which is accomplished by the animal body. Delusive perception and hallucinations are examples of this kind of mistake. The datum of perception is given in the mixed mode and it is only then that conceptual analysis can be applied in an effort to test the adequacy of perception.

> In the mixed mode, the perceptive determination is purely due to the bodily organs, and thus there is a gap in the perceptive logic—so to speak. This gap is not due to any conceptual freedom on the part of the ultimate subject. It is not a mistake due to consciousness. It is due to the fact that the body, as an instrument for synthesizing and enhancing feelings, is faulty, in the sense that it produces feelings which have but slight reference to the real state of the presented duration.[18]

Error is not the result of the intervention of thought but, rather, its likelihood is increased by the absence of reflection. Whitehead cites the example of the dog in Aesop's fables that lost the meat it was carrying because it grasped for the image of the meat in the water.[19] This error was not brought about by mental activity so much as by its absence. The dog did not stop to think about the symbolic reference involved. It is in this sense that the potential for error is involved in the perceptual form of symbolic reference. The two modes of perception function dependably, but either a faulty combination of the two or the absence of effective conceptual analysis can result in grave error. Conceptual analysis can be a corrective because it provides for discriminating the two basic modes in

17. *PR*, p. 262.
18. *Ibid.*, p. 274.
19. *Sym*, p. 19.

their relatively pure form. This allows a partial check on the already accomplished symbolic reference.[20] The absence of error depends on the lack of a developed sense-perception in the lower organisms. Where there is no presentational immediacy, there can be no interpretation at all and therefore no mistakes. The low-grade organisms merely conform to the deliverances of causal efficacy.[21]

Whitehead makes a good deal of the fact that error is not simply a destructive development. Error is the occasion for the progressive emergence of sophistication and freedom in the life of organisms. It is the "schoolmaster by whose agency there is upward evolution."[22] Even the development of consciousness can be seen as closely related to the frustration of error. In consciousness, the crucial factor is the contrast between what is and what might have been.[23] Error plays an important role in making that contrast apparent. To make mistakes on the very basic level of symbolic reference is a step which promotes the attainment of consciousness and various degrees of freedom. Therefore, Whitehead speaks appreciatively of error.

> We must not, however, judge too severely of error. In the initial stages of mental progress, error in symbolic reference is the discipline which promotes imaginative freedom. Aesop's dog lost his meat, but he gained a step on the road towards a free imagination.[24]

Whitehead's appeal to direct recognition in the two pure modes of perception is an important aspect of his doctrine of symbolism. He finds it necessary and possible to distinguish between direct knowledge, which is infallible, and the symbolic combinations which introduce the problem of error. Direct knowledge provides criteria by which the trustworthiness of

20. *Ibid.*, p. 10.
21. *Ibid.*
22. *PR*, p. 256.
23. *Ibid.*, p. 372.
24. *Sym*, p. 19.

symbolic references can be partially and tentatively evaluated.[25] Terminology presents a difficulty at this point because Whitehead calls this direct knowledge by a variety of names, suggesting that it is not knowledge in any formal or precise sense. It is an awareness of dependable and decisive contact with other actualities. It is recognition, or simply experience. "What you have experienced, you have experienced."[26] It is to be found by attending to the two basic modes of perception in their pure form. It is also to be had in the higher forms of symbolic activity in which the two components involved must always be intrinsically capable of direct recognition.[27] According to one of Whitehead's explicit definitions, it is "conscious recognition of a percept in a pure mode, devoid of symbolic reference."[28]

The discrimination of the pure modes of perception is the result of conceptual analysis. What is given on the most basic level of awareness is the already synthesized product of the two modes. Conceptual analysis proceeds to distinguish and separate the data as given by each of the fundamental modes. "Thus the result of symbolic reference is what the actual world is for us, as that datum in our experience productive of feelings, emotions, satisfactions, actions, and finally as the topic for conscious recognition when our mentality intervenes with its conceptual analysis."[29] We begin with the symbolic combination which is the result of pre-reflective interpretation and then we can proceed to factor out the pure modes of perception from the complex datum of experience. If some form of direct recognition is found to disagree with the symbolic combination, then error has been discovered and can potentially be corrected in future interpretations. No matter how sophisticated our train of symbolic reference, it is always subject to some kind of check by tracing it back to the two pure modes of perception. We discover error when "some 'direct recognition' disagrees,

25. *Ibid.*, p. 7.
26. *Ibid.*, p. 6.
27. *Ibid.*, p. 10.
28. *Ibid.*, p. 19.
29. *Ibid.*, p. 18.

in its report of the actual world, with the conscious recognition of the fused product resulting from symbolic reference."[30]

Direct knowledge in the mode of causal efficacy is closely tied to our awareness of our bodies. It is "existential" in the sense that it makes use of our concrete encounter with reality as its point of reference. Here it can be said that we have "infallible" experience.[31] There may be many questions about what it is that we are experiencing, but we are at the very least certain that we are experiencing something. The vividness of memory and the intimacy of the bodily organs combine to give us a degree of certainty that is unsurpassable. Whitehead puts it descriptively in an example of a lost traveler. "A traveler, who has lost his way, should not ask, Where am I? What he really wants to know is, Where are the other places? He has got his own body, but he has lost them."[32] In this sense, the body provides us with a criterion that enables us to test our symbolic interpretations in a partial way. The causal efficacy that is felt so insistently in our own involvement in the concrete interaction of the process allows us to make a relative distinction between our own bodies and the world around them, so that some correction can be given to our symbolic references to other actualities and objects. We have one distinction given in the mode of causal efficacy that can be taken with existential certainty. "The differentiation of the world into the animal body which is the region of intimate, intense, mutual expression, and the rest of nature where the intimacy and intensity of feeling fails to penetrate."[33] This distinction makes us certain of our experiences of other actualities, even though their distinctive features are vague and indefinite.

Presentational immediacy also provides a kind of limited certainty that is simply not attainable in the mixed mode of perception. Taken by itself, this mode of perception provides accuracy and precision within its own context. That context is,

30. *Ibid.*, p. 19.
31. *Ibid.*, p. 6.
32. *PR*, p. 259.
33. *MT*, pp. 98–99.

of course, abstract and does not tell us how these characteristics and relationships should be applied to the actualities
given in causal efficacy. In other words, what we perceive in
presentational immediacy is certain. We do not make errors
until these relatively abstract characteristics and relationships
are attributed to concrete actualities. The certainty given in
this mode of perception is the infallibility of appearances and
abstract relationships.[34]

The limitations of our direct knowledge are obvious. In
causal efficacy we are aware of the concreteness of our involvement with a world of actualities, but we know very little
about the nature of our companions. In presentational immediacy we have extensive relationships and clearly perceived
characteristics, but we are not so sure that these appearances
have reference to the real world or just how this information
should be interpreted. The certainties provided by the two
pure modes are not adequate by themselves to keep our trains
of symbolic reference on the right track. So the appeal to direct
experience must be supplemented by an adventuresome and
pragmatic appeal to future occasions of confirmation. We never
get to the place where we can dispense with symbolism or the
tentative probes of the future that it allows. But that symbolism
always has some points of direct confirmation. "All human
symbolism . . . is ultimately to be reduced to trains of this
fundamental symbolic reference, trains which finally connect
precepts in alternative modes of direct recognition."[35]

It is important to notice a certain lack of clarity in Whitehead's claim that direct knowledge is available in the pure
modes of perception. Whitehead's general position on the
impossibility of complete abstraction comes to bear on this
issue. Any abstractive emphasis is going to retain some connection with the complex from which it is taken, so the assertion that direct recognition is available in the two pure modes
seems to refer to an approach toward an asymptotic limit.
Whitehead is not saying that infallible and pure perceptive

34. *PR*, p. 261.
35. *Sym*, p. 7.

experience is possible in a strict sense, but that we can approach that ideal and find significant correctives for our symbolic interpretations. This is why the approach to the pure modes is arduous, and why examples are difficult to produce.

> Great care is required to distinguish the two modes. In order to find obvious examples of the pure mode of causal efficacy we must have recourse to the viscera and to memory; and to find examples of the pure mode of presentational immediacy we must have recourse to so-called 'delusive' perceptions.[36]

So the certain and infallible experience that is described in Whitehead's philosophy is highly qualified and limited. Direct experience is not the simple starting point in our conscious encounter with the world, but it is a partial means of testing our interpretations which can help us to cope with our environment and our future. The pragmatic appeal to the future and the role of reason are of great importance in productive interpretation. Reason in the means whereby we can discriminate the relatively pure contributions of causal efficacy and presentational immediacy in both the present and future checks on our experience. Indeed, the function of reason is intimately related to the use of symbols. "It is the task of reason to understand and purge the symbols on which humanity depends."[37] In order for reason to fulfill this function, it is necessary that the mixed mode should allow, at the very least, a partial discrimination of direct and reliable factors. Whitehead makes it quite plain that in the context of practical activity complete purity of the perceptive modes is neither possible nor necessary. We have, then, knowledge that is certain in two limited areas which cannot be the total basis for action or interpretation. The certainty we do have can only be productive in its recombination with the 'probabilities' of symbolic reference. Our interpretations are confirmed by their contribution to survival and self-satisfaction.[38]

36. *PR*, p. 186.
37. *Sym*, p. 7.
38. *Ibid.*, p. 80.

The way in which Whitehead describes the functioning of science suggests both the need for seeking pure and certain knowledge, as well as the difficulties and limitations involved. He sees scientific observations as intended to take place in the pure mode of presentational immediacy. "In this way accuracy is secured, in the sense that the direct observation is purged of all interpretation."[39] Yet, we are aware from other comments by Whitehead that observations and theory are inextricably intertwined. Whitehead has written that, "Every scientific memoir in its record of the 'facts' is shot through and through with interpretation."[40] And, theory has its primary mode of reference in causal efficacy. "All scientific theory is stated in terms referring exclusively to the scheme of relatedness, which, so far as it is observed, involves the percepta in the pure mode of causal efficacy."[41] Keeping these two modes separate seems like a very difficult matter, and variation of abstractive emphasis very likely provides the best way of understanding what Whitehead has in mind. Thus, even the rigorous attempts of science to separate the two pure modes results in an isolation that is only relative and partial. What is available as comparatively direct knowledge seems to be a kind of optimum emphasis which enables us to distinguish quite clearly between "factual" and "theoretical" considerations, even though in practice they are always influenced by one another.

The justification of symbolic reference between the two modes of perception turns out to be a much more complex affair than Whitehead's assertion of direct knowledge might first suggest. In spite of the availability of relatively direct knowledge in limited areas, experience always remains a "baffling mixture of certainty, ignorance, and probability."[42] We begin with a complex of symbolic interpretations which may be in grave error. "Symbolism . . . may induce actions, feelings, emotions, and beliefs about things which are mere notions

39. *PR*, p. 257.
40. *Ibid.*, p. 22.
41. *Ibid.*, p. 257.
42. *Ibid.*, p. 313.

without that exemplification in the world which the symbolism leads us to presuppose."[43] We cannot get entirely outside this complex of symbolic interpretation to give it the kind of rigorous testing and analysis that could satisfy all doubts and questions. Yet, within our symbolized environment, we can press our interpretations toward two poles of limitation in which diverse factors provide a relative check on the interpretations involved. Even in the middle of a buzzing world of experience, we can factor out two relatively certain points of reference to assist us in correcting our errors and reaching productive satisfaction.

Our present capacity for testing symbolic reference is increased by the process and its transition from past to future. Not only can we remember the tests we made in the past, but we can also anticipate the kind of checks which will be available in the future. In this way, the productive but partial justification of symbolic reference shares in the forward thrust of the creative process. What is only partial and tentative in the moment can be applied to events which are still in the process of development. Our knowledge, like the process is "on the way." The temporal movement of the "process" from past to future multiplies the opportunities for testing symbolic references against direct recognition. The justification of symbolic reference is not dependent on the immediate occasion, and the limited perspective that it affords. If that were the case, isolated instances of confirmation would give an instantaneous confidence in symbolic interpretations, but no basis for relating the confirmations attained with either past or future. In Whitehead's view, each immediate occasion of direct recognition can be fitted into patterns of connection with past confirmations which approximate modes of stability of the process. There is a wide range of historical accumulation which assists in the pursuit of present justification and suggests patterns for future occasions of confirmation. Whitehead describes the cumulative resources of confirmation in this way:

43. *Sym*, p. 6.

The mere interrogation of immediate consciousness at one immediate moment tells us very little. Analytic power vanishes under such direct scrutiny. We have recourse to memory, to the testimony of others including their memories, to language in the form of the analysis of words and phrases—that is to say, to etymology and syntax. We should also consider the institutions of mankind in the light of an embodiment of their stable experience.[44]

On the basis of experienced stability in the past, with careful but limited checks in the two modes of perception, and with definite expectations in regard to the future, we turn our tentative and probable symbolic references into impressive pragmatic achievements. Consciousness, conceptual analysis, direct recognition, and a pragmatic appeal to the future combine to justify the confident and adventuresome use of symbols.[45] But that confidence never gets to the point where all possibility of error is excluded in practical matters. Therefore, it must be accompanied by a continued willingness to criticize the application of symbols by appeals to direct recognitions. While the justification of symbolic reference is pragmatic, the practical applicability of symbolic interpretation is based on instances in which the productive character of such interpretation is evident.

So much of human experience is bound up with symbolic reference, that it is hardly an exaggeration to say that the very meaning of truth is pragmatic. . . . still it *is* an exaggeration, for the pragmatic test can never work, unless on some occasion—in the future, or in the present—there is a definite determination of what is true on that occasion.[46]

Ultimately, the goal of attempts to justify symbolic references is to get the body of the percipient into a position where direct recognitions will support the projected and tentative interpretations. This way, the two pure modes of perception continue to be of primary importance in the pragmatic assessment of the success of interpretation. "Beyond the body, the appeal is to

44. *FR*, p. 77.
45. *Sym*, p. 49.
46. *PR*, p. 275.

the pragmatic consequences, involving some future state of bodily feelings which can be checked up."[47]

The discrimination of patterns involved in the inherited data of experience, and their extrapolation to characterize the indirectly known and indeterminate, are important features of Whitehead's doctrine of symbolic reference. This projection is understood as fundamental in perception. It provides a basis for understanding more sophisticated modes of symbolic activity. It gives to all symbolism a derivative character, based on the immediate past and the relatively stable patterns of experience. Such derivation is combined with a provisional extension of discerned patterns to characterize the present, generic relationships, and the expected shape of future experience.

The definiteness of symbols is the result of abstractive emphasis, based on analogies in experience. The very possibility of symbolic activity is dependent on pervasive similarities between actualities, which enable them to participate in wider patterns of coordination and to be apprehended as functional parts of organic wholes. It is on such similarities that the very existence of structured societies and enduring entities is based.[48] Dominant characteristics, shared by an aggregate of actual entities, make possible their mutual contribution to a larger organic unity. Such societies of actual occasions are given a common definite structure by a massive, average objectification of their members and the practical elimination of their detailed diversities. It is in this manner that they are able to endure, with some stability, as their environment changes. Whitehead calls this coordination "transmutation." It functions so that congenial uniformities overwhelm a particular nexus, giving it definite character and structure.[49] Organic relationships are constituted

---

47. *Ibid.*, p. 272.

48. The very notion of order in the physical world involves the dominance of certain characteristics in a nexus of actual entities. Members of ordered societies share a common characteristic by virtue of their inheritance. Because of this common character, these members impose upon each other the conditions that lead to that likeness. "Thus in a society, the members can only exist by reason of the laws which dominate the society, and the laws only come into being by reason of the analogous characters of the members of the society." (*PR*, p. 139.)

49. *PR*, p. 154.

by dominant analogies in various grades of increasing generality. The consequence is a hierarchy of organic systems in which the patterns of the whole and the character of the parts are interdependent.

As analogy is fundamental in the coordination of societies and enduring entities, so it plays a crucial role in the perception of definite patterns and characteristics.[50] The body, in its fundamental role as the organ of experience, is sensitive to dominant similarities. On the basis of such analogies, the initial abstractive emphasis which produces the definite data of sense perception is possible. A multitude of physical feelings are coordinated into a definite pattern, characterizing specific regions of the presented locus. In the external world, and in our own most intimate experience, diverse pulses of energy are translated (or transmuted) into coordinated patterns by simplifications and unifications based on analogies. These larger patterns of coordinated activity are not simply collections of smaller components, but their being together in a specific manner gives to that society or its characterization a new context of significance. The whole is greater than the sum of its parts.

For Whitehead, then, our definite perceptions and the enduring entities perceived are based on pervasive analogies. Similarities are not arbitrary introductions, but they are efficacious in the emergence and coordination of actual entities. They are given in the very constitution of the ordered process, providing a basis for our discrimination of the more significant features of the actualities which we encounter. They are experienced threads of connection which enable us to look to the present and the future from a perspective of experienced order and direction. They allow us to assume that contemporary actualities will normally reflect a continuation of the immediate past, and to expect that some stable patterns of order will be effective in the future.

50. By analogy, here, I mean a similarity which is qualified by differences which are real, but which can be excluded as of negligible relevance in respect to a specific interest or context of significance.

The derivation of our definite perceptions by analogical approximations is an important clue for the treatment of symbols on any level. Symbols are specialized tools for dealing with a reality that exhibits continuous development and pervasive relativity. Thus, one cannot expect a one-to-one correspondence of definite symbols with our most concrete experience. By the same token, it can be expected that the interpretation of symbols will only allow a qualified and tentative precision. Symbolic activity relies on both simplification and projective application. Analogy is fundamental for both. In a rhythmic fashion, it is the basis for the definite apprehension of the determinate, and also the means whereby the future is anticipated. The combination of these roles makes perception a process of discrimination, projection, and justification which can never be reduced to a final and completely precise grasp of reality. There are no discriminated factors in experience which do not point beyond themselves to other factors and various levels of coordination. Whitehead puts it concisely. "No fact is merely itself."[51] Its essence is not independence but "connectedness."[52] It leads beyond itself through the analogies that bind it to its universe and to the future.

The recognition of the fundamental role of analogy in perception gives to all experience the character of partial penetration. From the very outset, experience exhibits the dynamic aspect of reality, even as it presents relatively stable structures. Man's grasp of reality must reflect the transition from a settled past toward the potentially surprising future. The force of this demand is evident in Whitehead's words:

> We are in the present; the present is always shifting; it is derived from the past; it is shaping the future; it is passing into the future. This is process, and in the universe it is an inexorable fact.[53]

For this reason, all knowledge and expression must somehow hold together an emphasis on both completion and growth.[54]

51. *MT*, p. 13.   53. *Ibid.*, p. 73.
52. *Ibid.*   54. *Ibid.*, p. 66.

Perception, knowledge, and expression are all characterized by their reference to further penetration, pressing beyond the relatively stable and precise in the venturesome exploration of analogies. That which is definitely given and taken for granted becomes a temporary base for the expansion of our experience and the modification of our symbols. We are led from the clearly discriminated to the conditions on which its character depends, which can be the guide for pragmatic investigations of the future. As Whitehead has said: "Whenever we attempt to express the matter of immediate experience, we find that its understanding leads us beyond itself, to its contemporaries, to its past, to its future, and to the universals in terms of which its definiteness is exhibited."[55]

Thus, Whitehead finds both analogy and projective extrapolation playing important roles in all experience. Beginning with perception, man is always involved in a process of approximation and estimation. He proceeds by imaginative leaps, based on the conformity of his definite perceptions to the past and the partial grasp of various grades of relatively stable coordination.[56] This does not mean that on the most fundamental level perception has a hypothetical uncertainty about it. Both the derivation of data and their projected application are given by the body as adequate and appropriate. Whitehead's analysis merely suggests that behind the definite data of perception and its apparent dependability is a long train of interaction and interpretation. The body, in its treatment of sensations, is involved in selective and interpretive activity from the beginning. Its role in man's encounter with his environment does not so much resemble direct transmission of a single message as it does conversation and dialogue.

Interestingly, modern psychology and physiology provide considerable support for this view. First of all, the time lag involved in the causal transmission of percepts through the nervous system to the brain and the observable effect of distance on our perceptions makes room for intervening activities.[57] Secondly, studies of the way perception takes place have indi-

56. *AI*, pp. 247–248.   57. Brain, *op. cit.*

cated that very complex chains of selection and combination are involved. The body and its organs can be understood as the locus of many cumulative exchanges of information in which selection, projection, and confirmation are continuing components of one process, resembling conversation. Dr. J. Bronowski has provided a summary of some of the research supporting this point of view in his volume, *The Identity of Man*. There he describes the role of the body, its sense organs and even individual neurons as reflecting rudimentary forms of data interpretation and simplification. "Our senses doctor their messages before they reach the brain."[58] For instance, the eyes of various species of animal select different shapes and movements as relevant to their type of organism.

> The eye does not respond to this single flash or that. It tries from the outset to find a pattern in what it sees, and the pattern it looks for is the shape of things. For example, the inner connections in the cat's eye make it sensitive to sharp edges. The frog's eye is more sensitive to edges if they are moving, and to quickly changing or moving contrasts of light and shade.[59]

In the studies of Horace Barlow on the rabbit, Bronowski finds it more surprising that preferences are built not only into the eye as a whole, but into its single neurons. Some neurons will observe downward and not upward movements. Others do exactly the opposite. Still others observe fast movements of objects and disregard the slower motions. Others do just the opposite. Bronowski's conclusion is that the message received by the brain is no neutral picture but an accumulation of interpretations and instructions. "There is, as it were, a continuous conversation between the brain and the senses."[60] It would seem that the polar interplay, described by Whitehead, between the two modes of perception is more than mere speculation about the way in which perception might take place. On the

58. J. Bronowski, *The Identity of Man* (Garden City, N.Y.: The Natural History Press, 1965), p. 30.
59. *Ibid.*, p. 31.
60. *Ibid.*, p. 35.

basis of biological and psychological evidence, Bronowski is led
to adopt a model for knowledge that is very close to Whitehead's, and he expresses it in a way that Whitehead might well
have chosen. Bronowski writes:

> No knowledge can be certain that continues to expand with us as
> we live inside the growing flesh of our experience. . . . Nature
> is a network of happenings that do not unroll like a red carpet
> into time, but are intertwined between every part of the world;
> and we are among those parts. In this nexus, we cannot reach
> certainty because it is not there to be reached; it goes with the
> wrong model, and the certain answers ironically are the wrong
> answers.[61]

It is in this sense that the most fundamental levels of perception can be seen as polar processes in which the "products"
of abstraction and the "projection" of such symbols as instruments of approximation play correlative roles. The extrapolation of given data to regions that can only be reached by indirect
extension of analogical patterns is a method of discovery that
begins long before scientists and metaphysicians, by conscious
decision, set about producing and exploring their explicit
hypotheses.

The activity evident on the most basic levels of perception
provides Whitehead with the pattern for every form of symbolism. "Symbolic reference between the two perceptive modes
affords the main example of the principles which govern all
symbolism."[62] There must be two kinds of percepts so that one
can evoke the perception of a correlate in the other species and
precipitate upon this "correlate the fusion of feelings, emotions,
and derivative actions, which belong to either of the pair of
correlates, and which are also enhanced by the correlation."[63]
The species functioning as symbol is generally the more handy
and definite, while the meanings are usually drawn from a more
concrete level of experience. Thus, not only is the general pat-

61. *Ibid.*, p. 37.
62. *PR*, p. 274.
63. *Ibid.*, p. 274.

tern of symbolic activity preserved on higher levels, but the predominant direction of symbolic reference is also maintained.

The common ground that is required for symbolic reference varies in degree and type of conformity between symbol and meaning. In the perception of other actualities and the "external world," there is a high degree of direct causal conformity as the basis for almost automatic interpretation. As symbolism becomes more abstract and adds its own complexity, this causal relationship is reduced, allowing a greater degree of freedom in interpretation. The level of symbolism with which we are concerned—language—exhibits a reduction of this conformity to the point where a useful distinction in kind can be drawn. The ground for symbolic reference becomes somewhat artificial and conventional. This is not to say that language or other cultural forms of symbolism are simply arbitrary in their relation of symbols and meanings. But symbolism on this level is more dependent on the history of a people than on a natural resemblance of symbols and their referents.

Whitehead clarifies the distinction between the two levels of symbolism in a discussion of truth-relations.[64] He points out that truth-relations are dependent on circumstances in much the same way as a particular type of symbolic reference. In general, truth is the conformation of appearance to reality which parallels the common symbolic interpretation of sense-perception in reference to causal efficacy.[65] It is a matter of degree and type. It can be direct or indirect. It is the way in which appearances justify the decisions and actions of the experiencing subject.[66]

In this context, sense-perception is the culmination of appearance. Its projective character is hidden by the initial interplay which is governed by the body. However, when the question arises concerning the actual conformity of the data of sense-perception to the regions indicated, the problem of truth has been introduced. Thus, on the most basic level, the question of truth has to do with the conformity of affective tone in per-

64. *AI*, pp. 241–251.
65. *Ibid.*, p. 241.
66. *Ibid.*

ceived actualities and those who perceive them. "When a region appears as red in sense-perception, the question arises whether red is qualifying in any dominant manner the affective tones of the actualities which in fact make up the region."[67] It is Whitehead's view that there is generally a dependable conformity on this level that is based on a mysterious harmony in which the animal body and the external world have a tendency to be attuned.[68]

A second level of truth-relation depends on the bodily sensitivities of a particular species. In other words, appearances can be classified as "true" when they correspond with the normal experience of a well-conditioned member of the species. "Given these conditions of normality, the resulting appearance will be that proper to that species of animal under circumstances of that type."[69] The stop light can be said to be red, when in fact there are members of the species who do not see it that way.

It is the third level of truth-relations that illuminates cultural symbolism. Whitehead recognizes that it is not sharply separated from the second, but he considers the difference in degree as adequate to warrant the assertion of a difference in kind. On this level, the truth-relation is quite indirect and does not depend on any causal connection between symbol and meaning, other than cultural association. Using the term "symbolic" in a much narrower sense than is his usual practice, Whitehead calls conformity on this basis, "symbolic truth."[70] It is indirect in the sense that the symbols have virtually become signs. Truth is dependent on the conformity of subjective form in a specially conditioned set of percipients.

A set of adventitious circumstances has brought about this connection between those Appearances and those Realities as prehended in the experiences of those percipients. In their own natures the Appearances throw no light upon the Realities, nor do the Reali-

67. *Ibid.*, p. 245.
68. *Ibid.*, p. 251.
69. *Ibid.*, p. 247.
70. *Ibid.*, p. 248.

ties upon the Appearances, except in the experiences of a set of peculiarly conditioned percipients.[71]

On this level of "symbolic truth," most language functions. Music and ceremonial symbols are also examples that Whitehead uses.[72]

Thus, while Whitehead contends that there must be some grounds for the interpretation of symbols, he does not assert that a corresponding structure or direct derivative origin is always required. On the most fundamental levels of experience, symbols depend on these grounds for their productive interpretation, but on more sophisticated levels; structural conformity and genetic derivation give way to social conditioning. The grounds for symbolic reference are provided by the community and its tradition. Like his other distinctions, Whitehead does not allow this one to become a separation. He provides linguistic examples of structural conformity which qualify the distinction between natural and cultural symbolism. For instance, while in most language use the grammatical structure is not of great import as a "ground" for symbolic reference, in some uses of language it is decisive. Whitehead cites algebra as one instance in which the pattern of syntax is directly relevant. Algebra "endeavours to exemplify in its written structures the patterns which it is its purpose to convey."[73] Language evidently uses both natural and conventional elements in a fashion that does not allow for sharp discrimination.

In the main, language indicates its meanings by means of casual associations as they arise in human history. It is true that language strives to embody some aspects of those meanings in its very structure. A deep sounding word embodies the deep solemnity of grief. In fact, the art of literature, vocal or written, is to adjust the language so that it embodies what it indicates. But the larger part of what language physically presents is irrelevant to the meaning indicated. The sentence is a sequence of words. But this sequence is, in general, irrelevant to the meaning.[74]

71. *Ibid.*
72. *Ibid.*, p. 249.
73. *SP*, p. 116, cf. *Sym*, p. 2.
74. *SP*, p. 115.

The higher forms of symbolism are also characterized by an increase of conceptual activity. The initial polarity of perception is enhanced and promoted by the capacity of conceptual analysis to discriminate a wide range of factors for symbolic manipulation.[75] The penetration of our intuition is partially determined by the expectation of thought.[76] The result is that there is no neat distinction between mental and physical aspects of interpretive activity. Indeed, "much of our perception is due to the enhanced subtlety arising from a concurrent conceptual analysis.[77] While initial errors are not the result of conceptual intervention in the more complex stages of symbolism, the manner in which conceptual analysis is applied can produce its own forms of error.[78] From Whitehead's point of view, these errors are largely in the loss of connection between symbolic factors and their ultimate reference to concrete experience.

The manner in which language functions is generally on the basis of visual marks or sounds in the mode of presentational immediacy which are interpreted as referring to meanings which are in the mode of causal efficacy.[79] This is to suggest that the certainty available when language is considered in abstraction from its reference is to be found in analytic relationships between words and in the formal truths of logical symbols and mathematics. The rules of language and the relationships of words in syntax and etymology can be studied with a precision that is helpful but always deficient in regard to its appropriate symbolic reference. Whitehead may have something like this in mind when he suggests that analytic statements and simple mathematical equations are only tautologies, when considered apart from the process. In a wider context, other interpretive considerations must be brought to bear so that what is certain and definite in the mode of presentational immediacy is made somewhat vague and uncertain. The symbols can be arranged

75. *Sym*, p. 19.
76. *FR*, p. 79.
77. *Sym*, p. 20.
78. *Ibid.*, p. 42.
79. *PR*, p. 263.

with certainty in their own context, but there are always questions of interpretation which complicate the issue.[80]

Language and other more conventional forms of symbolism are made more indefinite by the fact that they involve what Whitehead calls a "double symbolic reference." "From things to words on the part of the speaker, and from words back to things on the part of the listener."[81] Add to this the wide-ranging variations in emotional attitudes and conceptual perspectives in one cultural community and there are clear reasons why language must be put on the level of indirect and symbolic truth. The symbols involved in these higher uses can have many different meanings for different persons.

> At any epoch some people have the dominant mentality of the past, some of the present, others of the future, and others of the many problematic futures which will never dawn. For these various groups an old symbolism will have different shades of vague meaning.[82]

The complexity and indefiniteness of the higher forms of symbolism provide a basis for Whitehead's claim that such symbols are primarily evocative. They call for an emotional response, some shared subjective form, but always leave room for flexibility in their interpretation. Such freedom can be increased so that "objective meaning" is minimal, as in the powerful symbolism of music interpretating a strong sentiment of patriotism or religion.[83] But the same kind of dependence on subjective form is effective in language uses that are more apparently "objective" in their significance. The objective and subjective aspects of language use cannot be set against each other in a radical way or separated as intrinsically different modes of symbolism. The symbols confront the responding individual with definite structures for apprehension, but their interpretation requires elicited feeling and some tacit reference

80. *MT*, pp. 123–129.
81. *Sym*, p. 12.
82. *Ibid.*, pp. 63–64.
83. *AI*, p. 249.

to the environment in which they are utilized.[84] The tension between the definite symbols and their actual interpretation permits reasonably accurate communication without making a conformal response automatic.

It is just this ambiguity that is both the strength and the weakness of symbolic activity. On the side of weakness, it suggests a radical choice between blind acceptance of symbolic constructions and the persistent rejection of symbolic activity in an appeal to brute fact. It is this apparent alternative that generates man's ambivalent attitude to language and symbols. Men want the blunt truth and not some symbolic substitute. Therefore, they always seek to get behind the symbols to direct recognition at the same time that their quest for raw experience is informed by symbolic structures. "Hard-headed men want facts and not symbols."[85] Their search for facts is motivated by the real fear that their symbols may have lost touch with reality. The life of men can be overpowered by symbolic accessories which have lost the corrective reference to concrete experience.[86] At the same time, the influence of symbolic interpretation on the facts discerned seems unavoidable. "Symbolism is no mere idle fancy or corrupt degeneration: it is inherent in the very texture of human life."[87]

Because reality is in the process of transition and development, the rejection of "symbols" for "facts" amounts to a reductive emphasis on the determinate and settled aspects of experience. Since only the past is settled, the appeal to facts can have its own distortive emphasis. It leads to a deterministic, static view of reality. Symbolism is therefore required by the dynamic and creative aspects of reality. What is needed, according to Whitehead, is not the rejection of symbolism or a naive acceptance of symbolic constructions as the real world, but a continued pruning and correcting of our symbols by reference to our most direct intuitions. Symbolism needs to be balanced with

84. *PR*, p. 403.
85. *Sym*, p. 60.
86. *Ibid.*, p. 61.
87. *Ibid.*, pp. 61–62.

a concern for "hard data" but it is misleading to think that it can either be eliminated or made so precise as to be final and certain. When men try either of these alternatives, the ambiguity and indefiniteness of symbolism creep back into their interpretations without benefit of criticism or conscious awareness.

It is this same ambiguity of symbols that is the source of their creative power in human civilization. Symbols allow for relatively stable social structures, in which both corporate interests and personal freedom are enhanced.[88] They give a stability to community life that provides a basis for the consideration of the creative innovations, which can only be grasped in contrast to existing structures. They limit the context of response without excluding novelty and freedom. Like the very order of reality, they make progress possible by the limitations they impose and the liberties they allow. They are evocative in the sense that they provide the stimulus for a response, without dictating the form of that response. "The response to the symbol is almost automatic but not quite; . . . the reference is not so clear as to be imperative."[89] The leeway that symbol structures allow makes them apt instruments for dealing with a changing reality on a level of evolution where freedom has emerged as a significant factor. Symbols themselves are not a problem for man. Difficulties arise only when the combination of confidence and criticism becomes unbalanced. Whitehead succinctly describes the attitude toward symbols which is required. "Those societies which cannot combine reverence to thier symbols with freedom of revision, must ultimately decay either from anarchy, or from the slow atrophy of a life stifled by useless shadows."[90]

Whitehead's recognition of a wide-spread and rudimentary symbolic activity in perception breaks down the sharp barrier that is often erected between statements of "fact" and statements which are more dependent on symbolic construction and human decision. All of the boundaries between levels of experience and symbolism are relativized. The limits of consciousness

88. *Ibid.,* p. 66.
89. *Ibid.*
90. *Ibid.,* p. 88.

and the language structures used to articulate factors given in consciousness are somewhat flexible and subject to increased penetration and expansion. Efforts can be made to transcend these limits in order to correct interpretation, extend the conscious grasp of the environment, and increase the capacity for expression. In Whitehead's perspective, there are no fixed limits as to what can be experienced, known, or expressed in linguistic form. Only complete knowledge is impossible in the sense that nothing more than our own feelings can be included in our experience in an exhaustive manner. Nevertheless, the extent of our partial grasp of realities and relationships can be increased. Multiple, but connected, levels of symbolic activity are so interrelated as to allow a wide variation of abstractive emphasis and, therefore, from within these symbolic structures it is possible to criticize, compare, and partially revise our interpretive forms. Such an activity from within the symbolic structures virtually expands their limits and transforms their content to conform more adequately with the realities and relationships which transcend such structures. While man cannot deal with reality apart from symbols, it is possible to stretch and shape our symbolic structures to approximate the contours of dynamic experience.

This understanding of symbolism opens the way for a more venturesome and flexible use of language. Projection and extension of patterns only partially given is the foundation of all symbolism, and not an unusually risky endeavor. This fact encourages us to press beyond every apparent limit in the confidence that knowledge and the capacity for expression can be increased and extended. The apparent barriers indicate where we have been and what has been discerned in a particular mode of interest. They do not determine future experience, knowledge, or expression. It is just by extending our interests beyond our grasp, that we are able to cope with a dynamic and expanding reality. Such extension is fundamental, even on the most basic level of human sense-perception, because our body projects data well beyond the limits of the determinate and directly given. It is to be expected then, that symbolism on every level will involve a similar projection beyond fixed limits of apprehension and expression.

Such an assault on limits is evident in assertions of metaphysical scope. On this level, assumptions that are relevant to all symbolic activity are made explicit. The risk that becomes apparent on the metaphysical level is analogous to the projection involved in all uses of language. In this way, the sharp distinction between what can be expressed with precision and that which cannot be articulated at all is modified. By pressing beyond apparent limits in the extension of given patterns, metaphysical assertions only reflect the tentative and projective character of all linguistic expression.

In a similar way, this understanding of symbolic activity supports the interdependence of analogical and literal modes of expression. Like other important levels of experience, language exhibits both a stable and a flexible aspect. Stable linguistic components—like syntax and dictionary definitions—present only half of the picture: they veil their own dependence on the discernment of analogies and on assumptions which can only be expressed analogically. In this perspective, univocal language is a truncated form of analogy which is highly useful in situations in which assumptions are shared and circumstances are fairly stable. When considered critically, its derivation on the basis of patterns given in experience and extended beyond their empirical base becomes evident. At the same time, in its application to concrete reality, univocal language requires interpretive assumptions that cannot be expressed with the same precision.

Thus, analogy is not a temporary or secondary linguistic expedient to be used only until it can be replaced with straightforward statements requiring no qualification. Experience is constituted by pervasive analogies, and its most adequate expression requires the type of qualification associated with interpretative models and illuminating metaphors.

Since this seems to invert the usual view, an illustration may characterize the change in perspective. Consider the question: "What time is it?" It sounds like an unequivocal answer is no problem at all. In a given context, the answer can be exact for all practical purposes, indicating the position of hands on the face of a clock. We respond immediately, with no second thoughts, no qualifications. However, there are some very important hidden assumptions which make this practical precision possible. Implicit recognition of arbitrary time zones, current methods of calculating time changes, and even some notion of the nature of time are involved. None of these considerations needs expression for ordinary purposes, but broader interests require their articulation even though it is necessary to resort to models and metaphors in order to grasp the general contours of the situation. With this in mind, all language can be said to be analogical in that it involves more than what is readily made explicit. An exclusive appreciation of linguistic precision and finality is a form of misplaced concreteness, which confuses utility with ontological and cognitive priority. Like the doctrine of "simple location," it can lead to a radically distorted view of the way in which things are "together" in the concrete situation.

In the perspective which Whitehead presents, language cannot be neatly classified as univocal, analogical, or equivocal. It is completely analogical, even though its productive use depends on provisional stabilities approaching literal significance. Words function between the limits of complete precision and radical equivocation. These limits are asymptotic in that words cannot function at the limit but only in approaching it. The continuum between those limits is characterized by analogical qualification, in various degrees of explicit indication. For maximum clarity of language, continuous attempts must be made to press toward both limits. As univocal precision is approached, expressions are used with suppressed, implicit qualifications in contexts where much can be taken for granted. Even many metaphors reflect such a concern for precision and their dual reference is fairly easy to translate into some combination of univocal expressions. However, moving toward the opposite limit, the polarity of experience and the analogical character of linguistic expression become more obvious. These expressions are less and less amenable to reduction to univocal discourse. Finally, they verge on equivocation and sheer contradiction, but they continue to function in a meaningful way by expressing a partial grasp of realities, and by maintaining the tentative and approximate character of all knowledge and expression. They are not strictly equivocal because they do assert relative differences and similarities, but specifying such meaning with precision is extremely difficult.[91] The analogy developed can be specified, but its application to experience remains somewhat open and provisional.

In this way, Whitehead provides a view of language in which dependable precision gives way to approximation and pragmatic sufficiency. This is all that is available, short of the analytic consideration of symbols in the pure mode of presentational immediacy. When language is used to articulate the complexity of concrete experience, it draws on provisional precision to give shape and content to its assertions. In this way, analogy colors all uses of language. Complete definiteness of meaning is not attainable because it is incompatible with an organic reality in which process and novelty are fundamental. An organic, developing universe calls for symbols which are used with qualified and tentative precision like that apparent in analogical expressions and hidden by so-called literal usage.

Whitehead's understanding of the scope and character of symbolic interpretation has several direct implications for the understanding of religious language. First of all, it suggests that an inclusive referential theory of meaning is possible which will maintain continuity between the assertions of religion and the more obviously empirical statements of science and common sense. Secondly, it establishes the hypothetical status of all religious assertions in their attempts to attribute some special

91. Whitehead does not use this kind of illustration, although it seems consistent with his view. William Alston does, and also calls attention to expressions which verge on the equivocal. He calls them quasi-metaphors, and stresses their combination of importance and resistance to literal reduction. "Quasi-metaphors are, in the epistemologically crucial respects, in the position of metaphors that cannot die. They have the characteristic indeterminacy of metaphors, but they lack the means, available for many metaphors, for removing this indeterminacy." He includes assertions about God and personal feelings in this class. (William P. Alston, *Philosophy of Language* [Englewood Cliffs, N.J.: Prentice-Hall, Inc., 1964], p. 105.)

character to their necessary referent. Thirdly, it indicates the patterns of confirmation that may be expected, suggesting that the centrality of religious claims veils the actual comparison of alternatives and the process of decision with respect to those alternatives.

Referential theories of meaning have been in disrepute because of narrow interpretations of the perceptual data reflected in the tendency to treat the relationship between symbols and meanings as a one-to-one symmetrical correspondence. Expressions with more than one meaning, and different descriptions of the same referent, raise questions about using that type of reference as a general explanation of significant linguistic expression.

In addition, the many important uses of language which obviously do not refer to empirical objects or sensations seem to require either an extreme limitation of meaningful discourse or the reification of emotional, imaginary, and conceptual factors. With a narrow interpretation of the perceptual data and a clear distinction between internal and external components of experience, reference is not a viable principle for a general theory of meaning.[92]

Other theories of meaning have been put forward that often run into difficulty for similar reasons. The so-called ideational theory, for example, seeks to identify meaning with components of man's inner world, the ideas and images indicated and evoked by linguistic symbols. This emphasis on internal correspondence tends to make external reference problematic. It also raises problems because of a tendency to utilize a symmetrical relationship between words and ideas.[93]

Moving in a very different direction, behavioral theories have attempted to correlate linguistic stimuli and public responses as the key to meaning. Here the internal aspects of linguistic communication make the reduction of the meaning relationship to the action-reaction syndrome difficult. Intentions, misinterpretations, dispositions, and other hidden factors complicate lin-

92. Alston, *op. cit.*, pp. 12–22.
93. *Ibid.*, pp. 22–25.

guistic activity so that any behavioral theory seems less than adequate.[94]

It is because of limitations involved in these three types of interpretation that the identification of meaning with "use" has been so attractive. This approach seems to provide both an inclusive and flexible way of understanding the significance of language. It allows empirical reference to be interpreted in a narrow way without explicitly denigrating any other use of language. However, this ready acceptance of diversity of function has its own dangers. It easily leads to the compartmentalization of the various language uses, insulating them from each other and making the common features of language difficult to understand. While this separation and isolation of language uses need not be attributed to Wittgenstein, it has been widely influential. In a recent study of Wittgenstein's thought and religious language, Dallas M. High describes such an influence: "Many followers and interpreters of Wittgenstein have notoriously treated the plurality of language-games as a division of language into autonomous, hermetically sealed, self-justifying strata of speech or levels of discourse in which 'every sort of statement has its own sort of logic.' "[95] Such a stratification implicitly assumes that different language games deal with unique types of data, coordinated only by the conventional structures of language. In this respect, the "use" theory builds on the same narrow view of perception as the other three types. This weakness becomes especially evident when some apologists for religious discourse rush to escape the rigorous demands for verification. The "use" theory is not only an easy answer, but in its extreme form it tends to destroy religious expressions by isolating them from other aspects of culture and experience.[96]

94. *Ibid.*, pp. 25–31.

95. High, *op. cit.*, pp. 114–115.

96. This would seem to be what James A. Martin, Jr., has in mind when he remarks: "Popular theological apologetics has sometimes moved too quickly and carelessly to the affirmation that all questions of the relation of theology to science are resolved through the simple recognition of differences of perspective. If there is *any* common subject matter, there is an obligation to show at just what points, if any, the perspectives converge." (James A. Martin, Jr., *The New Dialogue Between Philosophy and Theology,* pp. 114–115.)

The narrow interpretation of the perceptual data and the assumption of semantic symmetry are more decisive in all these theories than is apparent at first glance. Without careful qualification, these theories of meaning can easily undercut the very type of reference that is required by religious discourse. Their tendency to utilize sharp discontinuities can inform the understanding of all reality. That which is symbolized by clear-cut linguistic units of meaning—the word, the phrase, the sentence —can be seen as having a similar independence. In a like manner, a neat distinction between external behavior and internal intention as utilized in a theory of meaning can also be attributed to concrete reality. Or, the carefully drawn distinctions between different kinds of meaning can imply the ultimate division of experience into insulated compartments of diverse data. As Whitehead has often indicated, the abstract characteristics of linguistic symbols can be applied to that which is symbolized, with far too much precision. What is obviously discontinuous linguistically is subtly given ontological precedence.

To use any of these theories of meaning without careful qualification, places religious assertions in difficulty. Because religious expressions refer to an integrated experience as the context of human response, the acceptance of sharp distinctions and a symmetrical semantic relationship can be used to deny just the kind of reference these assertions require.

In contrast, Whitehead offers an inclusive theory of meaning which is based on a modified notion of reference. The theory is based on an increased range of perceptual data, the recognition that a sharp distinction cannot be drawn between the internal and the external aspects of experience, and the dependence of most symbols on an asymmetrical relationship with their meanings. [97] It provides the flexibility of the "use" theory with less

97. Urban's description of a referential theory is not unlike Whitehead's in its recognition of the diversity of "meanings" which words can indicate. "All words then 'stand for something'—have some reference, either determinate or indeterminate. The opposite of this can be maintained only by virtue of some very crude notion of 'standing for' or by some equally crude notion of the 'something' for which it stands. Some element of reference enters, for all civilized adults at least, into all uses of words, including that described as emotive and evocative. But this reference may be indirect and indeterminate." (Urban, *Language and Reality*, p. 192.)

risk of compartmentalization. It allows a distinction to be drawn between the language of religion and scientific observation, while tracing them to the same complex of data. Reference to discrete objects, sensations, and measurements is one kind of abstractive development from the initial empirical complex. Since it is based on selection, such a development only ignores residual connections. It does not obliterate them. Other modes of emphasis, such as the religious, can proceed from the same data, and the convergence with the scientific mode of abstraction can be indicated.

Since reference is asymmetrical, except when symbols are manipulated on a carefully maintained abstract level, it is not necessary to be troubled by words which have more than one meaning, or the reference to a single factor by more than one expression. The extension of meanings and accumulation of supplementary descriptions increases the utility and flexibility of both expression and understanding. Experienced factors can be dealt with from different perspectives without losing their identity or isolating different types of expression. Such an understanding of reference allows the articulation of emotional and conceptual connections without turning them into "things." It allows language to have reference to (or stand for) any component of experience without asserting the radical discontinuities that produce insoluble dilemmas and isolation. By not oversimplifying the correspondence between words and things, language and thought, or linguistic stimuli and public response, Whitehead's theory of symbolic reference provides a "referential" theory of meaning that has the advantages of the "use" theory, with some built-in protection against its weaknesses. It works for the articulation of emotions, observation statements, metaphysical descriptions and religious assertions. In each case there are components of experience which can be the basis for linguistic abstraction and reference. The contrasts in the data which are developed differently still provide for the convergence of diverse interests in the empirical complex and the connection of the accumulated abstractive emphases in the common linguistic structure. Meaning is thus identified with purpose, perspective, and use, but not at the price of separation from the perceptual data or the isolation of diverse uses of language. This is of special importance for religious discourse because it is directly concerned with the coordination of facts and values in the universe and cannot maintain its own utility and significance in the face of such discontinuities.

In this way, Whitehead's doctrine of perception, combined with his understanding of symbolic reference, establishes continuity across the entire spectrum of linguistic activity. It puts religious assertions in touch with the most exact manipulations of perceptual data and allows multiple types of qualified linguistic precision. However, no precision can break the integrating connections which maintain the reference of every abstraction to concrete experience.

Whitehead's doctrine of symbolic reference also establishes the hypothetical character of religious assertions. The asymmetrical relationship between abstract symbols and their more concrete meanings determines the provisional, projective form of all linguistic interpretations of experience. Since, on the most fundamental level of symbolism, projected data are referred to realities which do not exactly correspond to the symbolic structures, all linguistic interpretations can be considered hypothetical. From the very outset, they are based on the discrimination and projection of analogies in anticipation of further confirmation. Religious assertions are no exception. Insofar as they refer to reality and attempt to characterize the generic coordination of fact and value given in every occasion of experience, they are also provisional and hypothetical. They are dependent on the grasp of especially significant analogies and their extension well beyond the circumstances of their origin. While they may be extrapolated with confidence to characterize the universal context of significance, they are, in principle, tentative probes of the broadest dimensions of experience. The character of experience is such that all such extensions of symbolic formulations must be provisional. The insights on which they are based may be taken as certain in their own context, but their extension to the universal mode of coordination and their stabilization in linguistic forms give the assertions used an approximate and hypothetical character.

The hypothetical character of religious assertions is made necessary in Whitehead's system by the fundamental role he gives to analogical projection. The very fabric of experience is established by similarities in various grades of dominance. From perception up to the most sophisticated form of symbolic activity, connections are grasped by means of analogy, and the dynamic aspects of experience are dealt with by means of approximate projections. Instead of the accumulation of discrete data, experience is more fundamentally the tracing and extension of analogical patterns on the basis of some perspective of interest. On the level of sense-perception, such projections include the risk of serious error. If on that fundamental level we must live with the risks of approximation and projection, then no symbolic interpretation is free from similar possibilities. The only way this provisional aspect of interpretation can be avoided is by maintaining a strict level of abstraction so that interpretive reference is between symbols of the same type. Even then, when the broader picture is taken into account, the precision of symbolic relations indicates some qualification by reference to more concrete levels of experience. Thus, in Whitehead's scheme, it is impossible for religious assertions to be anything but hypothetical, insofar as they refer some special character to the universal coordination of fact and value. They may be trusted and successful hypotheses, adequate projections worthy of confidence and respect, but they are always in the form of tentative and projective interpretations.

In principle, then, the analogies utilized in religious assertions are illustrative, coordinating, and interpretive. They are not based on simple deduction or probability, nor are they reducible to the abstract precision of mathematical proportion. They are analogies projected to interpret concrete experience and therefore have an irreducible ambiguity about them. They are like metaphors in the raw, produced and utilized in concrete dialogue. They assert similarities for further investigation. They project patterns that have illuminated experience in the hope that they will continue to do so. In a strict fashion, they do not prove anything. Neither can their basis in evidence be clearly established. What they do provide is alternative ways of dealing with the significance of life itself. Thus to use the analogy of being is to assert the pervasive connection of derivation between all finite beings and God. It is not established on some characteristic which God and man share in exactly the same way, unless that characteristic is the participation of both in the same complex of experience. In either case, it does not allow the details of God's character to be deduced from it. In a similar fashion, to say God loves man is to assert that the generic coordination of experience is illuminated by this analogy, not that there is or can be conclusive evidence of its validity. It is a proposal that appeals to the total impact of experience. It is a means for seeking deeper penetration and increased satisfaction. It offers one possible stance for a continuing probe of the future. It is, in principle, an hypothesis put forward as the best interpretation of all the available and anticipated evidence. It can be acted upon, but its ultimate confirmation is always wrapped up with an appeal to further experience.

It can easily be seen how attempts to base all analogies on clear and distinct similarities which can be expressed univocally would be misleading with respect to the religious use of analogy. Raw metaphors are useful because they are not reducible to literal expressions, which eliminate the living connections. They enable us to deal with a dynamic and complex experience which is not constituted solely by determinate particulars and distinct qualities. The claim that meaningful analogies must allow some strictly literal expression is just another example of the fallacy of misplaced concreteness. It is another way of using the clear and distinct in a normative way, another way of treating discontinuity and differences in kind as the decisive features of experience. Of course, there is one univocal assertion involved in every analogy. It parallels the necessary reality of universal coordination. That is the assertion of similarity, but such a notion points to problems in *any* other univocal expression rather than contributing to the potential reduction of analogy to final precision. Once experience is seen as fundamentally continuous, analogy is the basis for intelligible expression, not a temporary substitute for literal predication. As long as reference is made to entities that are not completely transcendent or to wholes that are reflected in their parts, the venturesome use of projective analogies is a fruitful probe of experience, even if it must always be somewhat tentative and approximate.

It is the extreme extension of religious analogies that frequently obscures their hypothetical character and the relevance of empirical data. Religious assertions are so close to the core of the individual's life and so crucial as a background for narrower interpretations that their provisional nature is hidden by commitment and confidence. Since one must take some attitude toward the significance of life, assumptions of a religious type are involved in the pattern of coordination in which all narrower projections and confirmations are carried out. Some analogical projection or interpretation on this level is necessary, and this obscures the provisional character of the religious extension of analogies. This explains why religious assertions do not seem to be taken as provisional or critically evaluated. At least, when they are the analogical projections by which *we* interpret our own existence, their tentative aspects are usually thoroughly hidden in the confidence which their particular function requires. It is just other people's religious assertions that are obviously hypothetical, appealing for our interest and consideration. When accepted, religious alternatives are so crucial in the life of the individual that they are treated as far more certain and dependable than their projective form will strictly allow.

The fact that religious assertions do not appear to be hypothetical puts them on a par with at least two other types of symbolic interpretation. Sense-perception is the crucial illustration in Whitehead's scheme. On that level, interpretations are put forward as adequate and appropriate before criticism and evaluation can take place. Their hypothetical character only becomes apparent in the wake of commitment and initial acceptance. Since some perception of the environment must occur, no criticism can proceed until an initial interpretation has been made. The projected data are accepted and then discovered to be in need of further confirmation and correction.

The implicit power of metaphysical assumptions on all narrower fields of inquiry and expression provides another example of hidden projective activity. Since the generic patterns of experience must be interpreted in one way or another, there is no way to stand on neutral ground to assess alternatives. Instead, they must be compared from a position of bias. One can compare metaphysical models, but their importance in all critical reflection makes neutrality impossible, and conceals the provisional status of the accepted point of view.

Religious assertions are hypothetical in a similar way. These claims are so close to the core of the person's existence that they must be acted upon with a confidence that may veil the risk and the decision involved. Their provisional character is masked by the sequence in which some commitment as to the significance of life must precede the recognition and critical comparison of alternatives. In this perspective, it is possible to recognize the theoretical uncertainties involved in religious claims without denying that they do function as though they were certain and dependable. Whitehead thus provides a context in which one can affirm the truth of a religious assertion and, at the same time, recognize the possibility of error. After all, even our most trusted interpretations are, in principle, hypothetical projections subject to continuing appraisal. They are all qualified by the impinging future in which new evidence may be uncovered and convictions can be radically revised.

The understanding of religious assertions as being hypothetical is important because their apparent incorrigibility has been both a source of criticism and a defensive barrier against any critical evaluation. The association of particular religious claims with absolute certainty has suggested their tautological "emptiness" and the irrelevance of any kind of evidence. At the same time, the need for such certainty has often contributed to the conclusion that religious claims were merely comforting illusions. But if they can be taken as hypotheses, then the question of their "truth" and their relation to evidence can be taken seriously, even though final answers are beyond our reach.

Whitehead offers such an alternative, in which the referent of religious claims is dependable and necessarily available for characterization, but the claims themselves are open to criticism, correction, and reformulation. Religious assertions, like all other human claims about concrete experience, are a mixture of certainty, probability, and provisional projection. The grasp of generic coordination and valuation is valid, but the best characterization and expression of the religious dimension of experience is always situational and provisional. A model for religious extrapolation may be the best available in one situation, without precluding the adoption of another illuminating analogy in different circumstances. In this way, Whitehead is able to maintain the importance of religious assertions without absolutizing their particular formulations. This opens the way for the consideration of their truth and adequacy. Since they are hypothetical in form, some sort of evidence is relevant and methods of criticism and confirmation can be sought.

Once the hypothetical character of religious assertions is clear, and the tendency to hide it recognized, the type of confirmation available becomes evident. Whitehead's doctrine of symbolic reference suggests that critical evaluation is more complex and subtle because of the scope and importance of the claims. Since real neutrality in respect to the significance of life is not an option, confirmation of fundamental religious assertions depends on the comparison of alternatives rather than on strictly objective attempts to discover an exact correspondence between a single option and confirming evidence. Such a comparison need not rely simply on traditional or readily available options. It can also be an exercise in the creation of new alternatives, based on expanded insight and experience. When religious alternatives conflict, the choice between conflicting options may point to other alternatives which had not been discerned before, and which may include the best advantages of a number of approaches. The important thing is that the test is always between options on the same level, and not the comparison of a religious perspective with some very limited segment of experience treated in an independent fashion.

Given Whitehead's view of the perceptual data and his understanding of symbolic reference, it is possible to assess assertions of the broadest possible scope. But the closer these attempts come to the fringes of consciousness or the limits of experience, the more difficult it is to feign conclusive evaluation or describe the process of confirmation extensively. At the limits where the perceptual input, generic characteristics, and religious commitments must be considered, confirmation depends on the comparison of alternatives with one another and the exact procedures of such an evaluation are extremely difficult to discern. Since the choice is a forced decision between competing options, objectivity is out of the question and the change from one option to another is usually noticed after it occurs. Thus, explaining the reasons for the change or anticipating evidence that would warrant a change is somewhat different than with narrower alternatives. One simply has to say that a more illuminating option was discovered. The initial perspective had to give way to a better, or at least a more convincing, alternative. It is precisely the best alternative that is sought, not some perfect formulation of truth. Indeed, on this level of interpretation, the truth itself is the best interpretation available in a given set of circumstances, rather than some final and unchanging conformity between appearance and reality.

When such a comparison of alternatives takes place, it is not comparable to a laboratory experiment, a logical manipulation or the testing of a limited scientific theory. All of these experiences are relevant, but they are not decisive. As the whole is greater than the sum of its parts, so the totality involved in religious assertions is not simply constructed from accumulated details. The scope of religious assertions is such that no single event or series of events taken in their own definiteness can, by themselves, require the acceptance or rejection of a religious alternative. The events may be important, but how they are seen in the total context of life is as important as the events themselves. This can work against certain positivistic kinds of religious apologetics as well as against critics who argue in an analogous fashion. Unless all of life has a revelatory dimension, then no single instance of miraculous intervention can do much to illuminate the broad features of experience. Or, with respect to the critical use of a similar reliance on discrete events, no series of experiments can verify or falsify a religious assertion unless the very fabric of experience indicates its inadequacy. Miracles cannot be used by themselves to establish the faith any more than laboratory experiments can discredit it. But, if all of life elicits a sense of mysterious disclosure, then a particular instance of miraculous fulfillment may illuminate that mystery. In a similar way, what happens in any laboratory can make its contribution to a broad religious interpretation. Since religious assertions involve the metaphysical, it is widespread, recurrent experience that is finally decisive.[98] Religious alternatives find their verification against other interpretations of similar scope, not against narrow segments of experience. They are dependent on experience in all forms of abstraction, "at all temperatures."[99]

In this perspective, one cannot say that evidence is irrelevant to religious assertions, but only that no discrete events can decide the outcome directly. Evidence is relevant to religious assertions, but only as it contributes to a minor revision of an accepted alternative, or as it is itself coordinated in another religious option. If a minor revision cannot include the evidence in some fashion, then the adequacy of alternatives would need to be considered. The decision is not fundamentally about the conformity of the religious assertion to some discrete segment of experience—it is made with respect to the relative adequacy of comparable alternatives. Thus, one can choose between scientific materialism and Christian Theism, but no religious alternative is evaluated against an interpretation of more limited scope.

98. *PR*, p. 25.
99. *RM*, p. 53.

Any evidence counts for or against specific religious convictions, but not in a simple and conclusive way. Since religious assertions are metaphysical, they must illuminate all experience, and no experience can be simply ignored. Yet because the choice is between alternative interpretations, the evidence has only a kind of cumulative or total effect. When the evidence is sufficient—one way or another—the perspective itself is so radically changed that the transformation (conversion) takes place in a subtle fashion. The individual simply discovers that he is *not* able to affirm the old assertions since he sees life in a different way. Such transformations are not unknown in common experience, even though they may not occur with great frequency. Similar transitions can be seen in the modification of fundamental scientific paradigms and metaphysical modéls. Not every weighing of evidence is a controlled, explicit, logical exercise done in public. The body itself interprets its perceptual data, and the very living of life is a pragmatic investigation of our broadest hypotheses.

Thus, it is not surprising that some have thought religious assertions have no basis in evidence. Nor is it strange that those who have accepted the truth of certain religious claims feel their certainty must eliminate all attempts to treat them as provisional. Since they are accepted as the best option, because their illuminating power is persuasive in the face of man's total experience, they may be held in spite of some evidence, without losing their empirical relevance. In this regard, they have much in common with other broad interpretations. Religious assertions are confirmed by their adequacy in the dynamic tensions of concrete existence. They are verified by their superiority over any other available option, in terms of the satisfaction, zest for life, and the sustaining power they provide for a high estimate of some relative coordination of values. They are not tested in the laboratory, although what happens in the laboratory is relevant. They are not evaluated on the basis of their sheer descriptive power like metaphysical models, but they utilize such descriptions. They are proved in the course of life itself, in their capacity to maintain a perspective on life's significance which cannot be conclusively established by any neat analysis of discrete segments of experience, including a single human life, or the history of one people. They never escape the risk of faith (projection) which is commensurate with life in a universe of pulsating and dynamic process.

When one is asked, "What would it take for you to reject a religious affirmation as false?", the appropriate answer is not to point to any single event or accumulation of events. Instead, admitting that one's belief is the adoption of a single alternative from among many, what can be pointed to is the possible discovery of an option which more adequately accounts for the significance of life in the face of all the evidence. In this sense, every event has its relevance to the religious alternative, but no single event or segment of experience need be decisive. Job's 'Though he slay me, yet will I trust in him," is not a sheer rejection of evidence but the articulation of a point of view based on an insight into the total significance of life which makes discrete events—even death—capable of interpretation which neither discounts their force or allows them to stand alone, as the sheer self-sufficient facts which demand the role of conclusive norms.[100]

Take, for example, the assertion "God is love." When this expression is used religiously, as the articulation of existential significance and not as a mere theoretical description of a metaphysical factor, it is said with a confidence that seems to deny the relevance of both evidence and criticism. But on closer analysis, it is a projective hypothesis put forward as one religious option. It refers to a metaphysical component of experience which can be characterized in various ways. It attributes to that factor a loving relationship to contingent realities which is approximated by our best understanding of human love, perhaps as discerned in the life of Jesus. It is an analogical assertion that makes no pretense of knowledge of God from his perspective. It only asserts that God, insofar as he is involved in every human experience, can best be characterized by the paradigmatic extension of certain acts of human love. This is

100. Job, 13:15.

not expressed as a deductive certainty or as a calculated probability. It is not the result of enumerating instances of joy and weighing them against those of pain and boredom. But it is related to evidence and put forward in anticipation of further confirmation. It would be falsified, or at least made unintelligible, if there were no human experiences of love. If there were nothing in our experience that enabled us to understand human love, then the analogical extension of these insights would be impossible. If the love of another person has never been a factor in experience, then the claim "God is love" is not likely to evoke confidence. If accepted, it is chosen from competing alternatives because it seems true. It illuminates life in a more adequate way than any other option.

The expression "God is love," when used religiously, is more than a policy statement indicating how one chooses to behave.[101] It does indicate policy, but on the basis of some grasp of the universe, not in a merely arbitrary way. It expresses a "blik," a way of seeing things, but not without the claim that the chosen perspective conforms most adequately to the universal coordination of facts and values.[102] It is an expression of commitment, made on the basis of the total impact of experience. In this sense, it allows both confidence and criticism, both decisive commitment and the recognition that risk is involved in the rejection of other alternatives.

One competing alternative could be expressed in the words "Eat, drink and be merry, for tomorrow we die." This expression can also be a religious assertion, indicating the significance of human life in the context of the universe. It expresses the "triviality of the merely finite."[103] It is more obviously based on evidence since it takes the end of man's life so seriously, but its characterization of the significance of life on the basis of its abrupt conclusion is as much of a projective interpretation as

---

101. R. B. Braithwaite, *An Empiricist's View of the Nature of Religious Belief* (Cambridge: Cambridge University Press, 1955).

102. "Blik" is Hare's term, sometimes criticized for being simply an arbitrary perspective. (R. M. Hare, "Theology and Falsification," *New Essays in Philosophical Theology*, pp. 99–103.)

103. *MT*, p. 108.

any religious claim. It interprets discontinuity as the final clue to the significance of man's existence. It puts the life of man in a context of significance in which the whole is never greater than the sum of its parts; the value of human achievements are not somehow coordinated and conserved in the universe. Still, like more obviously religious claims, it is put forward as certain, even though it is hypothetical. It may be the most adequate interpretation of all the facts, but in its interpretation of the human plight, it also runs the risk of grave error. Its validity is not to be decided by any mere accumulation of facts, but only by its comparison with other interpretive options.

Religious assertions, then, whatever their specific content are like other truth claims in some very significant respects. They are based on concrete experience in its combination of selection and conformation. They are projective, provisional, and yet related to man's experience on the appropriate scale. They are interpretations, but not condemned to be sheer illusion. They are based on their capacity to illuminate all experience as a perspective in which man can live in the most productive and satisfying manner. Their importance in the living of life veils their hypothetical character and their style of confirmation so that some effort is required to notice just how their evaluation, confirmation or rejection comes about. But they require no more effort in this regard than the pseudo-scientific attempts to turn bare facts into the final arbiters of all knowledge and significance.

Whitehead thus presents an alternative in which religious assertions are kept in touch with every interpretation of experience, and yet maintain their own place as one level of symbolic reference. Religious assertions are given a definite place on the scale of interpretive activity, without denying their relevance to every narrower interpretation and their connections with all other uses of language.

7

RELIGIOUS COMMITMENT
AND EXPRESSION

Having explored several selected aspects of Whitehead's thought and their bearing on the problem of religious language, it is now appropriate to consider Whitehead's own views on religion and its peculiar modes of discourse. This adds another perspective on his thought and gives weight to the argument that Whitehead does provide the basis for an interpretation of religious language in which its cognitive dimension may be taken seriously. The examination of Whitehead's application of his philosophy to the special realm of religion should not suggest that his general system is independent of religious insight. For Whitehead, what is application in one perspective is the derivation of general principles from a limited range of evidence in another. Religion is not only a field of special interest to which the organic philosophy may be applied, but it is also one facet of human experience which contributes fundamental insights for philosophical elaboration.

By focusing on religion, the relationship of fact and value, as one aspect of the problem of religious discourse, is brought into the foreground of attention. Whitehead's contention that fact and value are reciprocal factors in all experience allows a parallel interpretation of religion in which its primary emphasis on ultimate values is kept in productive interaction with those aspects of human competence and wisdom which are more readily accorded the status of cognitive inquiry. At the same time, in this interpretation of religion, its linguistic expressions are also treated as involving both factual considerations and affective valuation. While it is not only this relationship of fact and value which is important here, it is this facet of the problem of religious discourse which is of primary interest in this chapter.

Whitehead develops his views on religion with a continuing concern to avoid over-simplification. Thus, single statements should be taken as parts of a broader interpretation and not used to force Whitehead's views into an alien mold. In keeping with his general understanding of language which denies any single statement the capacity for indicating precise meaning, Whitehead offers his descriptive statements as contributing to a cumulative, but also partial, grasp of the subject matter. Each single statement requires qualification by others of slightly different emphasis, as well as the recognition that the meaning of certain general terms is fixed by Whitehead's own system and not by some competing alternative.

For example, one expression of Whitehead's which is well-known and widely misconstrued is the description of religion as what the "individual does with his own solitariness."[1] This statement requires the balance provided when Whitehead also speaks of religion as "world loyalty" and of its topic as "individuality in community."[2] This ensures that terms like "individual" and "solitariness" are construed properly. They do not carry the meanings often given to them. Whitehead's own words indicate the need for caution in interpreting his views of religion as radically individualistic and without concern for social obligations. "There is no such thing as absolute solitariness. Each entity requires its environment. Thus man cannot seclude himself from society."[3] Whatever else Whitehead's reference to the solitariness of the individual may mean, it is clearly not a call for the simple rejection of communal relationships or responsibilities.

One of the most comprehensive descriptions of religion

1. *RM,* p. 16.
2. *Ibid.,* pp. 59, 86.
3. *Ibid.,* p. 132.

Whitehead offers is found in *Adventures of Ideas*. There it is asserted that religion is "concerned with our reactions of purpose and emotion due to our personal measure of intuition into the ultimate mystery of the universe."[4] This description suggests three features of religion that may be the basis for further discussion.

First, religion has to do with the response of men to the universe in which they find themselves. It involves present enjoyment as well as the anticipation of an ideal in a particular set of circumstances, but with some reference to the totality of things —the universe. It functions by relating the individual to the broadest reaches of his environment. For this reason various grades of generality can inform the consideration of religion, moving between the limits of the immediacy of individual experience and the articulation of the most general features of reality. In this respect, the polarity of religion, its combination of general and specific aspects of experience, is an important feature of Whitehead's description.

The ultimate dependence of religion on the individual's response is another emphasis of Whitehead's that is of crucial significance. Religion involves the existential decision whereby man contributes something to his own character.[5] It is an intensely personal matter, reflecting our purposes, our affections, and our intuitions. In contrast with the scientific form of interest it is concerned with our own emotions and immediate passions, not those of other people, or those that are only memories.[6]

A third feature of religion suggested by Whitehead is its utilization of some penetrating insight into the nature of the universe. Religion does not function in isolation from man's best knowledge of his environment, but rather depends on that knowledge and even influences it.

4. *AI*, p. 161.
5. Whitehead does not utilize the term "existential" in this way. Its current use to describe man's most intimate decisions with respect to his own life make it a very appropriate term for describing Whitehead's emphasis on personal immediacy and self-determination.
6. *PR*, p. 24.

These features of religion, as well as most of Whitehead's descriptions of this aspect of human culture, are intended to be very general. While recognizing that religion is never experienced in bare generic form, Whitehead intentionally seeks the broadest understanding of religion as a basis for comprehending and assessing the claims of particular religions.

For the most part, it is his desire to function as metaphysician and philosopher of religion, not as a theologian who explores the content and implications of a *particular* religious option. It is Whitehead's concern, insofar as it is possible, to let the issues between different religions remain open questions. Where he departs from this ideal, and his own system leads us to expect such departures, Whitehead is usually very careful to indicate that his empirical base has narrowed decisively, and that his interpretation has a more tentative and personal status. This does not keep him from using concrete illustrations of the human response that is appropriately called "religious." His favorite references to particular religions involve Buddhism and Christianity. Others which he uses include Islam, Judaism, tribal cults, Greek mysteries, and even the scientific commitment to the pursuit of Truth.[7] Whitehead's descriptions of religion are not properly construed unless both their generality and their anchorage in historical alternatives are recognized.

For Whitehead, religion reflects the polar combination of universal and particular factors, which characterizes all reality. Its power is based on its involvement in the concrete occasion with all its particular relationships, but such historic manifestations can be treated on various levels of generality without completely severing the ties with concrete experience. One can consider a religion in its impact on a single individual, as the faith of one cultic community, as a type of religion in one cultural milieu, or as manifesting characteristics which are common to all religion. Religion, then, as a subject for study, is a polar phenomenon which can be traced to its concrete origins or subjected to continued abstraction until the maximum level of generality is reached. In seeking a generic description of religion,

7. *Ibid.*, p. 24.

Whitehead finds that continued recognition of both of these poles is essential. There are certain features common to all religion, but they are only manifested in particular religions and specific human responses. The generic understanding of religion depends on, and leaves room for, a wide variety of historic religions, with their own peculiar insights and practices.

The significance of this polarity is apparent in Whitehead's assessment of the contribution of religion to civilization. He is able to combine the highest estimate of religion in general with a critical and modestly optimistic judgment of its actual contribution in any concrete set of circumstances. Religion is of universal importance, of transcendent significance, in the life of man because it expresses and influences the human capacity to pursue the ideal.[8] Its performance, however, all too often denies its promise. The ideals that dominate men's lives may be either uplifting or downgrading. Religion, in a similar way, is a disrupting and energizing form of motivation which leads upward and downward. It can be either good or evil,[9] but it is always important, more because of its potential as the dimension of life in which the battle between ideals is fought, than its consistent contribution to human nobility. In this sense, it is our "one ground for optimism" even though it is only "sometimes progressive."[10] Religion must also carry the shame of glaring failure as the "last refuge of human savagery."[11] Accompanied by crude fancies and barbaric practices in its emergence, it continues to suffer relapses toward the primitive. History gives abundant evidence in recurrent superstition, dogmatism, racial hatred, and bigotry that religion has frequently been the very enemy of progress.[12]

Despite this contrast of promise and performance, Whitehead still is cautiously optimistic about the evolutionary contribution of religion. He discerns a slow but steady development in reli-

8. *RM*, p. 17.
9. *MT*, pp. 26–27, cf., *RM*, p. 36.
10. *SMW*, pp. 171, 26.
11. *RM*, p. 36.
12. *Ibid.*

gion which is not vitiated by the many retreats toward the barbaric. The developing ideal form of religion he terms "rational
religion."[13] It is general enough to allow the inclusion of a
variety of specific religious insights, but specific in that it makes
evident the potential implicit in all religion. A religion is "rational" when it gives explicit recognition to the ultimate responsibility of the individual as well as to the universal scope of his
obligations and opportunities. When these two aspects of religion are recognized, the religious dynamic is directed toward a
coherent view of life in which all experience is related to religious faith and practice.

"Rational religion is religion whose beliefs and rituals have
been reorganized with the aim of making it the central element
in a coherent ordering of life—an ordering which shall be
coherent both in respect to the elucidation of thought, and in
respect to the direction of conduct towards a unified purpose
commanding ethical approval."[14] Buddhism and Christianity are
Whitehead's contemporary examples of rational religion because of their world-consciousness. They call men to seek
loyalties beyond the individuals he knows, his tribe, or the
boundaries of race and nation.[15] It is this movement toward
universal loyalties that makes the Bible the best available history of the development of rational religion.[16] It exhibits the
progressive emphasis on the importance of the individual and
records the prophetic challenges to the narrow loyalties of what
Whitehead calls "communal religion."[17] Whitehead is highly
critical of the social aspects of religion because of the tendency
of these "trappings" to usurp ultimate importance. However, it
should be kept in mind that these criticisms are directed against
the idolatrous misuse of social and communal relationships
which obscure the importance of the individual and absolutize
narrow loyalties.

13. *Ibid.*, pp. 28–32.
14. *Ibid.*, p. 30.
15. *Ibid.*, pp. 42–43.
16. *Ibid.*, p. 29.
17. *Ibid.*, pp. 37–40.

In Whitehead's view, religion has gradually emerged in nobler form and with greater clarity of expression.[18] "Religion can be, and has been, the main instrument for progress."[19] Its generic importance is not diminished by its checkered history and unpredictable future. This is one way in which Whitehead gives expression to the polar contrast between the general and specific aspects of religion. The general features ensure its continued importance. The special characteristics give definite shape and power to the distinctive historical religions. The two aspects can be distinguished, but not separated. The consideration of either one always retains some reference to the other. This polar contrast is clarified by a distinction Whitehead makes in respect to metaphysics. Metaphysics can be considered on the level of maximum generality where its notions indicate factors required by any experience whatsoever. It can also be seen as utilizing special insights derived from limited areas of experience and extrapolated in a tentative way to provide a more definite grasp of metaphysical coordination. On the one hand, metaphysics is "properly general" and highly "abstract."[20] On the other, it is the extension of selected experiences beyond their origins to refer to the most general contours of experience. In its most general aspect, metaphysics depends on man's average experience. In its more special aspect, it relies on "occasions and modes of experience which in some degree are exceptional."[21] The two levels of metaphysics require each other. They function together much like the connotation and denotation of a term combine to give both sense and reference. A similar polarity is involved in Whitehead's treatment of religion. In keeping with Whitehead's ontological principle, the generic features always derive from historic manifestations. At the same time, every positive religion includes a drive toward the universal extension of its insights, which cannot be denied in its entirety.

18. *SMW*, p. 171.
19. *RM*, p. 36.
20. *SMW*, p. 156, cf., *RM*, p. 31.
21. *AI*, p. 299.

In recognizing this polar aspect of religion, Whitehead provides a basis for the appreciation of practice and theory as correlative emphases in religious commitment. While involvement in a particular form of ritual and devotion can be based on extremely narrow interests and involve a very limited development of conceptual implications, nevertheless, this practice of religion includes implicit insights and presuppositions of much broader significance. The ritual generates myths that reinforce and explain its emotional satisfaction. Gradually, the myths become doctrines which extend the implications of religion toward wider generality. Finally, religious insights make their own contribution to metaphysical descriptions. A major illustration of this latter development is the metaphysical import Whitehead finds in the early Christological formulations. He sees the thinkers of Alexandria and Antioch as "groping after the solution of a fundamental metaphysical problem . . . arising in a very special form in their attempt to state the content of their religious faith."[22] The resulting expression of the mutual immanence of the finite and the infinite is an instance of a contribution offered by religious doctrine for utilization on the level of metaphysical description.

Not only does the practice of religion give shape to theoretical explanations, but the development of the theoretical side of religion has its own impact on the manner in which insights and practices are maintained. Theories of the broadest scope verge on metaphysics and fix the meaning of general terms used in religious expression. More specific doctrines and dogmas enhance and emphasize religious insights so they may be shared more fully within the religious community and expressed to some of those outside. Thus, religion can be described as both the "art and the theory of the internal life of man."[23] Whitehead's description of the interplay between concrete experience and conceptual generalization as the pattern of the religious dynamic illuminates the combination of practice and theory.

22. *Ibid.*, pp. 167–169.
23. *RM*, p. 16.

Religion starts from the generalization of final truths first perceived as exemplified in particular instances. These truths are amplified into a coherent system and applied to the interpretation of life. They stand or fall—like other truths—by their success in this interpretation.[24]

Religion thus begins in concrete experience and returns to it. It generates theory, but the theory must gain continued support from extended experience. When theories become broad and explicit enough, their potential contribution to metaphysics become evident. Religion produces its own models for coordinating the entire range of experience.

Rational religion appeals to the direct intuition of special occasions, and to the elucidatory power of its concepts for all occasions. It arises from that which is special, but it extends to what is general. The doctrines of rational religion aim at being that metaphysics which can be derived from the super-normal experience of mankind in its moments of finest insight.[25]

Whitehead understands the dynamic motivation of religion as fluctuating between emotional involvement and conceptual generalization. Religion develops insights, drawn from particular relationships, as a vision illuminating all of life. In turn, it infuses those concrete circumstances with the recognition of universal implications. It focuses man's impetus toward the ideal by reconciling the emotional and conceptual drives. In this function religion has the power of a "transforming agency."[26] As Whitehead describes it, "Religion is an ultimate craving to infuse into the insistent particularity of emotion that non-temporal generality which primarily belongs to conceptual thought alone."[27] Without this motivation, emotional enjoyment and conceptual anticipation attain such a balance that tedious conformity and mediocrity result. Religion resists such a balance by providing powerful insights which raise man's inter-

24. *Ibid.*, p. 120.
25. *Ibid.*, p. 31.
26. *Ibid.*, p. 15.
27. *PR*, p. 23.

ests above his own immediate concerns. "It is directed to the end of stretching individual interest beyond its self-defeating particularity."[28]

The place of religion in culture is established by this movement between particular experience and conceptual generalization. Religion functions between the special sciences and philosophy, and yet is in touch with both of them. Based on a limited selection from experience, it is comparable to a scientific interest or some other specialized concern. "But on its other side, religion claims that its concepts, though derived primarily from special experiences, are yet of universal validity, to be applied by faith to the ordering of all experience."[29] In this aspect, religion is comparable to metaphysics.

The special sciences depend on exclusive attention to a certain genus of facts.[30] As a relatively narrow interest, a science can afford to limit its concern to those factors which allow dependable and precise symbols. Religion also originates in a selection from the same complex of empirical data, but its emphasis is radically different. It is 180° out of phase with the scientific interest, focusing on just those factors that science seeks to exclude—purpose and value. Whitehead's description makes the contrast clear.

> Remember the widely different aspects of events which are dealt with in science and in religion respectively. Science is concerned with the general conditions which are observed to regulate physical phenomena; whereas religion is wholly wrapped up in the contemplation of moral and aesthetic values. On the one side there is the law of gravitation, and on the other side the contemplation of the beauty of holiness. What one side sees, the other misses; and vice versa.[31]

Science can then be said to be primarily concerned with facts, while religion focuses on values. Experience, however, will not allow a final separation of fact and value, so the two fields

28. *Ibid.*
29. *RM,* p. 31.
30. *PR,* p. 14, cf., *ESP,* pp. 120–121.
31. *SMW,* p. 165.

are characterized by a common source of data and a relative divergence in emphasis. They go their apparently separate ways from a single point of departure, they are never completely out of touch along the way, and they find another point of contact since the insights of both must be included in the generalizations of metaphysics. As an inclusive interest which attempts to reverse the process of abstraction, philosophy cannot exclude either the facts of science or the values of religion. It cannot neglect the "multifariousness of the world."[32]

Whitehead sees the diverse emphases of science and religion on facts and values as the two fundamental modes of abstraction in which all man's wisdom is based. The scientific emphasis on discrete observations makes the multiplicity and divisibility of experience primary. Scientific disciplines themselves multiply and the accumulation of experimental data results in a "knowledge explosion" of diversification and specialization. The religious interest in values, in a contrary fashion, persists in attempting to express an apprehension of the ultimate coordination of things. The values which are given emphasis imply a wider order of relative values which is finally seen to include the entire universe. However, since fact and the sense of importance are inextricably bound together in concrete experience, neither science nor religion can simply ignore the other. Value judgments influence the methods of the scientist, as well as the utilization of his discoveries.[33] In a similar way, questions of value cannot be pursued productively without the consideration of definite conditions and realistic possibilities. In this way, the scientific and the religious understanding of the world each "exhibit the impress of the other."[34]

This means that the apparent conflicts of science and religion actually express contrasts in the data of concrete experience. They can conflict because they refer to the same complex of experience. But that same common reference makes them mutually corrective. Their confrontation and disagreement do not

32. *PR*, p. 513.
33. *AE*, p. 153.
34. *SP*, p. 97.

call for a choice between them so much as for more penetrating insights and formulations.[35] Thus, an important factor in the development of religious thought is its interaction with science.[36] The success of the special sciences is even taken as one mode of evidence for religious convictions.[37] Science also provides persistent criticism of religious ideas. In its turn, science has benefited from the convictions of religion—at least on some occasions. Whitehead claims that religious faith in an ultimate order and harmony at the base of things has undergirded the entire modern scientific enterprise.[38] Religion also exercises a corrective influence on the scientific preoccupation with discrete experiments, definite results, and divergent disciplines. "Religion insists that the world is a mutually adjusted disposition of things, issuing in value for its own sake. This is the very point that science is always forgetting.[39]

Religion and philosophy are also intimately related. The thrust of religion toward the universal extension of its insights is an impetus for philosophic reflection. At the same time, philosophy adds a critical dynamic to religion.[40] It presses for the recognition of the metaphysical implications involved in religious convictions and by doing so it brings them to the light of criticism. It does this for the sciences as well, but their chosen limitations allow them to function without the explicit extension of their insights to metaphysical generality. Because of its emphasis on values and their universal coordination, religion requires the development of its widest implications in order for it to retain its power. As Whitehead describes it:

> Science can leave its metaphysics implicit and retire behind our belief in the pragmatic value of its general descriptions. If religion does that, it admits that its dogmas are merely pleasing ideas for the purpose of stimulating its emotion.[41]

35. *AI*, p. 140, cf., *SMW*, p. 165.
36. *SMW*, p. 171.
37. *RM*, p. 138.
38. *SMW*, pp. 24–25.
39. *RM*, p. 138.
40. *AI*, pp. 24–25.
41. *RM*, p. 83.

It is only in productive relationship with both science and philosophy that religion can retain its claim to deal with truth. Its mutual interaction with these two modes of human interests, however, requires that changes affecting any of them shall be reflected in the others. The historical problem for all three has been their failure to see the tentative character of their own formulations.[42] If any of them is subject to change—and science has provided the most obvious example that one of them is— then, at least with respect to their precise formulations, they must all be open to corrective and clarifying revision. "You cannot shelter theology from science, or science from theology; nor can you shelter either of them from metaphysics, or metaphysics from either of them."[43] This insight led to Whitehead's attack on religious dogmatism in *Science and the Modern World*.[44] It also informs his critical appreciation of dogmatic formulations, properly held, in any field of interest, including religion.

Our purpose for exploring this polar aspect of religion has been to prepare the way for seeing religious language in Whitehead's perspective; now we can attempt to do that.

Whitehead seems to give clear justification to two distinct types of religious language which are yet interdependent. On the one hand, language is used to express the emotions and insights connected with the special experiences and particular practices of a concrete religious alternative. On the other, language is used in the theoretical or doctrinal development of those special insights toward their widest implications. The polarity of the general and the particular, as it is reflected in religion, results in two major emphases in religious expression. Just as religion is both art and theory, from its very earliest stages its use of language reflects both practical and explanatory aspects in various degrees of development. Generally, one can discern in a particular use of language some dominant interest, either in the special origins, power, and identity of religious

42. *SMW*, p. 168, cf., *FR*, p. 49.
43. *RM*, p. 76.
44. *SMW*, pp. 161–172.

insights or in the relation of that particular alternative to the broader dimensions of human experience and wisdom. Some expressions have obvious practical utility for the reinforcement of faith by involvement, others clearly indicate the conceptual development of those insights toward generality, and the gradual introduction of criticism that this allows. Of course, there are expressions that are useful in both ways, but the distinction between the two types of religious discourse is still legitimate. The practical and theoretical are implied by each other. Nevertheless, they do reflect a divergence in emphasis.

It is also true that at their limits the two types of language verge on secular discourse in a manner that prohibits a sharp boundary between religious language and other important forms of expression. These limits are roughly indicated by the concrete experience of value itself and by the convergence of religion and metaphysics at the point of maximum generalization.

The fact that Whitehead's philosophy justifies two interrelated and interdependent types of religious discourse is important because it reflects both the affective and the cognitive dimensions of religious discourse. This allows religious doctrines to retain the emotional power of concrete religious involvement at the same time as they express a relatively definite conceptual content and lay claim to truth. Conversely, this polar view of religious language gives to practical and cultic religious expressions an implicit conceptual content and some connection with the more rigorous structures of understanding which man develops. Whitehead's view ensures that religious claims to truth will be taken seriously as they are kept in potentially critical contact with other forms of human expression It suggests that the quest for religious truth is promising, both in respect to the concrete involvement in religious "faith" and in the articulation of that faith in relation to the "knowledge" of both science and philosophy.

Fortunately, Whitehead also provides examples of religious discourse across the entire spectrum. However, it should be recognized that the interpretation of these illustrations is not necessarily Whitehead's own.

Since religion gives emphasis to the value dimension of concrete experience, the type of expression that gives the most concrete example of the origin of religious discourse is the simple affirmation of value, experienced here and now. At least, it is this type of discourse which must be involved on the level of religious practice, and developed into a more explicit religious commitment. Whitehead's description of the genesis of this level of religious discourse makes evident both its potential for religious development and its availability for utilization in respect to other cultural interests.

> Our enjoyment of actuality is a realization of worth, good or bad. It is a value-experience. Its basic expression is—Have a care, here is something that matters! Yes—that is the best phrase—the primary glimmering of consciousness reveals, Something that matters.[45]

This concrete expression of value-experience is a rudimentary religious articulation. It illustrates the origin of religious insight in concrete experience, and its intimate connection with every secular development of that same experience. There is no insulated and isolated religious experience which can be developed into a strictly esoteric vocabulary or jargon. Religious experience is, instead, a dimension of man's common experience, and its expressions verge on the secular from the very outset. "Here is something that matters" parallels both the "alleluia" of ritual and the "eureka" of scientific discovery.

It is expressions of this type which become the source sayings of the great religious traditions. There is a slight move toward theory, in that *what* is important requires some articulation. These sayings are involved in ritual and the primitive generation of myth. Later, reinforced by tradition and elaborated by communal interpretation, they themselves become sources of religious insight and commitment. They carry the power of concrete religious intuition, expressing the immediate and emotional involvement of the original experience. This is

45. *MT*, p. 159.

the case, whether the preserved accounts involve the actual words of a religious leader or the report of a paradigm experience. Whitehead illustrates this concrete level of religious expression by describing the sayings of Christ.

> The reported sayings of Christ are not formularized thought. They are descriptions of direct insight. The ideas are in his mind as immediate pictures, and not as analyzed in terms of abstract concepts. He sees intuitively the relations between good men and bad men; his expressions are not cast into the form of an analysis of the goodness and badness of man. His sayings are actions and not adjustments of concepts. He speaks in the lowest abstractions that language is capable of, if it is to be language at all and not the fact itself.[46]

Whitehead's use of the words of Jesus to exemplify expressions of concrete religious insight reflects his judgment that the greatness of Christianity is its openness to development, maintained by its explicit reference to history. It does not begin with a finished system of general principles which are to be maintained in changing circumstances, but it finds its inspiration in historical experiences and leaves their interpretation open to a systematic development of provisional and progressive character. Christianity originates in a notion about the world derived from the sayings and actions of unusually perceptive men. Its fundamental source expressions point to concrete experience, not to a developed system of doctrine. While they include metaphysical presuppositions which can be made explicit, the appeal is not to a formulation but to the "fact" of concrete insight.[47] Thus, "Here is something that matters" on the lips of a man among men is the type of language on which the edifice of religion should build. "In the Sermon on the Mount, in the Parables, and in their accounts of Christ, the Gospels exhibit a tremendous fact."[48] In Whitehead's view, it is in this appeal to history that religion must find its inspiration.

46. *RM*, p. 56.
47. *Ibid.*, pp. 50–51, 84.
48. *Ibid.*, pp. 51–52.

Close to the source-sayings and their expression of immediate intuitions are the cultic expressions involved in the practice of religion, or other linguistic forms utilized by individuals in their appropriation and reinforcement of religious insight. In the traditional religions these language forms reflect the importance of a "living" community for the maintenance and interpretation of the original intuitions.[49] Whitehead calls these expressions of second-level religious use "intermediate representations" to indicate their distance from the concrete intuition as well as their partial conceptual and critical development.[50] They do not have to be linguistic forms of symbolization, but they would include liturgical formulations, some scriptural passages, hymns, catechisms, and various types of "popular religious literature."[51] Their concreteness may be that of an emotional expression of praise or they may verge on abstract doctrine. In every case, however, these intermediate expressions live off the power of concrete insights, remembered or re-enacted. They are the artistic tools of the religious life, but they require the criticism of further conceptual development, and continued reference to their concrete origins. "Religions cannot do without them; but if they are allowed to dominate, uncriticized by dogma or by recurrence to the primary sources of religious inspiration, they are properly to be termed idols."[52]

Moving toward the theoretical emphasis, the explicit conceptual content of religious expressions becomes more and more decisive. These are the doctrines, or dogmas, of religion which attempt to put all of life in a coherent perspective on the basis of religious insight. They have some of the power of concrete insights, but they also draw on man's critical faculties. Just as the practical expressions of religion have an implicit conceptual content, the theoretical formulations retain power to affect man's pursuit of ideals. Doctrines have a motivating and transforming power, despite their generality. "A religion, on its

49. *SP*, p. 75.
50. *RM*, p. 141.
51. *Ibid.*
52. *Ibid.*, p. 141.

doctrinal side, can thus be defined as a system of general truths which have the effect of transforming character when they are sincerely held and vividly apprehended."[53]

These theoretical religious expressions draw out the implications of special religious intuitions for purposes of reinforcement, communication, explanation, illuminating extension, and criticism of fundamental religious beliefs. Their rudimentary form is myth.[54] Their development is exemplified in the Christian tradition by the transformation of "Jesus is Lord" into the dogma of the pre-existent son of God.[55] In this way, what is of concrete importance is progressively related to the universal dimensions of experience. Thus, the doctrines that express how the "complex world is to be expressed in the light of the intuitions fundamental to the religion" are characteristics of theoretical religious expressions.[56] They are like the theories of science in their thrust toward generality, attempting to formulate precisely the truth of religious disclosure in just the same way as scientific "dogmas" articulate with rigor the truths given by the senses.[57]

It is at this point that the theoretical expressions of specific religion can be pressed to the level of generality where they can be called metaphysical. They are *not* metaphysical in the most general sense that any experience requires them, but they *are* metaphysical in the sense that they are extended to characterize the widest features of experience. The doctrines of sophisticated religion aim at being an adequate metaphysics derived from special insights.[58] This metaphysical level of religious discourse provides both its limit and another vague boundary between the secular and religious use of language.

The ambiguity involved in the metaphysical elaboration of religious insight is illuminated by Whitehead's di-polar doc-

53. *Ibid.,* p. 15.
54. *Ibid.,* p. 23.
55. This example is not Whitehead's, but my own.
56. *RM,* p. 134.
57. *Ibid.,* p. 57.
58. *Ibid.,* p. 31.

trine of God. God has functions in experience that are secular as well as religious.[59] God can be treated in a strictly metaphysical fashion as the ground of order and novelty effective in every occasion of experience, or he can be considered with respect to experiences of special disclosure, which are preserved and interpreted in the great religious traditions. The descriptions of the influence and character of God as discerned in particular circumstances are properly termed "religious expressions." By extrapolation, they are used to characterize the entity which is at the base of all experience and in that function they are metaphysical. It is these descriptions which represent the theoretical extreme of religious expression, even as they verge on philosophy.

When the metaphysical factor, to which all religious claims must ultimately be referred, is considered in strict abstraction, this is what Whitehead calls the "primordial nature" of God.[60] On this level, statements about God or the universal coordination of value become metaphysical in the most general and proper sense. However, God as a metaphysical factor in experience must be characterized by utilizing selected insights drawn from religion or explicitly secular modes of experience. It is this fuller characterization of God that Whitehead refers to as his "consequent nature" and which is dependent on particular circumstances of interaction between God and the world. This distinction directly parallels Whitehead's treatment of generic and particular religion. Indeed, the interdependence of the two natures is also adumbrated by the polar relationship of the practical and theoretical aspects of religion. What can be said about God in a general or primordial sense is drawn from man's "average experience," those characteristics made manifest in any man's attempt to deal with the religious dimension of experience. What can be said about God in his concrete involvement or consequent nature is comparable to the claims of the positive religions. Whitehead's own description of God as a metaphysical factor and as illuminated by special insights makes the parallel plain.

59. *PR*, p. 315.
60. *Ibid.*, pp. 521–522.

There is a metaphysical need for a principle of determination, but there can be no metaphysical reason for what is determined. . . . What further can be known about God must be sought in the region of particular experiences. . . . In respect to the interpretation of these experiences, mankind have differed profoundly. He has been named respectively, Jehovah, Allah, Brahma, Father in Heaven, Order of Heaven, First Cause, Supreme Being, Chance. Each name corresponds to a system of thought derived from the experiences of those who have used it.[61]

The importance of Whitehead's di-polar description of God, for our purposes, is that it supports both practical and theoretical uses of religious language. Whitehead's discussion of the primordial nature of God indicates the possibility of using the most precise language about God, even though this means a high degree of conceptual generality and a certain deficiency in concrete content. God is not an exception to the principles of metaphysics, but he is the factor in experience which most fully exemplifies the character and coordination of reality.[62] In this sense, God can be spoken of more literally than any other factor in experience.[63] It is our assumption about the ultimate mode of coordination that informs every description and expression. One can talk about the object of all religious doctrines as the source of order and novelty with the confidence that such a factor is required by any occasion of experience. The fact that God can be treated in this metaphysical way provides a basis on which more specific religious descriptions can be understood, compared, and even evaluated. If there is a factor in the experience of all men to which religious convictions refer, then communication between sects and individuals is not out of the question with respect to the meaning of particular religious alternatives. Because God can be spoken about with some precision on the metaphysical level, it is the truth of religious claims which should be the primary issue, not the importance of this type of assertion.

61. *SMW,* p. 161.
62. *PR,* p. 521.
63. Hartshorne, *op. cit.,* pp. 133–147.

When Whitehead describes the consequent nature of God, his appeal to insights which are properly termed "religious" is explicit. He focuses on the Galilean origins of Christianity and describes God's consequent nature in an admittedly "imaginative" manner. Descriptions, on this level, are only images and not precise metaphysical principles. "The image—and it is but an image—the image under which this operative growth of God's nature is best conceived, is that of a tender care that nothing be lost."[64] God is characterized in a more tentative and almost religious way as "infinite patience." "He is the poet of the world, with tender patience leading it by his vision of truth, beauty, and goodness."[65] Here there is no demand for literal accuracy, but there is a profound concern for the appropriate analogy. This is Whitehead's own exercise in doing metaphysics on the basis of a special and limited selection of experiences. This is metaphysical discourse which is also the extension of specific religious insight to the limits of generality. It is put forward as one alternative way of characterizing God in addition to the three speakers and positions given a platform in Hume's dialogues. It is based on Whitehead's own experience, the vision that moved him with profound emotion and feeling. Whitehead's characterization of the consequent nature of God can be traced to its origin in the Christian tradition. Its source-sayings are Jesus' use of the metaphor "Father" as a description of God, the phrase "The Kingdom of Heaven is within you" and the elaboration of the theme "God is love" in the fourth Gospel.[66]

It does not emphasize the ruling Caesar, or the ruthless moralist, or the unmoved mover. It dwells upon the tender elements in the world, which slowly and in quietness operate by love; and it finds purpose in the present immediacy of a kingdom not of this world.[67]

64. *PR*, p. 525.
65. *Ibid.*, p. 526.
66. *RM*, p. 70.
67. *PR*, p. 520.

It should be kept in mind that while God can be said to have two natures, they are not grasped in separation. God is apprehended in concrete experience and treated in two different modes of attention; the one focusing on generic features of the divine role, the other concerned with God's specific involvement in one strain of history, one set of circumstances. The two natures of God thus reflect divergent but inseparable emphases, much in the same manner as practical and theoretical aspects of religion and its expression have been seen to imply each other.

Whitehead's treatment of religion, insofar as we have considered it, justifies two emphases in religious expression—the practical and the theoretical. It provides an interpretive context in which both of these types of religious discourse can be connected with secular expressions, either on the level of concrete experience, or on the level of maximum generalization. It thus provides two ways of speaking about God. It gives reference to both, so that diverse religious intuitions can be intelligibly expressed, compared, and assessed. By maintaining a relationship of mutual implication between practical and theoretical expressions, the affective power of religious discourse and its potential contribution to man's knowledge are both illuminated.

In this way, Whitehead shows how the pursuit of linguistic precision and the maintenance of fidelity to the concrete religious insights are compatible. The quest for linguistic adequacy has its place both in the exercise of man's broadest critical powers and in the life of "faith." The two types of precision actually contribute to each other. The concern for the most accurate and powerful religious formulations for practice and reflection is not a threat to the mystery of disclosure, the majesty of God, or the rigors of rational inquiry. The polarity of experience and the limitations of language make that certain. The exact language that is used in the practice of religion is qualified by its exclusive interest in the insights of a particular religion. The even more precise language utilized to extend religious insights to an explicit metaphysical level, is qualified by its concern for relationships and generality. Both types of language are only "exact" in a provisional and partial manner. They both have reference to an empirical dimension that allows only partial discernment and description. Thus, religious assertions can be made relatively precise in their own right and also compared and assessed in respect to alternative descriptions of their referent. Criticism, conceptualization, and practice, function together to give increased penetration of insight and the confident use of definite formulations on many levels of generality without necessarily making those expressions final or exhaustive.

The generic reference of religious assertions is crucial for Whitehead's interpretation. It fixes the type of claim expressed in religious discourse, even though it does not give a basis for final and certain judgments about which religious alternative is most adequate. When the type of claim is evident, one can hope to weigh the relevant alternatives. But, unless the general assessment of man's experience requires an ordering factor, man's religious assertions are left without denotation, they have nothing to describe and attempted comparison is useless. Whitehead puts it this way: "For nothing, within any limited type of experience, can give intelligence to shape our ideas of any entity at the base of all actual things, unless the general character of things requires that there be such an entity."[68]

It is in attempting to establish the generic character of religious claims that Whitehead identifies religion with the "solitariness" of the individual. He was not content to make evident the complexity of religion in its empirical and cultural relationships. He also wanted to show just how religion is based in universal factors in human nature and on identifiable intuitions available to every man. He saw this as essential if particular religious claims were to be considered with the seriousness that he believed they deserved. In clear anticipation of contemporary problems with religious assertions, he addressed himself to the question of the "meaning" and "truth" of religious beliefs. His series of lectures published as *Religion in the Making* was addressed primarily to this problem. Faced with widespread

68. SMW, p. 156.

disagreement concerning the nature of religion as well as the validity of any particular religious claims, Whitehead set out to show how all religion is grounded in factors given in every occasion of experience which make possible man's apprehension of, and comprehension of, any of the other factors given in his encounter with the environment.[69]

In attempting to articulate the generic characteristics of religion, Whitehead put forward a view that is, in certain respects, reminiscent of Augustine and Luther. It is also similar to the more recent and explicitly existential approach of Paul Tillich. Man's situation is not one in which he can be religious or non-religious, a worshiper of God or an atheist. Instead, the choice is between alternatives that are all essentially "religious." Religion reflects and influences the ultimate choice which every man must make in determining the shape of his own existence. By an intimate decision in respect to the relative significance of available ideals, each man contributes something to his own destiny. Religion is not like other aspects of life in which disagreement and apparent uncertainty result in irrelevance or suspended judgment.[70] It has to do with man's existential decision to lead one kind of life, rather than another. Such a decision may be made by default, or in a positive and reflective way.

Thus, religion is the development, on the human level, of the germ of freedom that Whitehead attributes to every actuality. Man is a contributor to his existence, and not just the recipient of a determined inheritance. This self-determination is always partial and relative, but in man its combination with consciousness and thought make it of decisive importance. Since all men have this freedom to modify the endowment of the past, and because they contribute to their own character—whether or not they are reflective about it—there are universal factors in human nature with which religion may be identified. Religion is the integrating power of "love" (Augustine), "trust" (Luther), or "ultimate concern" (Tillich). Every religion gives

69. *RM*, pp. 7–8, 13–14.
70. *Ibid.*, pp. 14–15.

expression to man's limited freedom and influences its disposition. This is true, even of primitive "communal religion" which Whitehead sees as obscuring man's personal responsibility in a coercive social conformity. *Some* religious alternative is manifested in the life of every man, even those who count themselves as without religious commitments. Insofar as they exercise any control over their own lives, they reflect a religious response to the world in which they find themselves.[71]

It is in this context that Whitehead made his famous assertion: "Religion is what the individual does with his own solitariness."[72] This is first of all a generic description of what is common to all religion, and implicit in apparently divergent forms. It does not describe a specific alternative, that is, *what* to do with one's "solitariness." Secondly, this description depends on two different meanings of the term "solitary," neither one of which is compatible with an extremely individualistic interpretation of religion.

The primary meaning of "solitariness" in this description is informed by Whitehead's own metaphysical scheme. It refers to those immediate aspects of experience which are beyond exhaustive penetration and control. It is the manner in which every individual transcends his environment without being separated from it. It is not solitariness in the sense of being alone, but rather in the sense of appropriating the data of experience in one's own way. Man must accept his endowment from the past, but *how* he deals with it is essentially an immediate, personal, and ultimately private affair. No external circumstances can deprive him of this freedom to contribute to his own character. No information can fully determine his choice. No method of inquiry can discover exhaustive explanations behind such a decision. It is wrapped in the secrecy of a unique perspective which requires some ordering of alternatives without completely determining the order. It is in this sense that Whitehead describes religion as a matter for the "solitary individual,"

71. *Ibid.*, p. 15.
72. *Ibid.*, p. 16.

always more than a "communal" affair. It has to do with the very "formation of the experiencing subject."[73]

It is the case, obviously, that men are profoundly influenced by their environment and their heredity, including the people with whom they associate and the ideas and arguments which they consider. But religion, in its most general sense, cannot be limited to those types of response which make communal or explicit ideological systems decisive. Whitehead insists that the ultimate reference of religion is to man's internal life, his existential commitment to be one kind of person, rather than another.

> In the long run your character and your conduct of life depend upon your intimate convictions. Life is an internal fact for its own sake, before it is an external fact relating itself to others. The conduct of external life is conditioned by environment, but it receives its final quality, on which its worth depends, from the internal life which is the self-realization of existence.[74]

The importance of sophisticated or "rational" religion is that it makes the existential reference of religion explicit and seeks to influence men in a manner appropriate for those who ultimately make their own decisions. It is no longer simply the pressure of the group toward conformity which is decisive, nor the coercive concern for preservation, but the persuasive power of ideals in a universal perspective is recognized as the proper religious mode of influence. Every religion expresses man's disposition of his own freedom in response to the universe, but only in the highly developed religions does the importance of the individual's choice and the universal scope of ideals become apparent in doctrine and practice. This is the reason that Whitehead seems so highly critical of the social aspects of religion. They may obscure both the importance of the individual and the universal dimensions of the context of his significance "To attach that co-ordination of value to a finite social group is

73. *PR*, p. 24.
74. *RM*, pp. 15–16.

a lapse into barbaric polytheism."[75] Once this is established, Whitehead is quite willing to recognize the contribution of the social features of religion to the generation and expression of penetrating insight. His stress on the solitariness of the individual as the generic locus of religion does not require the rejection of the opportunities and responsibilities found in finite social groupings.

There is, however, a second sense of solitariness which is involved. This is the meaning of the term which is more common, suggesting isolation from other people and independence of community ties. This is important in Whitehead's understanding of religion because some experience of radical self-consciousness seems to be required for profound religious insight. At least, if religion is to develop into the recognition of individual responsibility and universal obligation, the sense of facing life alone is needed. The individual who is never alone with his own thoughts enough to recognize his freedom and responsibility could hardly be considered religious. Whitehead can claim, "if you are never solitary, you are never religious."[76] Perhaps this is a condition for being truly "human" as well.

With the importance of self-conscious responsibility in mind, it is easy to see why Whitehead did stress actual isolation from one's fellows as a factor in exceptional religious insight. Enjoying nature alone, suffering alone, or acting alone should contribute to man's firm and abiding religious intuitions. However, even being solitary in this usual sense is not the permanent denial of social obligations, or the irrevocable commitment to the life of a hermit. It is rather a means of gaining insight, the necessary impetus for transforming one's life in society and bringing narrow, arbitrary, and instinctive loyalties under judgment. Whitehead therefore takes note of the importance of actual solitariness in the paradigm experiences of the great religious leaders. As he sees it, these men made unusual religious contributions because they had experiences of loneliness, rejection, and radical isolation.

75. *SP*, p. 73.
76. *RM*, p. 16.

The great religious conceptions which haunt the imaginations of civilized mankind are scenes of solitariness: Prometheus chained to his rock, Mahomet brooding in the desert, the meditations of the Buddha, the solitary Man on the Cross. It belongs to the depth of the religious spirit to have felt forsaken, even by God.[77]

However, for Whitehead himself such existential pathos is but one stage in the religious life and only one source of insight. He describes in an almost Pauline manner the three stages through which religion runs as it develops toward fulfillment. Man moves from a sense of facing the unknown to an awareness of an angry God, until finally God is known as companion and fellow-sufferer. Religion may begin in solitariness, but it finds its fulfillment in relationship. "It is the transition from God the void to God the enemy, and from God the enemy to God the companion."[78]

What is seen clearly in moments of great religious insight, and given paradigmatic force in the great religious traditions is implied in the lives of all men. It is the universal responsibility of man for his own character that makes the widespread disagreement about religion less than fatal to its continuing importance for man. There is no way that man can avoid being religious in this general sense, and the particular path which he follows in his own development can be considered a religious alternative. Whitehead describes the necessity of religion by relating the character of a human being to the faith adopted. "Your character is developed according to your faith. This is the primary religious truth from which no one can escape."[79]

The ultimate identification of religion with existential freedom illuminates religious language. Such language must articulate alternatives in a way that allows some communication of definite content but does not preclude diverse interpretations in the exercise of man's freedom to choose his own character. Whitehead indicates that such discourse is truly sacramental, its explicit form and conceptual content do not fully determine its

77. *Ibid.*, p. 19.
78. *Ibid.*, p. 16.
79. *Ibid.*, p. 15.

influence. Religious assertions combine definite communication with an elusive, evocative power. They are sacramental in that they elicit an internal response without its being strictly determined by the definite formulation. They make a peculiar response possible at the same time as they protect the freedom of man to respond in his own way. They have a real effect on the internal experience of the interpreter, provided he is willing to be influenced. The language itself is sacramental in the traditional sense. "It is the outward and visible sign of an inward and spiritual grace."[80]

Some features of religious insight can be communicated in fairly precise fashion. Yet, the extent of such communication can never be exhaustive, nor its force strictly compelling. Since the religious insight is grasped by one person in a unique perspective, not everything about that insight can be put into words. At the same time, the reasons for affirming a particular religious alternative cannot be formulated in a completely coercive way. Thus, religious language may be highly useful and profoundly effective, but it always manifests a sacramental influence that is elusive and evocative.

Since religion does have to do with a metaphysical dimension of experience, dealing with factors that can be identified in the lives of all men, some communication of religious insight should be possible between *any* two individuals. At the very least, the type of claim should be recognizable, even if the origin, content and validity of a particular religious alternative remain vague or indeterminate. That is to say, the fact that one is asserting a religious claim with respect to the significance of one's own life should be evident, although the implications of that alternative and the reasons for its adoption are not explicitly and intelligibly developed.

In most cases, more than the mere type of claim should be communicable. Depending on the extent of shared experience and the availability of analogous intuitions for focused attention, it is possible to indicate the specific character of religious alternatives to those who have not yet adopted them. Such

80. *Ibid.*, p. 127.

descriptions cannot be exhaustive any more than any individual can articulate exactly how it feels to grasp the environment from his peculiar perspective. But, the point is, much can be expressed and communicated even with respect to our most intimate convictions. The extent of communication can be increased, depending upon the willingness of an interpreter to see things from a slightly different perspective than he can muster on his own. The Christian can point to specific stories, scriptures, historical events, and persons which inform that particular religious option. Similarly, Jews can indicate the history of their people, and the fundamental motifs that dominate that history. Or, in the case of some other alternative which may or may not bear the marks of formal religion, one can call attention to a type of experience and make explicit its elevation to the role of coordinating ideals.

What is crucial for this communication is shared experience. The best way to understand another person in respect to his deepest convictions is to stand very close to him, viewing the world from almost the same place and utilizing a similar conceptual and linguistic framework. Analogous definite experiences and relevant possibilities must be available to both persons. Then, insofar as experience allows diverse individuals to apprehend common data and entertain similar ideals, religious alternatives can be communicated with a great deal of precision. It is not necessary that the interpreter shall have given the same experience precedence in his existential coordination of ideals. But he must be able to focus on those experiences when they are suggested, and understand that they *could* be given the role of dominant ideals. In other words, given two persons who face similar possibilities for their own lives, the communication of the character of particular religious options should be possible, even though a complete grasp of any such alternative is only to be found by adopting it. As long as the key experiences and possibilities are available for recognition and emphasis, the religious alternatives that hinge on them can be partially communicated. Conversely, if those experiences are not given, communication is bound to fail. "You can only speak of mercy among people who, in some respects, are already merciful."[81] But no matter how intimate the relationship, no matter how much experience is shared, no expression of religious commitment could be formulated which would compel assent. Even though you could communicate the basic content of a religious alternative which exalts mercy, this does not mean you could persuade anyone to make mercy a dominant or even a decisively important ideal. Language can communicate the alternative. Persuading others to adopt it, indeed, is a far different matter.

Here, the sacramental character of religious assertions becomes crucial. Because religious assertions allow diverse interpretations, they appeal to man's freedom without depending on the words alone. They make a creative and novel response possible, but they do not demand it nor determine its precise nature. They appeal to the most intimate realm of decision, expanding the possibilities for the interpreter by calling attention to particular experiences and a specific religious alternative that may have gone unnoticed. In this respect alone, language has an influence that goes well beyond its definite content. It provides for the extension and reshaping of experience by the interpretation it allows, and the experiences indicated. By interpreting the religious assertion in terms of his own intuitions, the "recipient extends his apprehension of the ordered universe by penetrating into the inward nature of the originator of the expression."[82]

But religious assertions are more than interpretable. They are also creative in eliciting the very intuitions required for their own interpretation. By calling attention to intuitions that have gone unnoticed, they allow those intuitions to exert their own inherent persuasive and illuminating power. If they are illuminating, then insight is brought about by suggestions from without, even though it was available before being made the focus of attention. All that is required is the willingness to consider

81. *Ibid.*, p. 33.
82. *Ibid.*, p. 128.

the suggested intuition. In sacramental terms, the "sign works *ex opere operato,* but only within the limitation that the recipient be patient of the creative action."[83]

In this sacramental sense, the significance of religious assertions cannot be confined to the definite and explicitly formulated. They always involve more than is obviously communicated. Something of the religious insight is communicated "in, with, and under" the definitely formulated assertion. It is this extended, elusive, evocative communication which protects the free response of the individual on this level, and at the same time makes religious discourse seem less dependable and precise than many other uses of language. The communication involved in religious expression is both definite and elusive. The expression of religious alternatives functions as a kind of motivation, not in the conformal sense of mere reaction, but in the appeal to immediate intuitions which can generate and reinforce commitment.

This sacramental understanding of religious language is illuminated by the way Whitehead understands God as influencing man both through restrictive structures and by the persuasive appeal of ideals. God limits man's options through determinate structures and definite, exclusive possibilities, but, ultimately, when it comes down to the final character each man adopts, "The power of God is the worship He inspires."[84] Religious language has a similar dual influence on the interpreter. It reflects both the stability of determinate order and a dynamic appeal to freedom. Just as the structures of experience manifest God's relatively coercive power, imposing limitations on man's opportunities, religious assertions manifest a definite content and direct significance. Just as God's power is limited with respect to the final choice of the individual, religious assertions make certain responses possible but do not finally determine them. Different interpretations and "hardness of heart" are always possible. The word of God, or human words about God, may cut with the sharpness of a two-edged sword in prophetic

83. *Ibid.*
84. *SMW*, p. 172.

judgment and appealing promise, but it does not obliterate the freedom and responsibility of the individual; the "awful ultimate fact, which is the human being, consciously alone with itself, for its own sake."[85] Religious assertions can point to that freedom and appeal to it, but no expression can be so convincing as to destroy it.

The sacramental character of religious language clarifies all other uses of language in which human decision, the influence of community interests, and the reference to concrete experience may be obscured by utility and shared assumptions. All linguistic expressions are ultimately sacramental in their dependence on extralinguistic reality and exclusive human interests. Their appeal to man's interpretive freedom and immediate intuitions may be well hidden, but it is central. Not simply religious discourse, but expression itself is the "one fundamental sacrament."[86] The combination of conceptual and linguistic definiteness with affective appeal is more evident in religious discourse, but it is involved in every use of language which moves beyond the mere relationship of symbols on one carefully isolated level of abstraction. Religious language is sacramental in a pre-eminent, paradigmatic way that illuminates all other forms of linguistic interpretation. The sacramental power of religious discourse is evident in the history of religions. The expressions of myth not only express and explain the ritual, but they also generate and reinforce the purposes and emotions involved.[87] The source sayings and reports of the lives of great religious leaders are preserved and honored because of their peculiar evocative power.[88] The most precise dogmas or abstract doctrines retain this sacramental capability.[89] Even these highly systematized and generalized expressions of religious insight contribute to the transformation of character. Such precise forms of language used in the religious context are not sterile

85. *RM*, p. 16.
86. *Ibid.*, p. 127.
87. *Ibid.*, pp.23–25.
88. *Ibid.*, p. 56.
89. *Ibid.*, p. 15.

abstractions with no evocative power. They are not to be evaluated negatively just because they are highly abstract formulations. They assist in the identification and assessment of particular religious alternatives, and in so doing have their own sacramental appeal. They ensure that the content of faith is not lost in sheer equivocation.[90] They develop and sharpen the commitments of faith by utilizing the insights of a broader community and increasingly general descriptions. "What is known in secret must be enjoyed in common, and must be verified in common."[91] The development of dogma makes this common enjoyment and evaluation possible, even though using such dogmas apart from reference to their concrete origins is dangerously deceptive. When such originative and concrete connections are maintained, dogmas and doctrines have a powerful and positive role in religious commitment which ought not to be ignored.

> Every true dogma which formulates with some adequacy the facts of a complex religious experience is fundamental for the individual in question and he disregards it at his peril. For formulation increases vividness of apprehension, and the peril is the loss of an aid in the difficult task of spiritual ascent.[92]

In this way, in its sacramental appeal to man's ultimate freedom of interpretation, religious language epitomizes the elliptical character of all linguistic expression. It makes obvious what is easily obscured in many forms of communication. It ensures that the polarities of language are taken seriously on every level, including that of religious conviction. Language is a public structure with profound "private" implications. It requires both confidence in its definite structures and the recognition of its limited contribution to productive communication and dependable knowledge. When religious discourse is excluded from the context of significant language or cognitive expression, it is just such limitations that are easily forgotten.

90. *Ibid.*, p. 139.
91. *Ibid.*, p. 133.
92. *Ibid.*, p. 132.

The leap of imaginative interpretation is ignored in the wake of pragmatic success and apparently definite systems. Whitehead's sacramental interpretation of language makes such errors less likely, even as it calls for the recognition of the persuasive power of articulated religious alternatives.

Whitehead's general description of religion as the individual's exercise of his own capacity for self-determination is well-balanced by frequent references to the conditions which both limit and allow such freedom. Man does not choose his character in a vacuum, in some purely arbitrary fashion, but he makes this fundamental choice on the basis of his best insight and wisdom. The virtue of religion is, as Whitehead indicates, sincerity, but it is a penetrating sincerity which seeks the knowledge required by good intentions.[93] In choosing the character that he believes to be worthwhile, man is compelled to discriminate alternatives, compare them as ideals for his own life and assess their relative status in respect to some universal coordination.

Freedom, for Whitehead, depends on man's capacity to discern the structure of his circumstances as much as on his innate capacity to make some contribution to his own character. Without such discernment, freedom becomes empty and ideals cannot be responsibly entertained or adopted. Freedom cannot be absolute, but it lies between complete conformity to a given structure and chaos. The degree of freedom, the possibility of reflective consideration of alternatives, and the means of evaluating relative importance are the crucial considerations. Order itself can be as much of an aid to freedom as it is a limitation. As "restriction is the price of value," the order that sets limits is the condition of opportunity.[94] Order can, of course, demand such slavish conformity that choice becomes irrelevant. This is the case on many levels of reality. Even much of man's behavior must be understood as influenced by instinctive and inherited influences. To cry out for water in the desert is hardly a significant exercise of freedom. But, on the human level, the

93. *Ibid.*, p. 15.
94. *SMW*, p. 160, cf., *RM*, p. 109.

conditions of life do not determine its final significance. There is a difference of degree that makes *all* the difference.[95] Compared to the animal's enjoyment of the given order and instinctive utilization of structure, man can study the conditions of his existence, gaining an understanding which enables him to exercise the power of self-determination. This capacity for understanding the context of his decisions distinguishes man from the animals. It is the basis for both freedom and religion.

> The animals enjoy structure. They can build nests and dams: they can follow the trail of scent through the forest. The concrete realized facts, confused and intermixed, dominate animal life. Man understands structure. He abstracts its dominating principle from the welter of detail. He can imagine alternative illustration. He constructs distant objectives. He can compare the variety of issues. He can aim at the best. But the essence of this human control of purposes depends on the understanding of structure in its variety of applications.[96]

Understanding something of the conditions in which he exists, man is open to a new kind of motivation—the persuasive power of ideals which appeal to his own judgment. Whitehead's reference to the cleansing power of belief, the transforming effect of general truths, the impact of intimate convictions on character all point to the influence of relevant ideals.[97] In this sense, "intuition into the ultimate mystery of the universe" is the source of the religious dynamic.[98] It is not just man's decision which gives weight to his religious commitment, but he is moved by the truth of his fundamental intuition into the relative status of diverse ideals. Such a grasp of the ideal illustrates what Whitehead calls a "mode of causation, which is derived from a mode of thought."[99] It shapes the purposes and anticipation on which the worth of the human life depends.[100] It is not

95. *MT*, pp. 37–38.
96. *Ibid.*, pp. 104–105.
97. *RM*, p. 15.
98. *AI*, p. 161.
99. *MT*, p. 25.
100. *Ibid.*, p. 37.

only molecules and senseless forces that drive men forward, but what they think about their lives in relation to the universe is also a powerful motivating factor.[101] "The ideals cherished in the souls of men enter into the character of their actions."[102]

This makes the persuasive power of knowledge and truth an essential factor in religious commitment and expression. Religion is a way of knowing the universe, as well as a way of responding to it. Like all knowing, it utilizes symbolic processes which put discriminated factors in wider contexts of coordination and significance. It takes the life of man and refers it to the universe as a context of significance. It reflects both the appropriation of a place of importance in the universe and a surrender to a given order. Like all knowledge, it is both constructive appropriation and patient accommodation.

> It brings into our consciousness that permanent side of the universe which we can care for. It thereby provides a meaning, in terms of value, for our own existence, a meaning which flows from the nature of things.[103]

The significance that man finds in his own life is directly related to his understanding of his environment. He responds freely with a sense of responsibility which demands the selection of a response that is appropriate to his circumstances. He is persuaded by the relative status of the alternatives, at the same time as he chooses the direction of his life. His worth is wrapped up in this sensitivity to his surroundings, his "liability to persuasion" by the disclosure of ordered alternatives.[104] On this level, the truth is not coercive but allows both rejection and misunderstanding. Like the mode of perception on which it depends, causal efficacy, it is easily ignored or taken for granted. It hangs in the balance of freedom, "equally compelling recognition and permissive of disregard."[105] It demands some decision

101. *AI*, p. 146.
102. *Ibid.*, p. 42.
103. *RM*, p. 120.
104. *AI*, p. 83.
105. *RM*, p. 59.

with respect to this dimension of experience, but it does not require a self-conscious, critical, or appropriate evaluation of the options. Man must somehow find his place in the universe, but his conclusions need not manifest the most responsible and efficient use of his intuitive faculties. Whether the individual intends it or not, whether he uses his critical abilities or lets the choice slip by unnoticed, he does make a cognitive claim about the universe in the shape and direction he gives to his own character. Indeed, in very important respects, it is this level of cognitive activity that underlies the more definite and obvious types of knowledge. It is this understanding of the conditions of human significance which coordinates man's interests in more limited areas of inquiry. It makes scientific experiments worth pursuing, giving the discernment of accurate measurements and definite relationships a place of importance in a broad spectrum of interests. What man finds significant enough to notice and investigate reflects a concomitant estimate of his own significance in the coordination of the universe. It is this aspect of cognition which is properly termed "religious" and which is articulated in religious assertions.

Of course, even to claim that the term "cognitive" applies to that which transcends the definite organization of detailed factors in limited systems requires a radical revision of the prevailing notion of knowledge. It demands a shift in perspective not unlike the qualification of "simple location" and the recognition that all symbolic forms are only one-sided and abstract instruments. If this shift is not made, and knowledge is strictly identified with the apparently definite and precise, then religious intuitions are not cognitive in any strict sense and even the contribution of religious commitments to the specialized pursuit of relatively stable information is obscured. This can lead to the multiplication of diverse kinds of human wisdom, which are all relatively independent of one another. Some place may be given to the "know-how" and vision of religion, but its status tends to be inferior to the more precise modes of apprehension.[106]

106. Randall, *op. cit.*, pp. 123–134.

Whitehead offers another view of knowledge in which cognitive activity has many levels of diverse scope and character. But, in spite of their differences, these levels have much in common and mutually affect one another. For one thing, they are all projective in character, making absolute certainty unattainable in any interpretation of concrete experience. On all levels where knowledge involves the reference of symbols to more concrete factors, certainty gives way to approximation, the more or less adequate grasp of reality. The interpretation of sense perception is provisional knowledge. So are the scientific theories and coordinating patterns that are used to give significance to the details of experience. Even the choices of metaphysical models and religious analogies have this kind of cognitive character. Furthermore, all these levels of cognition are interrelated in organic fashion. They are reciprocally coordinated and interdependent. What is known on one level affects the others. Thus, the scientific theory chosen to articulate the arrangement of a genus of facts has an impact on the way those facts are discerned and understood. Conversely, the facts give shape to the theoretical interpretation, reinforcing it, calling for revision or demanding rejection. Similarly, the specific coordination of values grasped in religious insight has its influence on our understanding of more limited fields of inquiry, and vice versa.

This gives to knowledge itself a heuristic, pragmatic character. It combines relatively stable relationships with an openness to growth and correction. It includes mutually qualifying and corrective factors. It is open-ended, reflecting the unfinished aspect of reality. As a consequence, the truth must be identified with the most adequate interpretation of experience in a particular situation. What man knows is always qualified by his peculiar perspective on the future which is yet to be realized. Even if that knowledge does indicate its ultimate dependence on some universal mode of coordination, it never offers complete possession of its object.

Thus, if even our most precise forms of knowledge are limited by the purposes which inform them and by the anticipatory features of experience, the situation is quite different.

Religious insight can be given a cognitive status. It shares in the limitations and possibilities of all human inquiry because of its own special emphasis. It is intelligibly related to other forms of understanding since it draws on the same complex of empirical data and its dominant purpose can be compared with other modes of interest. If self-sufficient precision is not the norm for knowledge, then there is room for many different abstractive emphases as complementary modes of cognitive inquiry. The expressive emphasis that focuses on value and purpose is by no means the least important or decisive.

The key to this shift in the understanding of knowledge is Whitehead's use of organic process, rather than static substance, as a metaphysical model. The consequence is that knowledge is conceived in terms of growth and organic development, rather than as something that is determinate and complete—or constituted simply by arranging the well-defined details in exact relationships. Knowledge is not simply the grasp of determinate factors in definite patterns, but it is also the developing apprehension of a total environment, constituted by organic, evolutionary relationships. In this case it is possible on any level to seek the most adequate understanding of reality, for a specific purpose and in the face of particular circumstances. Every man's evaluation of his own significance in the world can be a claim with meaning, backed up by an intelligent assessment of the environment. That does not mean that such knowledge is completely certain in its details, or exhaustive in its vision. It is the explicit grasp of the transcendence of the universe which is implied in all our other modes of knowledge.

In Whitehead's perspective, all knowledge carries with it the recognition of its own qualification. It is knowing *what* you know and that you do not know everything, at the same time. It is the awareness of the selection of specific factors and modes of coordination with the simultaneous apprehension of the exclusion involved. That exclusion brings in the notion of transcendent reality. Together with the advance of the process, it also indicates the possibility of change and the provisional character of all our symbolic interpretations. Thus knowledge always includes a reference to the transcendent and as yet indirectly accessible. It is the partial grasp of mystery and the tracing of relative distinctions. It thrives on the projection of illuminating analogies and the development of novel interpretations. It is as dependent on the discernment of significant "wholes" as on the grasp of "details." It even requires a vague sense of the "totality" in which all interpretation must take place and against which all knowledge must be achieved. Understood organically, knowledge is the grasp of the finite and the infinite in a single occasion of experience. It involves at least the implicit claim that experience is *more* than what is definitely apprehended and explicitly articulated.

The cognitive claim involved in religion is initially just this very general notion of transcendence. It is based on the profound intuition that life is more than the bare facts of successive experiences. This grasp of the transcendent is implicit in all human life and evident in the positive religions. It receives maximum emphasis in sophisticated or "rational" religion as the claims of faith are pressed to universal scope. As Whitehead describes it: "The importance of rational religion in the history of modern culture is that it stands or falls with its fundamental position, that we know more than can be formulated in one finite systematized scheme of abstractions."[107] This appropriation and expression of transcendence, without the capacity to characterize it exhaustively, is the identifying feature of the religious dimension of experience. It is also a kind of knowledge which Whitehead compares to the way men can be said to know their intimate friends. Knowledge of their character exceeds all attempts to systematize or formulate it. "We know more of the characters of those who are dear to us than we can express accurately in words."[108] In an analogous fashion, our knowledge of this universe in which we live is not exhausted by the neat systems of information or precise symbolic formulations that man creates.

---

107. *RM*, p. 137.
108. *Ibid.*, p. 123.

If the awareness of transcendent coordination can be considered a cognitive claim, then as the formulations of religion develop this insight, they too are assertions of knowledge. To say that life is *more than* the descriptions of physical science, *more than* bodily sustenance, *more than* precise statistical calculations is to give some indication of the context in which human freedom is exercised. It represents a part of our awareness of our environment just as much as assertions about trees, stones, and sub-atomic particles. The religious expression, "Man shall not live by bread alone," symbolizes the carefully discerned character of the human situation, not merely fleeting emotion or sheer imagination. It contributes to the articulation of the coordinated possibilities which are a part of man's immediate circumstances. It is knowledge which makes possible the responsible exercise of freedom on the human level.

Such broad claims concerning transcendent coordination have implications for every human endeavor. Their impact is not simply upon some esoteric religious realm, but they affect any human interest in which freedom is somehow implicated. While conditioned behavioral responses may not be affected by religious knowledge, certainly any conscious and intentional focus of attention must find its place in some wider coordination of values. The very need to determine how long and how hard one will concentrate on specific data makes the selective interests involved a significant choice in respect to the use of time and energy. In the long run, such a decision contributes to the shape of one's character in the context of universal obligations. Thus, the cognitive claims involved in religion have implications for every pursuit to which man may dedicate himself by conscious decision or by the weight of habit. When knowledge is conceived in terms of the organic model, contrasts and partial exclusions become more important than final exclusion and inclusion. As a consequence, knowledge from one area has connections which give it some impact on the other aspects of inquiry.

The expressions of religion can be expected to symbolize transcendence in whatever form the situation requires. Whitehead's description of religion in *Science and the Modern World* is a classic expression of this kind. It is constituted by a series of phrases which might seem to cancel each other out, but which in fact point to the dialectical character of human existence in the living tension between the finite and the infinite, the actual and the possible. Whitehead puts this sense of the transcendent superbly:

> Religion is the vision of something which stands beyond, behind, and within, the passing flux of immediate things; something which is real, and yet waiting to be realised; something which is a remote possibility, and yet the greatest of present facts; something that gives meaning to all that passes, and yet eludes apprehension; something whose possession is the final good, and yet is beyond all reach; something which is the ultimate ideal, and the hopeless quest.[109]

These are not sheer contradictions. They are intelligible and persuasive expressions of the transcendent quality of experience. They symbolize the pervasive qualification of the finite by a transcendent order. They express a cognitive claim about the universe in which man finds himself, and within which he must contribute to his own destiny.

The transcendence here articulated cannot be conceived after the non-organic model. It, too, is a factor in the process grasped in experience and affected by the course of events. It is transcendence relative to the determinate and definitely apprehended, not some reality separated from concrete experience. As a consequence, this apprehension of the transcendent can protect man from treating any abstractions too lightly, as well as from taking them as ultimate. It can keep him from rejecting all partial knowledge for the sake of some unattainable ideal. At the same time, it will not allow the elevation of the definite and determinate aspects of experience to a final and exhaustive characterization of reality. It prohibits even the implicit acceptance of the world as a given structure in which nothing new can happen so that freedom is merely an illusion. With respect

109. *SMW*, p. 171.

to the results of special modes of inquiry, it maintains an openness to new insights and revised formulations. In this way, the grasp of transcendence undergirds the search for the connections and purposive influences which are not readily apparent or easily distinguished.

Thus, the cognitive contribution of religious insight is not the recognition of sheer transcendence. It is rather the vague grasp of the immanence of the infinite in the finite. It is not simply the awareness of something beyond the definitely given, but rather the recognition of a transcendent reality partially given in the experiences at hand. The religious dimension of experience, in this sense, discloses an interdependent universe in which flux and stability, mind and body, or values and facts cannot be neatly separated. It gives powerful indications, in the many particular forms of religion, that all reality is somehow coordinated in reciprocal and progressive relationships. By bringing the "other" into the picture and setting the topic of religion as "individuality in community," this dimension of experience does make a real contribution to man's understanding of the environment in which he lives.[110]

Up to this point, religious experience yields only a very vague but powerful knowledge of some transcendent reference for further interpretation. By itself, it is really only a component factor of knowledge, the awareness of some reality which must be characterized in one way or another. Such characterization is what requires intuition into the relative order of values. The cognitive intent is to symbolize the coordination of values which is effective in the universe. This requires the selection and projection of analogies which are put forward as the most adequate indication of the transcendent coordination.

These special insights are claims about the shape of man's environment and the relative significance of his alternatives. They are subject to some validation, both corporate and private. The really crude and savage models are quickly seen, by most men, as false representations of a universe that could bring forth and sustain man as a creature capable of persuasion and

110. *RM*, pp. 84–86.

altruistic love. The choice between the relatively successful models is more difficult. Nevertheless, these claims, at least in broad analogous types, can also be understood as having cognitive significance. They are put forward as ways of understanding the context of human decision and existence.

On this level, Whitehead's assessment of certain models in the Christian tradition is relevant. Positively, he sees the life of Christ as an authentic disclosure of the character of the transcendent coordination of value. In its circumstances, in its particular train of history, this life illuminates the relative nobility of man's alternatives. It is capable not only of communicating an understanding of the noblest ideals, but also of evoking a response in man to their authenticity. Whitehead describes the model in terms that are indeed moving.

> The Mother, the Child, and the bare manger: the lowly man, homeless and self-forgetful, with his message of peace, love, and sympathy: the suffering, the agony, the tender words as life ebbed, the final despair: and the whole with the authority of supreme victory.[111]

In contrast to this model, Whitehead is critical of the use of the ruling Caesar as the key to religious interpretation. This analogy is not the most adequate, by an means. It is misleading with respect to the relative order of values, and completely deceptive in its attribution of *all* power to god.[112]

These analogies are judged, as are all interpretations, by their adequacy on their own level and scope of reference. Whitehead takes assertions of this type, i.e., God is revealed in Jesus, the Galilean, very seriously, as claims based on experience and extended to illuminate further experience. They are claims about the character of the context of realistic alternatives in which each man must find his own significance. The problem of truth here is similar to all other levels of interpretation where man must evaluate his extended analogies on the basis of broader experience. Since the universe has a character to be

111. *AI*, p. 167.
112. *Ibid.*, pp. 167–169.

intuited and approximated, the process of developing religious knowledge is not unlike the progress that is discernible in other areas. Whitehead compares it with science, for instance:

> Progress in truth—truth of science and truth of religion—is mainly a progress in the framing of concepts, in discarding artificial abstractions or partial metaphors, and in evolving notions which strike more deeply into the root of reality.[113]

Unless there is some basis in experience for man to "know" his alternatives and discern relative differences between better and worse religious interpretations, then it seems that both freedom and responsibility are without meaning. Somehow, the significance of man in the universe is wrapped up in his capacity to develop religious knowledge as the basis and interpretation of his own ultimate decisions. Making this knowledge completely definite, exhaustive, or final is impossible, but this is a difficulty that is tacitly shared with all other forms of human knowledge. Like interpretation on every level, religious knowledge is a combination of certainty, probability, and projective reference. The insights into the transcendent mode of coordination are powerfully convincing in their own context, and they have an empirically necessary referent. It is the more precise and abstract extrapolations of those insights that run the greatest risk of error or disproportionate emphasis. Thus, knowledge on the religious level is not merely relative in an arbitrary sense, but it is dependent on particular circumstances and limited in its definite formulations to relative distinctions and approximations.

With respect to the language of religion, Whitehead's view of cognition allows it to communicate a partial but powerful grasp of transcendent coordination and pervasive interdependence. These aspects of experience are apprehended as certainly as our sense of our own identity. Their expression in words can be equally dependable in its reference to the relatively stable factors on which all other experience depends. But

113. *RM*, p. 127.

this transcendent reference to the ultimate coordination of the actual and the potential, facts and values, is not usually given alone. It is tied in with some kind of particular description of the divine factor in human experience. Thus, religious assertions normally combine necessary reference with some projective characterization which is relative to a particular situation and potentially in need of revision, both in terms of its fundamental analogies, and the forms in which they are expressed. However, since man can remember insights that seemed valid in other situations and reinterpret the formulations that were adequate in those circumstances, religious assertions out of the past or drawn from distant situations can still be relevant expressions of authentic insight into that which is of transcendent and abiding significance. One is not trapped within his own perspective with no possibility for suggestion from without. Nor must one conclude that there is no dependability in religious insight and expression that can be communicated from one situation to another. Religious expression, our own or someone else's, can communicate illuminating truth about the human situation, but it does so in a context of relativity and development, not in a world where everything is known completely or not at all, expressed with peak precision once and for all. If nothing else, man's freedom and the impinging future persist in limiting the finality of such expressions.

In its attempt to characterize the transcendent mode of coordination, we can expect language to seem paradoxical. Since it must make its own qualification explicit in order to indicate the proper referent, both positive characterization and its limitations must be expressed. In this respect, religious assertions are like metaphysical descriptions. They must make both their transcendent reference and their projected analogies evident, and at this point language tends to break down.

Whitehead explains such apparently equivocal statements as contrasts, rather than contradictions. Because of their metaphysical scope, they involve reference to concrete experience, and this qualifies their radical opposition in a manner similar to Whitehead's understanding of linguistic identities at the

other extreme. Just as tautologies cannot be considered as completely empty and balanced in their ultimate reference to concrete experience, so the most radical contrasts man can express
on the metaphysical level ultimately turn out to be relative
distinctions which need not imply strict contradiction. Take, for
example, the series of apparently conflicting assertions Whitehead puts forward in *Process and Reality* when discussing the
relation of God and the world.

> It is as true to say that God is permanent and the World fluent,
> as that the World is permanent and God is fluent.
> It is as true to say that God is one and the World many, as that
> the World is one and God many.
> It is as true to say that, in comparison with the World, God is
> actual eminently, as that, in comparison with God, the World is
> actual eminently.
> It is as true to say that the World is immanent in God, as that
> God is immanent in the World.
> It is as true to say that God transcends the World, as that the
> World transcends God.
> It is as true to say that God creates the World, as that the World
> creates God.[114]

These are "antitheses," but the apparent salf-contradictions
"depend on neglect of the diverse categories of existence."[115]
When understood in relation to concrete and inclusive experience, there is a "shift of meaning which converts the opposition
into a contrast."[116]

Similarly, one can understand the assertions of religion in
Whitehead's scheme so that apparently blatant equivocation
does not completely destroy linguistic significance. Expressions
about what is "real, and yet waiting to be realized," or "the
ultimate ideal, and the hopeless quest," are not without reference or cognitive significance. They point to a transcendent and
universal factor in experience which can only be indicated by
the explicit combination of assertion and qualification.[117] In a

114. *PR*, p. 528.
115. *Ibid.*, p. 528.
116. *Ibid.*, p. 528.
117. *SMW*, p. 171.

more limited area of inquiry, they would be contradictions, but because of the scope of these claims, the abstract precision of equivalence or contradiction is not decisive. In this paradoxical fashion, religious assertions are able to communicate the knowledge of a transcendent reality by bringing judgment on all definite formulations, including themselves. They make evident what is obscured in most uses of language—that our symbols require both "reverence" and "revision."

In describing religion as based on man's intuition into "the ultimate mystery of the universe," Whitehead suggests that there is a religious component of knowledge and a correspondingly significant way of articulating that mode of insight. There is a religious way of knowing and describing the world. It contributes to the unification and qualification of all human knowledge. By doing so it helps to free man from bondage to his own symbolic formulations and definite abstractions. It reminds us, persistently, that none of our important and useful distinctions can be pressed to the point where they destroy the unity of experience or deny its creative advance. There may be significant differences between "knowing how" and "knowing that," between faith and certainty, between knowing persons and knowing things, between "believing in" and "believing that," but none of these distinctions can be pressed to radical separation. At the very least, religious experience expressed linguistically ought to communicate this qualification of our precise distinctions, and for that alone it would deserve the status "cognitive."

Of equal significance are the specific analogies offered as characterizations of man's place in the universe. They describe real alternatives with diverse consequences. They express claims about man's circumstances which can be tested in living and dying. The fact that they resist conclusive proof and final confirmation does not deny their contribution to knowledge. Indeed, they encourage us to reconsider the *kind* of knowledge available in a dynamic and evolving universe.

This would seem to be the thrust of Whitehead's interpretation of religious cognition. Such knowledge is reflected in linguistic formulations, but in ways that are always limited. This enables Whitehead to distinguish between the validity of the fundamental concrete insights and their relatively adequate linguistic expression. His treatment of religious truth is not simply relativistic, reducing all options to the lowest common denominator, but he allows for both confidence and criticism. Knowledge, for him, does not preclude the combination of existential certainty on the one hand, and a critical awareness of the possibility of error on the other. The grasp of religious truth is not thereby vitiated by the recognition that man can be wrong in his most fundamental interpretations. Indeed, it is just this risk that enables us to take religious claims seriously. What this amounts to is a call for a continued openness to "repentance" in language use, whether it is "religious" or "secular." Our religious formulations must be under judgment in the same way as the lives of individuals and the structures of institutions. This should reinforce honest criticism in every area of life.

In his own interpretation of religion and its language, Whitehead does provide a scheme in which religious experience and expression can be understood as both affective and cognitive. He carries through the implications that have been discerned in more general facets of his thought. By doing so, he illuminates the important connections between cultic and theological language, as well as between the expressions of religion, science, and philosophy. He recognizes the sacramental power of linguistic expression, and its paradigmatic form in the assertions of religion. He articulates both the need for, and the character of, religious knowledge so that even words about God can have cognitive significance in their interdependence with man's other modes of wisdom and expression.

8

WHITEHEAD'S

CONTRIBUTION

Utilizing several diverse, but overlapping, perspectives on Whitehead's philosophy, this study has sought to demonstrate the relevance of his mature thought in respect to the problem of religious discourse. An attempt has been made to expose the resources available in the organic philosophy for the interpretation of religious assertions as having both affective power and cognitive significance. Since it is the cognitive aspect of religious language that has been the focus of criticism, it is this feature of religious discourse that has received the larger share of attention. Implications of Whitehead's position have been developed, but some additional concluding reflections are in order. These summary remarks give cursory answers to several questions. Just what is the significance of Whitehead's contribution to the discussion of religious language? Where does his work fit alongside some other efforts to deal with this problem? What are the specific directions for positive theological development that his work seems to suggest?

Surely, Whitehead's contribution and this interpretation will have to stand on their own merit. Also, the limited scope of this study restricts the development and comparisons that can be undertaken at this juncture. In the spirit of Whitehead's own work, this need not be seen as a deficiency. There is no advantage in trying to decide these matters in any final way. It must remain to be seen what Whitehead's contribution will be. Where it reinforces or supplements other points of view, well and good. Where it generates contrast and conflict, that can mean a shift in the direction of inquiry that will lead well beyond Whitehead and any other approach now available. In other words, the case for Whitehead's alternative need not be treated as an argument for exclusive or final attachment to his system or his terminology. The discussion of religious language is not comparable to a popularity contest where one candidate must win and all the rest lose. Instead, it is an effort to move our corporate understanding forward, and this can utilize a multitude of resources. These resources are not less important if they are only stepping stones to further achievement.

Ultimately, it is not what Whitehead says that matters most. Nor is it crucial that he should be credited with the resolution of certain problems. What is decisive is that our ability to cope with life is enhanced. Whitehead may help us in this respect, but similar and complementary insights can be gleaned from others as well. The recognition of the potential in Whitehead's approach does not entail the wholesale rejection of all other contemporary proposals.

This needs to be said here because of the very obvious limitations of this study. For example, all the variations in linguistic modes of philosophy have not been taken into account. They may offer many constructive suggestions for dealing with religious discourse and there simply is not space here to attempt to give them the credit they may deserve. Instead, the focus here has been admittedly on the more positivistic aspects of the linguistic movement and their parallels in the general culture. This has been done for at least two reasons: first, it sets the basic problems of religious discourse in the sharpest way, the way they are most easily noticed in common experience; and second, it allows Whitehead's alternative to stand out in the boldest relief. It is this contrast in alternative interpretation that can arouse both interest and critical comparisons. It has also been the contention here that reductionist influences continue to inform the analysis of religious discourse in a potent, but subtle, manner. Wherever the question, "What exactly do you mean?" is raised in such a way that the complexity of life is arbitrarily excluded from significant consideration, or relegated to the neglected background, something like positivism is at work. However, this need not suggest that all linguistic philosophers are positivists or that they are unaware of the tacit effect that narrow empirical assumptions can have in apparently moderate and modest styles of linguistic analysis. In many ways, themes that Whitehead picks up for emphasis are also evident in the work of men like John Austin, John Wisdom, and the later Wittgenstein. Insofar as this is the case, the mutual reinforcement of "process" and "linguistic" modes of thought ought to be recognized and appreciated.

It is also true that this has been a very one-sided analysis of Whitehead's thought. By intention, only certain aspects of Whitehead's work have been explored. This not does indicate that the work of others is to be disregarded or treated as without implications for the problem of religious discourse. Let Whitehead be studied from as many angles as possible. His own system requires such progressive and cumulative analysis. Like experience itself, Whitehead's philosophy provides a "field day" for diverse types of inquiry.

The contribution of Whitehead can be summarized in a way that hopefully will be suggestive of further development. Let these claims stand as conclusions for extended testing and exploration.

First, it should be very clear that Whitehead offers a wealth of resources for the understanding of language in general, and religious language in particular. He belongs in the conversation along with Wittgenstein, Heidegger, Austin, and all the others. There should be no question about the direct bearing of Whitehead's philosophy on linguistic issues or, for that matter, about the dependence of his metaphysics on a serious analysis of language. No explicitly linguistic philosopher pays greater attention to linguistic activity or derives more from its analysis.

Furthermore, it should also be apparent that selected aspects of Whitehead's thought, as they have been singled out in this study, have immediate relevance for the interpretation of the language of faith. Specifically, Whitehead's discussions of metaphysics, the perceptual data, symbolism, and religion all raise critical questions in this area and suggest possible solutions. Their importance does not depend solely on the adequacy of Whitehead's total scheme, but they each have some value in their own right. What finally counts are the practical results of including these diverse possibilities in the actual discussion of the issues. Given the diagnosis of the times, religious language is problematic, and Whitehead provides a whole range of resources that must be considered as potentially therapeutic.

At the very least, Whitehead puts forward an alternative for the interpretation of religious language which deserves wider recognition alongside of more influential and well-known positions. In keeping with Whitehead's own approach, even if his alternative requires radical revision or final rejection, its very contrast with other interpretations can bring increased insight. For in the most crucial situations, merely the awareness that alternatives can be articulated changes the situation decisively. On the level of metaphysical assumptions and religious convictions, this is pre-eminently true because their scope is so broad. Particular options tend to parade as necessary and without rival just because they provide a framework for other decisions. Thus, in respect to religious discourse, even the presentation of an interesting alternative has constructive significance.

It should also be admitted, at this point, that a fundamental problem with Whitehead's thought is the radical shift in perspective, which it requires. For some, the appreciation of organic categories with their emphasis on relative distinctions and provisional interpretations is extremely difficult. It runs against many prevailing modes of thought. It stands against certain powerful attitudes and expectations. It can therefore readily appear to be an unrealistic option. Whitehead's philosophy requires such a change in point of view that the relevance, suggestiveness, and potential of his alternative is easily neglected. However, if alternate points of view are at all helpful, Whitehead's contribution is not diminished by such difficulties.

In a similar way, there are those whose theological convictions will not permit them to see Whitehead's alternative as a platform for a significant defense of religious assertions. Their commitment to the absolute transcendence of God, or to the certainty of religious claims, may make Whitehead's approach seem like the denial of central religious affirmations. Or, the tendency to reject metaphysics as an arrogant human activity inherently opposed to divine revelation leads to the same result. It can be recognized that Whitehead's approach is not compatible with every understanding of religious faith. Where there is real conflict with religious convictions a potentially helpful challenge is offered that could lead to modifications on both sides of the discussion. However, one cannot expect that either philosophers or theologians who are hesitant about looking again at their basic experience are likely to be impressed or helped by what Whitehead has to offer.

A second contribution of Whitehead can be found in the specific answers that he gives to central issues involved in interpreting religious assertions as cognitive. Whitehead's philosophy can be seen as a viable basis for understanding religious discourse as both cognitive and affective just because it does offer potential solutions to the crucial contemporary criticisms of this mode of expression. At each focal point of criticism, Whitehead's thought provides a counter-argument that leaves room for significant religious assertions about God, based on man's concrete experience of his identity and environment. For each phase in the argument against the cognitive status of religious assertions, Whitehead either suggests a way around the difficulty or indicates that the criticism builds on assumptions similar to those attacked. Or put another way, when the question of how religious language might be cognitive is raised from different angles, Whitehead offers corresponding suggestions for explanatory response. His answers are not always fully developed, nor are they strictly compelling in terms of logic or probability. They are suggestive in their appeal to concrete experience, and there certainly are enough problems in other philosophical positions to encourage us to take repeated and careful looks at the initial complex of data. Whitehead's answers are attractive just because they do not minimize the intricate and evolutionary character of the empirical data. They do not ignore the deceptiveness of abstract thought or the potential distortion involved in the use of precise symbolic formulations. Neither do they minimize the problems of fantasy and projection. They do give shape to a positive alternative which mitigates the fundamental criticisms of the cognitive interpretation of religious discourse.

There is the issue of the relationship of religious assertions and metaphysics. This problem can be raised explicity or in a subtle manner that automatically denigrates any attempt to speak about the universe as an integral reality. Or it can be raised by the apologists for religion who too quickly claim that a particular form of faith is compatible with any metaphysics whatsoever.

When this problem is raised, Whitehead calls for the recognition of metaphysical decisions involved in every use of language. The issue is transformed from *whether* we should make claims about all of reality to *what* claims are most appropriate in a situation where neutrality is not an available option. Whitehead indicates that the apparently troublesome metaphysical dimension of religious discourse may actually be an asset. It lays bare assumptions about the "whole" of reality which are hidden from criticism in most other modes of expression.

Here Whitehead can be seen as reinforcing a growing willingness to take the metaphysical implications of religious discourse seriously. For instance, William Hordern in a helpful attempt to defend the personal encounter analogy as the basis for the cognitive significance of religious assertions goes to great lengths to recognize that statements of faith do make ontological claims. They are therefore in some sense metaphysical.[1] What Whitehead adds is a clearer emphasis on the metaphysical implications of other forms of discourse. Every expression depends on implicit decisions about the nature of reality. In respect to Hordern's argument, this would make some difference because

1. Hordern, *op. cit.*

one might not be so quick to praise the humility or neutrality of analytic philosophy. To accept certain of its fundamental distinctions as final carries more prescriptive freight than Hordern recognizes. His willingness to celebrate the disjunction between analytic and empirical statements tends to weaken his own case for a personal knowledge that is not divorced from our physical experience.[2] If the metaphysical weight of these distinctions had been considered, along with the ontological implications of religious claims, Hordern might have been able to meet the powerful criticisms of the encounter analogy more adequately.[3]

Another crucial question that has been developed in this study has to do with the content of the perceptual data. There are those that still claim perception only offers discrete factors of one kind or another.[4] Or, at least, they utilize sharp distinctions that rely on a fundamental discontinuity in human experience. Here Whitehead offers a significant alternative. Recognizing the roots of all language activity in the basic data of perception, Whitehead finds a much richer empirical base. When narrow assumptions about the empirical data are put forward, Whitehead offers a corrective emphasis which is not without persuasive power. On his terms, it is much more likely that a case can be made for the fundamental role of "personal" knowledge like that which is decisive for religion. If perception does indicate continuities and the exclusive power of interest, then all knowledge can be understood as more provisional. Every cognitive claim is at some point dependent on human valuation. Partial penetration, adequate appropriation, and heuristic considerations are then more decisive than any exact correspondence of our symbols with fragments of experience. While this gives strong emphasis to the role of purpose and interest in our experience, it need not result in a purely arbitrary treat-

---

2. *Ibid.,* p. 34.
3. Ronald W. Hepburn, *Christianity and Paradox* (New York: Pegasus, 1966), pp. 24–59.
4. Peter Geach, *Mental Acts,* ed. by R. F. Holland (New York: Humanities Press, 1964), pp. 20–23. While this discussion is not theological it does indicate the persistent influence of interpretations of the data which give arbitrary emphasis to some kind of really separable intuitions.

ment of the concrete data. It supports a pragmatic, contextual epistemology, and that may well be what our circumstances require; indeed, all that they will allow.

This move of Whitehead's is especially important when narrow interpretations of the empirical input are introduced in subtle ways, like the elevation of clear-cut distinctions to normative status. For instance, the statement "The universe is not a thing, but the class of all things" may seem to be an effective argument against treating the holistic assertions of religion as intelligible.[5] Things supposedly are perceived while the universe —at least in its totality—is not. The presuppositions about the perceptual data in this kind of approach need to be made explicit. When they are, the importance of Whitehead's alternative becomes apparent. If the universe is taken as only the class of all things, an implicit precedence is given to particulars in experience which makes all relationships ultimately problematic. The whole is only equal to the sum of its parts, with no reality of its own. In such a perspective it should not be surprising that statements about God are in difficulty. But it is not because they are metaphysical in scope and thus not grounded in the primary data, it is because they clash with one interpretation of the perceptual input. They conflict with the fundamental perspective that informs the criticism. By calling our attention to this fact, Whitehead provides a way of dealing with this sort of approach to religious discourse.

While there is not as much attention given to this perceptual question as its importance would seem to warrant, there are other attempts besides that of Whitehead to recover concrete experience as a basis for religious expression. The work of John E. Smith is one outstanding example.[6] He subjects the empirical assumptions involved in the analysis of language to careful scrutiny. Like Whitehead, he sees the problems that arise when one attempts to defend or interpret religious cognition in a basic framework that is alien to the very notion. Smith calls for the

5. Robert W. Jenson, *The Knowledge of Things Hoped for* (New York: Oxford Univ. Press, 1969), p. 17.
6. Smith, *op. cit.*

recognition of complexity and continuity in the empirical data. For him, religious experience is a dimension of every experience, and therefore connections are given in the initial data for further development and articulation.[7] With men like Smith in mind, Whitehead can be seen as contributing to a broader movement toward the recovery of experience as a resource for both the religious interpretation of life and the critical understanding of the assertions of faith.

The use and interpretation of analogy is another issue that has been emphasized in this study. Here Whitehead again shifts the grounds for discussion, but in a way that can be seen as responsible and intellectually respectable. The use of analogy is not something superficial in human knowledge and expression. It is not an option that comes in only after our precise knowledge and literal modes of expression have been developed to their limits. Nor is it merely congenial to some people who prefer "soft" data. It is the basis for any knowledge or expression whatsoever. All language is grounded in the discernment and projection of analogies, so the highly symbolic character of religious discourse is not in itself a problem. Metaphor and myth are far more decisive in human understanding and expression than is usually assumed. The choice of analogies is what is decisive, and certain religious alternatives may well be in trouble here. That is, they may give precedence to less than adequate models. However, Whitehead helps us to see how every use of language faces this same kind of risk in that the choice of basic analogies is unavoidable. The question becomes which analogies are more adequate, not whether or not analogy is dependable. We must look for the mythical and metaphorical components involved in any use of language. In this sense, Whitehead opposes attempts to achieve a fully "demythologized" or "literal" translation of religious assertions. He stands in the tradition of those who limit our possibilities to a kind of re-mythologization.

Here there are apparent conflicts with some of those who

7. Ibid., p. 55.

have offered recent constructive interpretations of religious discourse. Robert Jenson's approach to analogy is one of these.[8] Without giving a complete treatment of Jenson's position, it is possible to note his rejection of analogy as an appropriate way of understanding religious, or as he prefers it, theological discourse.

Jenson's argument is that, in contrast to our normal uses of language, analogy requires that we mean more than we say. In his discussion of Aquinas, the shift to analogy comes when we recognize that our mundane assertions about objects must be stretched to refer to God.[9] This leads Jenson finally to reject analogy explicitly. "If we are about to say something about God that if pressed we will have to explain in terms of 'analogy,' 'picture,' 'symbol,' or the like, we will not say it."[10] Such a rule against the use of analogy muddles what is otherwise a very lucid and potentially helpful discussion. For Jenson himself resorts to analogy in order to buttress his eschatological interpretation of the discourse of faith. He introduces the notion of dramatic coherence as a way of understanding the kind of confirmation that can be anticipated for theological claims.[11] Surely this use of analogy is even more helpful when it is recognized as such.

Here again Whitehead offers another route. He moves beyond both Thomas Aquinas and Robert Jenson by indicating that we always mean more than we say, so that no statement can be a literal expression in the strict sense. Analogy is not brought in when the language about objects gives out, but it is seen as fundamental in our use of language about anything. As a consequence, analogy is not an option, it is a necessity from the very outset. By the same token, exact knowledge and precise expression are always qualified by the limitations of underlying analogies.

Jenson's failure to appreciate the fundamental role of analogy

8. Jenson, *op. cit.*
9. *Ibid.* pp. 88, 91.
10. *Ibid.,* p. 238.
11. *Ibid.,* pp. 149–154.

contributes to his unwillingness to discuss more fully the generic aspects of religious discourse or its referent, God. The particular Christian alternative on which he focuses is isolated from any comparison or real criticism. Whitehead's understanding of analogy has the advantage that it allows both the appreciation of particular religious commitments and some analysis of their general features. Jenson is left with the story of Jesus and he has few resources to relate that story to the God question in its more general dimensions. This need not take away from other features of his discussion which are very illuminating and sometimes even quite similar to Whitehead's process-oriented approach. But on the question of analogy he and Whitehead diverge radically, so Jenson's work therefore provides a real contrast.

The fourth basic problem involved in religious discourse has been described as the relationship of fact and value. Where this has been turned into a sharp disjunction in some discussions of language, Whitehead relativizes this distinction in his persistent emphasis on interdependence. Judgments of fact and judgments reflecting values cannot be strictly isolated. Description and prescription somehow inform each other in the interplay of experience and the development of interpretation. By locating religion in relationship to other components of culture and by basing it in the existential commitment of the individual, Whitehead shows how diverse interests can utilize the same complex of data and contribute, corporately, to an integrated and dynamic complex of knowledge. Religion and science will not allow total separation, nor can faith and knowledge be relegated to independent arenas of operation. Whenever this kind of compartmentalization becomes the dilemma on which religious discourse is stretched beyond the breaking point, Whitehead's alternative is directly relevant.

Here, again, there are parallels with Whitehead's approach which reinforce and supplement his own position. For instance, Dallas High interprets the later Wittgenstein as moving in a direction that seems quite compatible with Whitehead.[12] The

12. High, *op. cit.*

emphasis on language as a form of life in which decisions are always important restricts the compartmentalization of fact and value, science and religion, in a manner that is very similar to Whitehead's own approach. High will not accept the claim that "Every statement has its own kind of logic" because this tends to remove the critical tension between the various modes of expression.[13] He discusses the role of decision and "belief" as a part of the human condition in which all language must function. He views these acts of faith as affecting both the interpretation of "facts" and the religious attempt to articulate man's values. High describes the dependence of the whole context of language on selective commitments in a way that could well be a summary of Whitehead's own general position,

> "belief acts" are a part of our ordinary speech, our ways of getting along, and our being in the world. Moreover, the acts of believing which are made explicit by our speech serve as guides to the whole context, framework, and vision of a civilization in which man finds himself capable of speaking, knowing, and recognizing what it is to be in the world.[14]

Thus, in several ways, Whitehead provides ways for meeting the central criticisms of religious language. By the directions he moves, if not by more explicit connections, he puts himself in touch with the broad discussion concerning the significance and status of religious assertions. He is linked with what other scholars are saying by compatibilities and contrasts with his own point of view. A very few of these points of contact have been indicated here merely to assist in placing Whitehead in the context of this continuing inquiry.

Another contribution Whitehead makes can be seen in the possibilities for theological development that his work suggests. Whitehead's treatment of language amounts to a kind of natural theology that limits but does not dictate the particular superstructure of faith to be built upon it, or expressed by means of it. It is compatible with any number of alternatives, but there

13. *Ibid.*, p. 206.
14. *Ibid.*, p. 144.

are also those options that are excluded by his approach and those which might claim its constructive support. Therefore it is important to take notice of the directions in theological or religious development which receive some direct impetus from Whitehead's philosophy. If these broad directions have special importance to a positive religion, such as Christianity, then the usefulness of Whitehead's philosophy for that particular faith perspective is appreciably enhanced.

In order to build constructively on Whitehead's work, the inherent risk of religious faith must be taken into account. The important status that Whitehead gives to religious assertions is directly dependent on the chances of error and success that these claims involve. They can be taken seriously just because they can be treated honestly, with full awareness of the context of change, finitude and fallibility in which they arise. Insofar as they do make claims about the purposive coordination of the universe, religious assertions are projections which simply cannot avoid the possibility of grave error, or the need for radical revision in the face of new experiences. They are broad hypotheses on which men wager their very lives. Reflecting some specific posture toward future developments, they share in the risk that goes with any form of prediction or conjecture. This need not take anything away from the certainty of practical commitment. It does not contradict the fact that men hold their religious convictions to be true. It only requires honesty about the kinds of certainty that are available in historical circumstances. One can be confident enough to act and live without escaping from those conditions of human existence which, in principle, always make mistakes possible.

Indeed, when the projective character of religious claims is recognized and their risk acknowledged, the importance of such convictions becomes more apparent. The stance one assumes in respect to the universe affects, at least in a small way, the very character of the future. What man anticipates makes a real difference in his actions and also in the consequences that follow from them. Even fantasy and wishful thinking have their effects. In this sense, a self-conscious appreciation of the projection involved in religion is not a denial of its importance, but a way of taking it seriously. Since there can be no escape from some holistic interpretation of life which includes the future, the lack of finality in religious claims is not a debilitating defect. The recognition of risk does not destroy the power of religious convictions unless absolute certainty is a central feature of a particular religious faith. The recognition of the theoretical possibility of error is all that Whitehead's natural theology requires. However, it also allows a much more positive appreciation of risk as the necessary counterpart to freedom and creativity. Any theological development that would stress the adventuresome aspects of faith should find his work especially congenial.

There are some outright apologetic advantages that go with a theological move in this direction. A whole series of modern critics of religion, including Feuerbach, Marx, and Freud, have focused on the projective aspects of religious faith as a major defect, or at least as a feature of religion that ought to be honestly recognized. The possibility that religion may be merely wishful thinking, illusory, or escapist has turned into a powerful argument against taking any religious claims as important. The damage seems to have been compounded by those stalwart defenders of the faith who have attempted to maintain a privileged position for their religion. By encouraging a self-conscious recognition of the risks involved in every form of faith, Whitehead changes this kind of debate into a potentially fruitful dialogue. If all the parties in the discussion make similar "faith" projections and run the risk of being wrong, they can afford to listen to each other, and perhaps even learn from one another. They may still disagree about any particular faith, but there would be increased possibility for understanding, respect, and communication.

By openly accepting the risks of faith, the possibility of gross error and some productive grasp of truth are both left open. It works two ways. Faith may be only fantasy in a particular instance, but in other forms it could also be an appropriate response to the human situation and a reasonably accurate characterization of the impinging future. The anticipatory character of religious faith is not, in itself, a difficulty. Everything depends on the adequacy of particular expectations. By making all faith claims vulnerable, Whitehead provides one way for taking any religious conviction seriously.

The relevance of this theological tack can be illustrated by relating it to two religious alternatives presently available. Humanism is one, with its ethically oriented attempt to identify religion with man's ideals. The other is the widely publicized "theology of hope," with its emphasis on apocalyptic eschatology. Both of these options stress the future in its potentially fulfilling and qualifying power. Both of them depend on some clues given in present experience which can inform man's anticipation and action. The difference between them turns in part on the relative certainty of their claims. Humanism gives precedence to man's constructive activity and the contingencies that go with human decision in an evolutionary context. The school of hope puts more weight on the future that God is bringing in under his power. The future is often absolutized in a way that tends to denigrate human effort and evolutionary developments. In the first instance, man is responsible for the future and confidence depends on unpredictable human actions. In the second alternative, certainty is an important factor because God somehow knows "the end of the story." Looking only at these two options, one seems to be faced with the choice between sheer contingency and some kind of determinism.

If the risk inherent in all religion is taken seriously, there is the possibility for at least correlating man's decisions and God's activity. The evolutionary and eschatological emphases do not have to be seen as mutually exclusive. God works through human decisions in persuasive yet effective ways which do not destroy all freedom. At the same time, an apocalyptic approach to eschatology might be sustained, provided one does not claim that this interpretation of the future escapes the risk of human decision and error. Even radically apocalyptic views are tied to other very human expectations insofar as it is always man who makes some judgment about the validity of revelatory or proleptic events. In this sense, what comes out of the evolutionary process cannot be totally divorced from the coming of a Divine future.[15] By taking the pervasiveness of existential risk as basic, Whitehead provides for more productive understanding, comparison and criticism between such religious alternatives as humanism and the theology of hope.

Another direction for theological development that Whitehead undergirds is the concern for ecological interdependence. This has ramifications on at least three levels; the relationship of the individual to the community of faith, the relationship of a particular religious group to society in general, and the relationship of man to his natural environment. In each case, the problem is one of giving due weight to specific identities, without cutting them off from the very conditions of their emergence and sustenance. Whitehead provides a conceptual scheme and an understanding of linguistic distinctions in which reciprocity between individuals and their environment is a fundamental feature of experience, not something tacked on after all the unbridgeable bifurcations have been established. This stress on reciprocity and the relativity it involves sets the stage for any theology that wants to take both personal piety and social concerns as equally important. In Whitehead's perspective, the individual and the community can readily be interpreted as two interdependent foci of significance. The individual has a genuine importance but not in isolation from his relationships. This would reinforce religious convictions which take the community of faith or even the institutional church as an intrinsic factor in religious commitment. However, it would not allow the absolutizing of the church anymore than the strict individualizing of the faith. Reciprocity provides a continuing check and balance system so that the emphasis is relational. It provides a dialectic in which one does not have to choose between the spiritual transformation of the individual and the social reconstruction of society. They may both be goals, resting on the same religious faith.

15. Carl E. Braaten, *The Future of God* (New York: Harper & Row, 1969), pp. 29–30.

Moving further, the nature-history split which has been so influential in modern times is also qualified by this relational point of view. There is a reciprocity between man and nature that cannot be denied in the evolutionary process. One simply must deal with man's many environments at the same time as one considers the peculiar human aspects of the temporal process. Just as scientific statements about natural phenomena cannot be divorced from religious assertions of valuation, so many's physical surroundings and his intimate history can be seen in effective interdependence. When one considers the faltering theological attempts to give ecological concerns their due within a framework that does not make interdependence fundamental, the relevance of Whitehead's contribution should become obvious. For example, the acceptance of philosophical and theological arguments against natural theology has contributed directly to our disregard for the natural environment. Attempts to exalt nature without somehow finding God in it seem contrived, at best. Whitehead's natural theology offers a way of once again including nature positively in our religious interpretations, both epistemologically and ethically. Not only does he provide resources for the understanding of religious language, but the interpretation he encourages opens the way for particular religious commitments which might generate and sustain an appreciation of environmental considerations. As the natural environment manifests increasingly the effects of technological culture such an approach seems more and more necessary. In this sense, Whitehead opens the way for a theology with both natural and technological implications. His is a "systems" approach which is aptly suited for the realities of a sociotechnic age.[16]

One might also note that this emphasis on reciprocity also undergirds the use of certain dialectical distinctions in theological development. In this perspective, God's persuasive redemptive work in the life of the individual can be affirmed at the same time as God's coercive involvement in the struc-

16. Herbert W. Richardson, *Theology for a New World* (London: SCM Press Ltd., 1968), p. 1.

tures of nature and politics is recognized. One can talk about such things as law and Gospel, church and state, creation and redemption without facing untenable choices between these facets of man's situation. Conversely, the ambiguities of a religious interpretation of man's situation are more readily maintained. Such claims as Luther's *simul justus et peccator* can be given emphasis without being construed as sheer contradiction. As in Whitehead's treatment of language distinctions are relativized, so in the use of his work one can maintain contrasts and creative tension where others find only disjunctions, contradictions, and dilemmas. This does not make distinctions themselves unimportant, it only keeps them in the context of concrete experience. One does need to make choices, but such decisions do not have to be absolutized so that the very process of decision is made unintelligible.

The confidence in linguistic assertions which Whitehead's approach encourages should also be mentioned here. Language can carry a lot of freight even though it need not bear all of the load itself. With the relativism that Whitehead espouses, there is a confidence in all linguistic formulations—including those of religion—that exceeds many other contemporary alternatives. Such confidence does not cut language free from its empirical base, nor does it preclude criticism and revision. It does indicate the power and utility of linguistic expression. The word becomes a central indication of man's interaction with an unfolding and all-encompassing environment. In respect to theological development, this implies an enhanced appreciation of doctrine in a day when this aspect of religious faith has been deemphasized. Since what is believed is of decisive importance, the attempts to express, clarify and communicate specific convictions about the meaning of life can take on new importance. Whitehead opens the way for theological developments which will once again find words as crucial instruments of faith, but without the dogmatic pretensions that have often accompanied such an attitude. Words generate, reinforce, and clarify religious experience. Preaching, doctrinal development, and liturgical expression may all benefit from Whitehead's estimate of the status of language. Provided they are not disengaged from their origins in concrete experience or cut off from the corrective power of future developments, these linguistic aspects of religion are given important emphasis by Whitehead's alternative. Any specific faith commitment that has a high stake in linguistic expression ought to find his work eminently useful.

Finally, Whitehead's approach to religious language suggests that persuasion in an admittedly pluralistic context will be the means whereby faith can be proclaimed, appropriated, and sustained. In the wake of religious imperialisms which have often battered opponents and potential adherents with absolute claims of truth, Whitehead provides a conceptual framework in which the appeal is to experience, not arbitrary authority. He encourages a much greater openness in the expression of faith. Alternatives are not easily written off just because they are not one's own, but they can be sympathetically appreciated on their own merit. This makes room for a more humble and honest approach to the question of religious commitment. Where success in the religious enterprise has often been seen as the plain defeat and rejection of competing alternatives, Whitehead allows for both genuine choice and the respectful recognition of a whole spectrum of options. He gives a constructive significance to pluralism that has been absent from most expressions of religious faith. If freedom and persuasion are decisive in religion, then the availability of alternatives is not just the complication of man's situation. Such opportunities are required for freedom to make sense, and they should also make evident the necessity of persuasive appeals rather than negative judgmental tactics. Truth and falsity in religion have too easily been set against each other as mere opponents. Whitehead's more relative interpretation mitigates this conflict without reducing all religious claims to their common elements. One is in a position to learn something from any man's faith, and no religious convictions can be put forward in an imperialistic fashion. Persuasion becomes the watchword in the communication of faith claims. The appeal of truth is to experience where individuals, in the last analysis, find out for themselves.

The proclamation of faith then is a descriptive account of experience which offers itself for further authentication in the lives of others. Doctrine and creedal statements stand also in a descriptive relationship to the experience of a community. They present themselves as capable of standing further tests in the ongoing process. They are positive appeals to experience, not threats requiring mindless compliance.

In these brief remarks, it should be possible to see some consequences of Whitehead's alternative in the styles of theology that can be developed upon it. It must be theology in which risk, reciprocal relations, a high regard for language and a commitment to persuasion are key factors. Such a theology will express itself with both confidence and humility. It will not pretend to have an absolute point of view which is invulnerable to the normal vicissitudes of human existence. Neither will it condone any sheer relativism which makes the very quest for significance irrelevant. There is risk and relativity in all religious conviction. Yet, the assertions of faith are not merely rhetoric, they are serious claims about reality in its fullest dimensions. As such they purport to be informative, corrigible expressions based on some cognitive but partial grasp of the human situation.

In challenging other approaches to language, in meeting the specific criticism of religious cognition and in opening certain routes for theological development, Whitehead needs to be heard more clearly in our contemporary situation. He may well provide the productive resolution of some painful frustration and debilitating confusion. It could be that he offers just the kind of clarity with respect to language that is clear enough for the challenges and opportunities at hand.

Index

274

Type, 11 on 13 and 10 on 11 Garamond
Display, Garamond